First World War
and Army of Occupation
War Diary
France, Belgium and Germany

34 DIVISION
Divisional Troops
Divisional Trench Mortar Batteries
and Divisional Ammunition Column
11 January 1916 - 31 July 1919

WO95/2448/3

The Naval & Military Press Ltd
www.nmarchive.com
Published in association with The National Archives

Published by

The Naval & Military Press Ltd

Unit 10 Ridgewood Industrial Park,
Uckfield, East Sussex,
TN22 5QE England
Tel: +44 (0) 1825 749494

www.naval-military-press.com
www.nmarchive.com

This diary has been reprinted in facsimile from the original. Any imperfections are inevitably reproduced and the quality may fall short of modern type and cartographic standards.

© Crown Copyright
Images reproduced by permission of The National Archives, London, England, 2015.

Contents

Document type	Place/Title	Date From	Date To
Heading	34th Division 34 T.H.D. IVL Trench Mortar Btts Jan 1916-1919 May.		
Heading	War Diary Of 34th Division Trench Mortar Batteries From January 28th 1916 to 30th Sept 1916 Jan to Sept Vol 1.		
War Diary	Blaringhem.	28/01/1916	28/01/1916
War Diary	Steenbecque.	01/02/1916	20/02/1916
War Diary	Erquinghem Lys.	21/02/1916	22/02/1916
War Diary	Armentieres.	23/02/1916	23/03/1916
War Diary	Ypres.	24/02/1916	07/03/1916
War Diary	Armentieres.	24/02/1916	06/04/1916
War Diary	Le Boudrelle.	07/04/1916	12/04/1916
War Diary	Morbecque.	13/04/1916	13/04/1916
War Diary	Tilques.	15/04/1916	02/05/1916
War Diary	Seninghem.	03/05/1916	07/05/1916
War Diary	Franvillers.	08/05/1916	19/05/1916
War Diary	Albert.	20/05/1916	19/08/1916
War Diary	Amiens.	21/08/1916	22/08/1916
War Diary	Steenwercke.	22/08/1916	24/08/1916
War Diary	Armentieres.	26/08/1916	30/09/1916
Miscellaneous	Report In Connection With The Firing Of The "Stokes" Guns And 1/1.2 and 3.7" Trench Howitzers.	15/03/1916	15/03/1916
Map			
Heading	War Diary. of 34th Division F.M. Btys. From 1st To 31st Oct. 1916 Vol 2.		
War Diary	Armentieres.	01/10/1916	31/10/1916
Heading	War Diary Of 34th Division F.M. Btys From 1st To 30th Nov 1916. Volume III.		
War Diary	Armentieres.	01/11/1916	30/11/1916
Heading	War Diary Of 34th Division F.M. Batteries. From 1st To 31st Dec 1916 Volume 4.		
War Diary	Armentieres.	01/12/1916	31/12/1916
Heading	War Diary Of 34th Division F.M. Btys. From 1st Jany To 31st Jany. 1917 Volume 5.		
War Diary	Armentieres.	01/01/1917	31/01/1917
Heading	Trench Mortars. Vol VI.		
War Diary	Armentieres.	01/02/1917	18/02/1917
War Diary	Neuf Berquin.	19/02/1917	19/02/1917
War Diary	Steenbecque	20/02/1917	20/02/1917
War Diary	Fontes.	21/02/1917	21/02/1917
War Diary	Cauchy-A La-Tour.	22/02/1917	22/02/1917
War Diary	Marest.	23/02/1917	23/02/1917
War Diary	Frevent Capelle.	24/02/1917	24/02/1917
War Diary	Arras.	24/02/1917	03/04/1917
War Diary	Arras.		
War Diary	'V' Day.	04/04/1917	04/04/1917
War Diary	'W' Day.	05/04/1917	05/04/1917
War Diary	'X' Day.	06/04/1917	06/04/1917
War Diary	'Q' Day.	07/04/1917	07/04/1917
War Diary	'Y' Day.	08/04/1917	08/04/1917

Type	Description	From	To
War Diary	'Z' Day.	09/04/1917	13/04/1917
War Diary	Arras.	14/04/1917	31/05/1917
War Diary	Arras.	25/04/1917	30/04/1917
War Diary	Arras.	01/06/1917	22/06/1917
War Diary	Tilloy-Les Hermaville.	22/06/1917	06/07/1917
War Diary	Ligny-Saint-Flochel.	06/07/1917	06/07/1917
War Diary	Peronne.	06/07/1917	11/07/1917
War Diary	Hervilly.	11/07/1917	16/08/1917
War Diary	A Day.	17/08/1917	17/08/1917
War Diary	B Day.	18/08/1917	18/08/1917
War Diary	Hervilly.	18/08/1917	18/08/1917
War Diary	C Day.	19/08/1917	19/08/1917
War Diary	Hervilly.	19/08/1917	19/08/1917
War Diary	D Day.	20/08/1917	20/08/1917
War Diary	Hervilly.	20/08/1917	20/08/1917
War Diary	E Day.	21/08/1917	21/08/1917
War Diary	Hervilly.	21/08/1917	21/08/1917
War Diary	E Day.	21/08/1917	21/08/1917
War Diary	Hervilly.	22/08/1917	22/08/1917
War Diary	F Day.	22/08/1917	22/08/1917
War Diary	Hervilly.	22/08/1917	23/08/1917
War Diary	F + 1 Day.	23/08/1917	23/08/1917
War Diary	G Day.	24/08/1917	24/08/1917
War Diary	Hervilly.	24/08/1917	24/08/1917
War Diary	H Day.	25/08/1917	25/08/1917
War Diary	Hervilly "I" Day.	26/08/1917	29/08/1917
War Diary	Hervilly.	29/08/1917	30/09/1917
War Diary	Doingt.	01/10/1917	08/10/1917
War Diary	Poperinghe.	09/10/1917	13/10/1917
War Diary	Gay Farm.	14/10/1917	24/10/1917
War Diary	Woesten.	24/10/1917	31/10/1917
War Diary	(N.R). Woesten.	01/11/1917	03/11/1917
War Diary	Sarawak Camp.	03/11/1917	11/11/1917
War Diary	Boiry Becquerelle.	11/11/1917	25/11/1917
Miscellaneous	Express digital copy service Order Details.		
War Diary	Boiry Becquerelle.	25/11/1917	10/02/1918
War Diary	Canettemont. (Sheet 51c).	11/02/1918	13/02/1918
War Diary	Canettemont.	13/02/1918	24/02/1918
Miscellaneous	Training Programme-For Week Commencing. Saturday 24th Feby 1918	24/07/1918	24/07/1918
War Diary	Canettemont.	25/02/1918	04/03/1918
War Diary	St Leger.	05/03/1918	22/03/1918
War Diary	Hendecourt Lez Ransart.	23/03/1918	31/03/1918
Heading	34th Divisional Artillery War Diary D.T.M.O. 34th Division. April 1918.		
War Diary	Gaudiempre.	01/04/1918	08/04/1918
War Diary	Erquinghem.	09/04/1918	13/04/1918
War Diary	Morbecque.	20/04/1918	30/04/1918
War Diary		29/04/1918	29/04/1918
War Diary	Morbecque	01/05/1918	10/05/1918
War Diary	Steenbecque.	11/05/1918	18/05/1918
Miscellaneous	Appendix 1.	11/05/1918	11/05/1918
War Diary	Steenbecque. C.29.d.5.1.	26/06/1918	30/06/1918
War Diary	Steenbecque. C.30.d.8.0.	01/07/1918	06/07/1918
War Diary	Pera Camp (Haandekot-Area) Sh/27.	06/07/1918	15/07/1918
War Diary	Para Camp. Haandekot-Area. Belgium. Sh/27.	15/07/1918	31/07/1918

War Diary	Oulchy-Le-Chateau. Trench Sheet 1/40,000.	01/08/1918	05/08/1918
War Diary	(Map Sheet) Hazebrouck 5 A.	06/08/1918	07/08/1918
War Diary	Borden Camp. K.3.d.8.5.	08/08/1918	08/08/1918
War Diary	Borden Camp K.3.d.8.5. (Ref Sheet 27) 1/40,000.	09/08/1918	12/08/1918
War Diary	E.10.a.5.4. (Ref Sheet 27) (1/40,000).	12/08/1918	22/08/1918
War Diary	Sh 28/ A.27.a.2.6.	23/08/1918	31/08/1918
War Diary	A.27.c.2.6. Sh 28/1/40,000.	01/09/1918	05/09/1918
War Diary	L.2.d.6.6. Sh 27 1/40,000.	06/09/1918	10/09/1918
War Diary	L.29.b.5.2.	10/09/1918	15/09/1918
War Diary	L.29.d.9.2.	15/09/1918	18/09/1918
War Diary	Refce Map. Sheet 27.	19/08/1918	20/08/1918
War Diary	Sh 28/ B.1.a.4.4. Brewery Camp.	20/09/1918	30/09/1918
War Diary	Kemmel.	01/10/1918	04/10/1918
War Diary	Cafe Belge.	05/10/1918	10/10/1918
War Diary	N.3.a.2.1. Sh/28.	10/10/1918	11/10/1918
War Diary	Hallebash Corner Sh 28/N.3.a.2.1.	12/10/1918	16/10/1918
War Diary	Basseville Cabaret.	17/10/1918	21/10/1918
War Diary	M.9.c. 45.35. Lauwe (Sh 29).	21/10/1918	24/10/1918
War Diary	Rolleghem. N.25.d.3.5.	25/10/1918	28/10/1918
War Diary	Beveren Sh 29. (C.25.d.95.80).	29/10/1918	03/11/1918
War Diary	Wevelghem Sh 29. L.36.c.5.3.	04/11/1918	19/11/1918
War Diary	Stocq.	20/11/1918	22/12/1918
War Diary	Falisolle.	22/12/1918	26/12/1918
War Diary	Falisolle (Ref Sheet Namur. 8).	23/12/1918	31/12/1918
War Diary		29/12/1918	29/12/1918
War Diary	Falisolle.	01/01/1919	29/01/1919
War Diary	Falisolle.	01/01/1919	23/01/1919
War Diary	Lundorf.	04/02/1919	24/03/1919
War Diary	Hennef.	10/05/1919	15/05/1919
War Diary	Weingarts Gasse.	22/05/1919	28/05/1919
Miscellaneous	G.		
Heading	34th Division 34th Divl Ammn Column Jan 1916-1919 Jly.		
Heading	34th D.A.C. Vol I Jan Jan 16 Dec 18.		
Heading	War Diary Of 34th Div. AM, Col. R.F.A. From Jany 11th 1916, to Jany 31st 1916.		
War Diary	Codford.	11/01/1916	11/01/1916
War Diary	Southampton.	11/01/1916	11/01/1916
War Diary	Havre.	12/01/1916	13/01/1916
War Diary	St. Omer.	14/01/1916	14/01/1916
War Diary	Arques.	14/01/1916	23/01/1916
Heading	War Diary Of 34th Divl. Ammunition Coln R.F.A. From Feb 1st 1916, To Feb. 29th 1916.		
War Diary	Estaires.	04/02/1916	19/02/1916
War Diary	Steenwerck.	19/02/1916	21/02/1916
Heading	34 Div A.C. Vol 3.		
War Diary	Steenwerck.	18/03/1916	18/03/1916
Heading	34th Divisional Ammn Column Vol II.		
Heading	War Diary Of 34th Divisional Ammunition Column From April 1st 1916 to April 30th 1916. 34 Div AC Vol 4.		
War Diary	Steenwerck.	10/04/1916	10/04/1916
War Diary	Le Petit Mortier.	12/04/1916	12/04/1916
War Diary	Steenwerck.	13/04/1916	13/04/1916
War Diary	Moulin Fontaine.	14/04/1916	15/04/1916
War Diary	Coulomby.	15/04/1916	16/05/1916

War Diary	Seninghem.	17/04/1916	22/04/1916
Heading	War Diary Of 34th Divl Ammn. Col. From May 1st 1916 To May 31st 1916. Vol 5.		
War Diary	Seninghem.	05/05/1916	07/05/1916
War Diary	Longeau.	07/05/1916	07/05/1916
War Diary	Lahoussoye.	08/05/1916	08/05/1916
War Diary	Bresle.	09/05/1916	09/05/1916
War Diary	Buire.	10/05/1916	25/05/1916
War Diary	Dernancourt.	27/05/1916	28/05/1916
Heading	War Diary Of 34th Divisional Ammunition Column From June 1st 1916 To June 30th 1916 Vol 6		
War Diary	Dernancourt.	01/06/1916	30/06/1916
Miscellaneous			
Miscellaneous	34th D.A.C. (Ammunition Supply June 1916) Appendix "B".	19/06/1916	19/06/1916
Miscellaneous	Appendix D French 75 Mm. A.mtn.		
Heading	34th Div. III. Corps. War Diary 34th Division Ammunition Column. July 1916.		
War Diary	Albert Area.	01/07/1916	01/07/1916
War Diary	Dernancourt.	01/07/1916	01/07/1916
War Diary	Becourt Wood.	01/07/1916	01/07/1916
War Diary	Dernancourt.	02/07/1916	06/07/1916
War Diary	Becourt Wood.	10/07/1916	10/07/1916
War Diary	Dernancourt.	10/07/1916	17/07/1916
War Diary	Becourt Wood.	18/07/1916	18/07/1916
War Diary	Dernancourt.	19/07/1916	20/07/1916
War Diary	Albert Area.	21/07/1916	21/07/1916
War Diary	Dernancourt.	22/07/1916	22/07/1916
War Diary	Albert Area.	23/07/1916	26/07/1916
War Diary	Dernancourt.	26/07/1916	26/07/1916
War Diary	Albert Area.	27/07/1916	31/07/1916
Heading	Appendices "G" & "H".		
Miscellaneous	34th D.A.C. Amtn Aest. July, 1916. Appendix G.		
Miscellaneous	Special Order Of the Day by Major General E.C. Ingouville Williams, C.B.D.S.O. Commanding 34th Divn. Appendix H.		
Miscellaneous	C.O.C. 34th Division Appendix H.	12/07/1916	12/07/1916
Miscellaneous	Headquarters, R.A. 111th Corps. Appendix H.	09/07/1916	09/07/1916
Miscellaneous	Appendix H Page 4.	11/07/1916	11/07/1916
Heading	34th Divisional Artillery. 34th Divisional Ammunition Column August 1916.		
Heading	War Diary Volume 8 Of 34th Divisional Ammunition Column From August 1st 1916 To August 31st 1916.		
War Diary	Albert.	01/08/1916	19/08/1916
War Diary	Frechencourt.	21/08/1916	21/08/1916
War Diary	Steenwerck.	22/08/1916	31/08/1916
Heading	War Diary (Volume 9) Of 34th Divisional Ammunition Column From Sept 1st 1916 To Sept 30th 1916.		
War Diary	Steenwerck.	02/09/1916	30/09/1916
Heading	War Diary (Volume 10) Of 34th Divisional Ammunition Column From Oct 1st 1916 To Oct. 31st-1916.		
War Diary	Steenwerck.	05/10/1916	31/10/1916
Heading	War Diary (Volume XI) Of 34th Divisional Ammunition Column From Nov 1st 1916 To Nov 30th 1916.		

War Diary	Steenwerck.	01/11/1916	21/12/1916
War Diary	Erquinghem.	22/12/1916	30/12/1916
Heading	D.A.C. Vol 14.		
War Diary	Steenwerck.	03/01/1917	13/02/1917
War Diary	Hazebrouck.	14/02/1917	14/02/1917
War Diary	Fontes.	15/02/1917	15/02/1917
War Diary	Frevin Capelle.	16/02/1917	16/02/1917
War Diary	Steenwerck.	19/02/1917	19/02/1917
War Diary	Steenbecque.	19/02/1917	20/02/1917
War Diary	Fontes.	20/02/1917	21/02/1917
War Diary	Antigneul Chateau.	22/02/1917	22/02/1917
War Diary	Antigneul Chau	02/03/1917	02/03/1917
War Diary	Bethonsart.	04/03/1917	04/03/1917
War Diary	Frevin Capelle.	08/03/1917	10/03/1917
War Diary	E17 Central.	11/03/1917	11/03/1917
War Diary	Herlinlevert.	12/03/1917	12/03/1917
War Diary	Frevin Capelle.	13/03/1917	18/03/1917
War Diary	Villers Brulin.	19/03/1917	20/03/1917
War Diary	E.16.b.8.1.	23/03/1917	24/03/1917
War Diary	E.16.b.	26/03/1917	29/03/1917
War Diary	E.16.b (51c).	01/04/1917	10/04/1917
War Diary	G.2.a.3.6. (51B).	11/04/1917	14/04/1917
War Diary	G.2.a. (51B).	14/04/1917	17/04/1917
War Diary	H.8.c. (51B).	18/04/1917	19/04/1917
War Diary	G.2.a. (51B).	20/04/1917	22/04/1917
War Diary	G.2.9.3.6. (51B).	23/04/1917	30/04/1917
War Diary	In The Field G.2.a.3.6.	03/05/1917	17/05/1917
War Diary	G.2.a.3.6.	19/05/1917	31/05/1917
War Diary	In The Field (G.2.a.3.6).	01/06/1917	30/06/1917
War Diary	Frevin Capelle.	01/07/1917	04/07/1917
War Diary	Monchiet.	05/07/1917	05/07/1917
War Diary	In The Field.	06/07/1917	06/07/1917
War Diary	Peronne.	09/07/1917	09/07/1917
War Diary	Hancourt.	10/07/1917	10/07/1917
War Diary	Q.13.d.8.8.	12/07/1917	25/07/1917
War Diary	K.35.B.9.4.	26/07/1917	26/07/1917
War Diary	Q.13.d.8.8.	30/07/1917	31/08/1917
War Diary	Q.19.d.9.6.	01/09/1917	01/09/1917
War Diary	K.35.b.8.2.	04/09/1917	04/09/1917
War Diary	Q.19.d.9.6.	04/09/1917	07/09/1917
War Diary	K.35.b.8.2.	10/09/1917	11/09/1917
War Diary	Q.19.d.9.6.	13/09/1917	29/09/1917
War Diary	Courcelles.	01/10/1917	07/10/1917
War Diary	Peronne.	08/10/1917	09/10/1917
War Diary	Crombeke.	10/10/1917	13/10/1917
War Diary	Boesinghe.	14/10/1917	26/10/1917
War Diary	Woeston.	27/10/1917	03/11/1917
War Diary	Crombeke.	04/11/1917	05/11/1917
War Diary	Steenvorde.	06/11/1917	06/11/1917
War Diary	Calonne.	07/11/1917	07/11/1917
War Diary	Labeuvriere.	08/11/1917	08/11/1917
War Diary	Bethonsart.	09/11/1917	09/11/1917
War Diary	Boiry St. Rictrude.	10/11/1917	29/11/1917
Miscellaneous	XIX Corps R.A. No. A. 2569. 34th Div. Arty No. 5 H.A. 24,25,27,28.	23/11/1917	23/11/1917
War Diary	Boiry St. Rictrude.	30/11/1917	07/02/1918

War Diary	Souastre.	08/02/1918	08/02/1918
War Diary	Etree-Wamin.	09/02/1918	01/03/1918
War Diary	Souastre.	02/03/1918	02/03/1918
War Diary	Hamelincourt.	03/03/1918	25/03/1918
War Diary	Bellacourt.	26/03/1918	28/03/1918
War Diary	Guidempre.	29/03/1918	31/03/1918
Heading	34th Divisional Artillery War Diary 34th Divisional Ammunition Column R.F.A. April 1918.		
War Diary	Guidempre.	01/04/1918	03/04/1918
War Diary	Bavincourt	04/04/1918	06/04/1918
War Diary	St. Hilaire and Ecquedecques.	07/04/1918	07/04/1918
War Diary	Haverskerque La. Corbie.	08/04/1918	08/04/1918
War Diary	Steenwerck.	09/04/1918	10/04/1918
War Diary	Outersteen.	11/04/1918	11/04/1918
War Diary	Morbecque.	12/04/1918	12/04/1918
War Diary	St. Sylvestre.	13/04/1918	13/04/1918
War Diary	Godewaersveld.	14/04/1918	25/04/1918
War Diary	Watou Area L.9.b.5.5.	26/04/1918	28/04/1918
War Diary	Watou L.7.d.	29/04/1918	30/04/1918
War Diary	Watou L.7.d. (Sheet 27).	01/05/1918	05/05/1918
War Diary	Watou L.7.d.	06/05/1918	06/05/1918
War Diary	Watou.	07/05/1918	08/05/1918
War Diary	Morbecque.	09/05/1918	10/05/1918
War Diary	Steenbecque.	11/05/1918	04/07/1918
War Diary	Rubrouck.	05/07/1918	05/07/1918
War Diary	Proven (Ponty Pool Camp).	06/07/1918	15/07/1918
War Diary	Proven.	16/07/1918	16/07/1918
War Diary	Chantilly.	17/07/1918	17/07/1918
War Diary	Survilliers.	18/07/1918	19/07/1918
War Diary	Lafresnoy.	20/07/1918	20/07/1918
War Diary	Viviers.	21/07/1918	23/07/1918
War Diary	La Grille Farm.	24/07/1918	28/07/1918
War Diary	Rozet Wood.	29/07/1918	02/08/1918
War Diary	Oulchy La-Ville.	03/08/1918	03/08/1918
War Diary	Rozet Wood.	04/08/1918	04/08/1918
War Diary	Boullarre	05/08/1918	05/08/1918
War Diary	La. Plessis.	06/08/1918	06/08/1918
War Diary	Esquelbecq.	07/08/1918	07/08/1918
War Diary	Watou.	08/08/1918	12/08/1918
War Diary	Hanndekot.	13/08/1918	31/08/1918
War Diary	Hamhoek.	22/08/1918	02/09/1918
War Diary	Rattlekot 27/K.23.d.4.4.	03/09/1918	05/09/1918
War Diary	Poperinghe.	06/09/1918	08/09/1918
War Diary	Reninghelst.	10/09/1918	12/09/1918
War Diary	Loye	13/09/1918	29/09/1918
War Diary	Kemmel.	30/09/1918	01/10/1918
War Diary	Kirtwilde.	02/10/1918	03/10/1918
War Diary	Cafebelg.	04/10/1918	09/10/1918
War Diary	Hallebast Corner.	10/10/1918	16/10/1918
War Diary	Gheluvelt	17/10/1918	19/10/1918
War Diary	Menin.	20/10/1918	21/10/1918
War Diary	Lauwe.	22/10/1918	24/10/1918
War Diary	Kiijtgat.	25/10/1918	28/10/1918
War Diary	Beveren.	29/10/1918	03/11/1918
War Diary	Kloefhoek.	04/11/1918	10/11/1918
War Diary	Esscher.	11/11/1918	12/11/1918

War Diary	Herthoek.	13/11/1918	15/11/1918
War Diary	St. Genois.	16/11/1918	16/11/1918
War Diary	Ellignies Les-Frasnes.	17/11/1918	18/11/1918
War Diary	Bouissons.	19/11/1918	30/11/1918
War Diary	Bouisson Oeudeghien.	01/12/1918	12/12/1918
War Diary	Bois-De-Lessines.	13/12/1918	14/12/1918
War Diary	Soignies.	15/12/1918	16/12/1918
War Diary	Houdeng.	17/12/1918	17/12/1918
War Diary	Lagasse.	18/12/1918	18/12/1918
War Diary	Chatelin Au	19/12/1918	19/12/1918
War Diary	St Gerrard.	20/12/1918	22/12/1918
War Diary	Mornimont.	23/12/1918	23/01/1919
War Diary	Mornimont and Sieglar.	24/01/1919	24/01/1919
War Diary	Sieglar.	25/01/1919	29/01/1919
War Diary	Lulsdorf and Zundorf.	30/01/1919	31/01/1919
War Diary	Zundoff Spich & Lulsdorf.	01/02/1919	12/02/1919
War Diary	Zundoff Lulsdorf Liebour Ranzel & Langel.	13/02/1919	28/02/1919
War Diary	Zundorf Langel Lulsdorf Ranzel Liebour.	01/03/1919	31/03/1919
War Diary	Zundorf. Lulsdorf & Ranzel.	02/05/1919	31/05/1919
War Diary	Lulsdorf. Zundorf & Ranzel.	01/06/1919	18/06/1919
War Diary	Hennef & Donrath.	19/06/1919	30/06/1919
War Diary	Zundorf Lulsdorf & Ranzel.	01/07/1919	31/07/1919

34TH DIVISION

3 FH.D IVL TRENCH MORTAR BTTS
JAN 1916-DEC 1916

1919 MAY

34TH DIVISION

Jan to Sept / Vol 1

Confidential
War Diary
of
34th Division Trench
Mortar Batteries

From January 28th 1916 to 30th Sept 1916

Army Form C. 2118

WAR DIARY
or
INTELLIGENCE-SUMMARY
(Erase heading not required.)

Instructions regarding War Diaries and Intelligence Summaries are contained in F.S. Regs., Part II. and the Staff Manual respectively. Title Pages will be prepared in manuscript.

Place	Date	Hour	Summary of Events and Information	Remarks and references to Appendices
	1916			
BLARINGHEM	28th Jan.		61st. Trench Mortar battery joined 34th. Division from the First Army School of Mortars. Billeted at STEENBECQUE.	
STEENBECQUE	1st to 8th Feby.		61st. Trench Mortar battery constructed a range at I.3.d. (sheet 36A.) and did a little practice shooting. Weather very wet. Moved billets to I.3.d.3.7. 2nd Lt. H.S.M. DARVILLE, O.C. admitted to Hospital. Battery was armed with 2" T.M's.	
	8th.			
	9th.		60th. Trench Mortar battery joined 34th. Division from First Army School of Mortars, and was billeted at I.3.b.5.8.	
	10th.		LIEUT. G.BURLINGHAM 7th. R.S.F. from 2nd. T.M.B. took over 61st battery. 60th. and 61st. batteries shared the guns (2") and did some work and shooting on the range.	
	11th.		The 34th. Division, including 60th. T.M.B. was inspected by FIELD-MARSHALL, LORD KITCHENER, K.G., Poured with rain all day. Half 61st battery left for ARMENTIERES.	
	15th.		60th. and 61st. batteries paraded at the range for inspection by the Divisional Commander (MAJOR-GENERAL E.C. INGOUVILLE-WILLIAMS,C.B.,D.S.O.) A few rounds were fired successfully. Weather still cold and wet.	
	17th		Football, 60th. V 61st. batteries. Air-raid on HAZEBROUCK.	
	18th		Remainder of 61st. battery left for ARMENTIERES, to be attached to 21st. battery (23rd.Division)	

1875 Wt. W593/826 1,000,000 4/15 J.B.C. & A. A.D.S.S./Forms/C. 2118:

WAR DIARY
or
INTELLIGENCE SUMMARY

(Erase heading not required.)

Instructions regarding War Diaries and Intelligence Summaries are contained in F.S. Regs, Part II. and the Staff Manual respectively. Title Pages will be prepared in manuscript.

Army Form C. 2118.

Place	Date	Hour	Summary of Events and Information	Remarks and references to Appendices
STEENBECQUE	FEB 19th		61st. battery took over from 21st. 60th. did some firing on the range . 61st. battery armed with 1½" guns.	
	20th	9-30 a.m.	60th. battery proceeded in lorries to ERQUINGHEM-LYS via SAINT-VENANT. Took 2 2" guns into trenches near BOIS GRENIER (LE BRIDOUX SALIENT), during the night	
ERQUINGHEM-LYS.	21st.		60th. battery received orders to take out 2" guns and take over 1½" guns of 12th. T.M.B. Rations precarious.	
	22nd	3 p.m.	The 2" guns of 60th. battery were handed over to 61st. who left in lorries, and pouring rain, for 5th. CORPS H.Q. 2nd. Army (YPRES.)	
ARMENTIERES	23rd	8 p.m.	60th. battery left ERQUINGHEM-LYS for ARMENTIERES and took over 61st. battery's billets I.c.1½.6. Snow, and very cold. 60th. battery took over 1½" guns in RUE DU BOIS SALIENT, in very bad condition. Attached to 103rd. Infantry Brigade.	
YPRES.	24th to 7th Mar.		61st. battery took part in the taking of the "BLUFF" at HOOGE. Corpl MACKENZIE won D.C.M., and the battery was mentioned in despatches.	
ARMENTIERES	24th to 29th.		60th. battery brought one more (3rd), gun into action and stood by ready to fire if required nightly. However, there was no action. Weather very bad.	
	MARCH 1st.	10 a.m.	There was a Trench Mortar display at Divisional bomb-school LA BOUDRELLE by commandant, First Army School of Mortars (MAJOR R.C.DODGSON, D.S.O., R.A.) 60th battery attempted to register, but not one out of 100 T-tubes would fit the vent. Guns taken out of action and sent to Base for repairs.	
	3rd.		Divisional Commander inspected the trenches. 2nd. Lt.J.W.G.WYLIE, 9th. H.L.I. joined 60th battery. Weather wet and cold, as usual.	
	4th.	4-45pm	Enemy shelled ARMENTIERES with 5.9"s	
	5th.		Work was commenced on one emplacement in the CHORD-LINE and on another in the salient.	
	6th.	9.p.m.	False gas-alarm in trenches. 70th. battery joined Division.	
	7th.	1.a.m.	Snow almost all day, but work continued. 61st. battery, only 13 strong, returned from YPRES. All guns were removed from trenches and thoroughly overhauled by Ordnance. 61st. battery left to be attached to 8th. Division near LAVENTIE, after receiving re-inforcements.	
	8th.		3 guns returned from Ordnance in the afternoon. Work progressed on the two new emplacements, and they were nearly completed.	
	10th.		Batteries were re-named as follows:- 61st. to be X/34th. 70th. to be Z/34th. 60th. to be Y/34th.	
	11th.			

WAR DIARY
INTELLIGENCE SUMMARY
(Erase heading not required.)

Instructions regarding War Diaries and Intelligence Summaries are contained in F.S. Regs., Part II and the Staff Manual respectively. Title Pages will be prepared in manuscript.

Place	Date	Hour	Summary of Events and Information	Remarks and references to Appendices
ARMENTIERES	MARCH 11th		70th. battery were at LE BRIDOUX SALIENT.	
	12th.		"X" battery's emplacements completed.	
	13th.		A bombardment of the hostile salient about GERMAN HOUSE was arranged, and 3" STOKES mortars were used for the first time in action. "X" battery co-operated, and so did Artillery, rifle-grenades (NEWTON) and 3.7" Mortars.	Ref:34th.G S./18/42. account appended
	14th. 4.27 a.m.		"X" battery fired 3 rounds in the morning.	
	16th.		"X" battery took part in a 10 minute bombardment of the hostile salient. 15 rounds fired. Some misfires prevented better results. The 3" STOKES BATTERY "101/2" also took part.	
	17th. 8.a.m.		Heavy shelling of CHAPPELLE D'ARMENTIERES about mid-day. Divisional Commander inspected trenches, and, incidentally "X" battery's emplacements. At this time "Z" battery were in action, and fired chiefly in retaliation. "Y" battery rejoined 34th. Division, not having been actually engaged in firing whilst with 8th. Division.	
	19th. 1.p.m.		Enemy shelled our support line from DEAD COW FARM to the ESTAMINET with 5.9", killing one of "X" battery's working party.	
	22nd 5.40 a.m.		"X" battery, in conjunction with 101/2 and 102/1 L.T.M.B's, bombarded hostile salient for ¾ hour. Results believed to have been excellent. 15 rounds 33-pdr were fired. Work was continued on dug-outs and emplacements.	
	24th.		Snow all the morning, and afterwards very wet. About this date "Y" battery bombarded BOIS BLANCS with 50 rounds 2", "Z" battery co-operating at LE BRIDOUX. 34th. division was transferred to 2nd. CORPS, 2nd. ARMY.	
	28th.5.p.m.		"X" battery again co-operated in a bombardment of the hostile salient at RUE DU BOIS, firing 21 rounds 33-pdsr.	
	29th		Weather fine. About this date "Y" battery bombarded CORNER FORT successfully.	
	APRIL 1 to 5th.		Weather fine; work continued on emplacements and dug-outs.	
	6th. 10a.m.		Enemy bombarded, our salient at RUE DU BOIS with light winged mortar-bombs, firing about 100 rounds. No damage was done. "X" battery retaliated with 10 rounds 33-pdr and 3 18-pdr.	
	11p.m.		In accordance with orders received from the G.O.C. 102nd Infantry Brigade, all guns and gun-stores were removed from the trenches back to the billets. The enemy fired a few light mortars whilst this was going on.	
LA BOUDRE-LLE.	7th. 9.p.m.		"X" battery was relieved by 7th. AUSTRALIAN INFANTRY BRIGADE T.M. BATTERY, and moved at night to the 34th Divisional Instructional School at LA BOUDRELLE.	

WAR DIARY or INTELLIGENCE SUMMARY

(Erase heading not required.)

Instructions regarding War Diaries and Intelligence Summaries are contained in F.S. Regs., Part II. and the Staff Manual respectively. Title Pages will be prepared in manuscript.

Place	Date	Hour	Summary of Events and Information	Remarks and references to Appendices
LA BOUDRELLE	APRIL 9th		"Y" battery came to LA BOUDRELLE from FLEURBAIX.	
	11th.		"Z" battery came to LA BOUDRELLE from BOIS GRENIER.	
	12th.		All three medium batteries were attached to the 34th. D.A.C.for rations and discipline.	
MORBECQUE.	13th.	8.a.m.	Parade for medium batteries. Marched, with 3 G.S.Wagons, to MORBECQUE via DOULIEU and VIEUX BERQUIN. Lost by the D.A.C. who failed to provide either rations or billets.	
	15th.	noon	Found by D.T.M.O. Four lorries were provided to take the batteries to TILQUES, via EBLINGHEM and SAINT-OMER. Reached billets at the BRASSERIE, near D.H.Q.in the afternoon.	
TILQUES.	16th.	6-45 a.m.	Commenced programme of training for all batteries, medium & light. Telephone course and gun-drill daily.	
	19th		Dug butts at a range near LES MARAIS. Firing with dummies.	
	20th		Kit-inspection.	
	22nd	12-30 p.m.	All three medium batteries were armed with 2" mortars. Grenade accident took place in one of the light batteries.	
	23rd	a.m.	Route-march.	
	24th	a.m.	Gun-drill and fatigues.	
		p.m.	Elementary examination on gunnery.	
	26th		Gun-drill and firing on the range. D.O.C. 34th. Division watched the firing of "X" battery.	
	27th	p.m.	Firing on range.	
	28th	a.m.	Routemarch.	
		p.m.	Inspection by A.A.& Q.M.G.	
	30th	3.a.m.	Reveille. Parade for Divisional Field Day at 4-15. a.m. Practised the advance for attack on SOMME FRONT. Gun-drill display befor G.O.C. 34th. Division and M.G.G.S. 2nd Army.	
		1-20	Returned to billets. Instruction in the use of NEWTON D.A. FUZE. Fatigues.	
	MAY. 2nd	3-0.a.m.	Divisional Field-day as before. Weather dull; one heavy shower of rain	
		1 p.m.	Returned to billets.	
SENINGHEM	3rd	4 p.m	3 medium batteries left for SENINGHEM.	
	5th	5-30	Reached excellent billets. Attached to 34th D.A.C. Weather hot	
	5th.	9-30	Route-march.	

Instructions regarding War Diaries and Intelligence Summaries are contained in F.S. Regs, Part II. and the Staff Manual respectively. Title Pages will be prepared in manuscript.

INTELLIGENCE SUMMARY

(Erase heading not required.)

Place	Date MAY	Hour	Summary of Events and Information	Remarks and references to Appendices
SENINGHEM	6th.	10-30 a.m.	"X" and "Y" batteries left for SAINT-OMER ; "Z" battery for WIZERNES. Heavy rain during morning. During the night loaded wagons for the 34th. DAC.	
	7th.	a.m.	Entrained for LONGEAU, near AMIENS (SOMME).	
		noon	Detrained. Rained hard. "X" battery proceeded to FRANVILLERS to be attached to 103rd Infantry Brigade. "Y" & "Z" batteries to FERME SAINT LAURENT.	
FRANVILLERS	8th.		Rations precarious, weather bad.	
	9th.		One officer per battery went round trenches at ALBERT with D.T.M.O. "X" battery moved to Fme. St. LAURENT.	
	10th.		Further inspection of trenches by various officers.	
	12th.		Selected about 13 possible positions. Fatigues.	
	17th.		Construction of a mortar-range commenced.	
	18th.		A Divisional School of Mortars was started under Capt'n. R.A. LLOYD-BARROW, R.F.A. "Y" battery went forward to ALBERT and trenches.	
	19th.		Work on the range continued. Fine weather.	
	20th.		"X" battery moved forward to ALBERT. "X" & "Y" batteries both billeted in the HOSPICE, also 8 men of "Z".	
ALBERT.	21st.		"X" battery relieved "Y" battery in the trenches opposite LA BOISSELLE, and fired 4 rounds. 2 duds. but excellent shots. Enemy active with mortars.	
	23rd.	a.m.	Four rounds fired into LA BOISSELLE during night.	
		7-30am	6 rounds fired at registered points. Considerable shelling both day & night.	
		4.p.m.	2 more rounds fired. Started a new emplacement in "LOCHNAGAR St".	
		9.p.m.	Remainder of "X" battery went into the trenches. Worked all night, except during heavy mortar fire, on emplacements in "KINGSGATE St" and LOCHNAGAR. H.Q. in "DALHOUSIE St".	
	24th	12-40	Bombardment of hostile trenches with 9.2" Seige-Howitzers. Enemy active with mortars, especially "oilcans". 4 rounds fired from LOCHNAGAR in retaliation.	
	25th.	noon	Enemy again active with mortars.	
		6-50am	ditto.	
		10-11am	We retaliated with 3 rounds from our 2 right emplacements. Rained all night.	
	26th.		The first newly trained D.A.C. personnel from the Divisional School took over the right sector from "X" battery	
	27th	noon	Enemy fired over some oil-cans during the night. Another bombardment of LA-BOISSELLE by our 9.2"'s. Enemy retaliated with 4.2"'s.	
		5-30.	More "oil-cans". We fired 3 rounds in retaliation from a new emplacement in "SCONE St".	

WAR DIARY
or
INTELLIGENCE SUMMARY

(Erase heading not required.)

Instructions regarding War Diaries and Intelligence Summaries are contained in F.S. Regs., Part II. and the Staff Manual respectively. Title Pages will be prepared in manuscript.

Place	Date	Hour	Summary of Events and Information	Remarks and references to Appendices
ALBERT.	MAY 28th.	a.m.	4 beds were put into position for a raid, in the craters.	
		10-40am	We retaliated for some "oil-cans" with seven rounds.	
		11-30pm	2 more rounds fired from SCONE STREET.	
	29th.	1.a.m.	2 more rounds from "SCONE St."	
		2-5pm	Fired one round ranging from new emplacement in the craters. Rained all night.	
	30th.	5.p.m.	Fired 2 more rounds ranging from crater-emplacements. Heavy shelling of SCONE St, in the evening. "Y" Heavy battery formed.	
	31st.	10a.m.	Continuous hostile shelling all day.	
		5-30p.m.	Carried in ammunition to SCONE St. until late.	
	JUNE 1st	12-30	Continued carrying in ammunition. Weather improved.	
		10-20	25 more rounds carried forward in the evening. Hostile shelling of "PERTH AVNE". for ¼ hour.	
	2nd		Half "Y" battery came into trenches.	
			Completed 180 rounds in left sector.	
	3rd	6.p.m.	"Y" battery relieved "X" battery. The latter returned to HOSPICE.	
		10-30	Enemy sent some 5.9"s into ALBERT.	
	4th	1 a.m.	Hostile raid in the right sector. R.F.A. detachment there fired 44 rounds. 2nd Lt MALTBY, R.F.A. wounded. Enemy shelled about HOSPICE with H.E. and "Lachrymatory". Began pushing forward ammunition for strafe.	
		9-30pm	Heavy shelling until midnight.	
	5th.	11-pm.	Hostile shelling of south-end of ALBERT, in retaliation for our raid.	
	6th.	12-30.	"Y" battery cut wire, and bombarded hostile trenches. Henceforward it was much quieter, and ammunition was carried forward daily.	
	10th.		Wet. "M". "O". "P" batteries formed from newly-trained D.A.C. re-assortment of personnel.	
	15th	11.pm.	Summer-time introduced.	
	16th		"X"/19 and "X", "Y" and "Z"/38. T.M.B's attached to the division. Batteries were organised into groups as follows:-	

Left	Centre	Right.
Z/34	M/34	V/34
X/19	X/38	O/34
Y/38	Z/38	P/34

X/34 in reserve for general duties. V/34 in action. 3 guns

WAR DIARY or INTELLIGENCE SUMMARY

(Erase heading not required.)

Instructions regarding War Diaries and Intelligence Summaries are contained in F. S. Regs., Part II. and the Staff Manual respectively. Title Pages will be prepared in manuscript.

Place	Date	Hour	Summary of Events and Information	Remarks and references to Appendices
ALBERT.	JUNE 24th		The great preliminary bombardment commenced, and henceforth batteries cut wire daily, firing about 900 rounds daily.	
	27th		2nd Lieut.W.M.LAKE, R.G.A. P/34 T.M.B. mortally wounded. Bombardment considerably increased in intensity.	
	JULY 1st	6-30	Finally bombarded.	
		7-30 a.m.	The assault. Henceforward the batteries spent all their time rescuing and tending the wounded, and several N.C.O's particularly distinguished themselves.	
	3rd		D.T.M.O. and 2/Lt WYLLIE took part in a bombing attack on LA BOISELLE, during which D.T.M.O. (Captn. D.H.JAMES) was severely wounded. 2 guns were taken over to the crater on the right in the evening but were not used.	
	4th		All except the heavy battery, "V" which was temporarily handed over to the 23rd DIVISION, were withdrawn from action.	
	6th		Moved to DERNANCOURT.	
	11th		Moved into billets in ALBERT, RUE D'AMIENS.	
	14th		Salvage fatigues near BECOURT CHÂTEAU.	
	17th		A course of telephones was started.	
	22nd		Moved back to FERME ST. LAURENT. G.O.C. 34th Division killed in action.	
	24th		Route-march.	
	28th		Range fatigues. Improved emplacement and put out some barbed-wire on the target.	
	31st		Moved to bivouacs near BOUZINCOURT. Attached to 34th D.A.C.	
	Augst 2nd	8-15	Route-march.	
		3.p.m.	Gun-drill	
	4th	7.a.m.	Route-march.	
	5th	7.a.m.	Route-march.	
	6th	10-30	Church Parade.	
	7th	6-15	Fatigues for D.A.C. Practice shooting for reinforcements at FME ST. LAURENT.	
		4.p.m.	Returned.	
	9th	7.a.m.	Route-march.	
	10th	2-30	Route-march.	
	12th	7-30	Fatigues for Signals R.E. in "SAUSAGE VALLEY" 3-30 p.m. Returned	

WAR DIARY
or
INTELLIGENCE SUMMARY

(Erase heading not required.)

Army Form C. 2118

Instructions regarding War Diaries and Intelligence Summaries are contained in F.S. Regs, Part II. and the Staff Manual respectively. Title Pages will be prepared in manuscript.

Place	Date	Hour	Summary of Events and Information	Remarks and references to Appendices
ALBERT.	AUGST 13th	10-30	Church Parade.	
	14th	9.a.m.	Parade for marching-drill. Accident in "Y" battery. 10-30. p.m. Rain.	
	15th	6-15pm	Fatigues for D.A.C.	
		9-30am	Route-march for remainder.	
		2-30pm	Gun-drill.	
	17th		"M", "O", "P" and "Y" batteries disbanded, and personnel reassorted. Weather unsettled	
	19th	11a.m.	"X", "Y", and "Z" batteries moved back to FRECHENCOURT. Great difficulty with the lorries owing to the mud.	
AMIENS.	21st	5.p.m.	Billeted in the village with the D.A.C.	
		noon	"X" and "Y" batteries proceeded to entrain at SALEUX near AMIENS, "Z" battery to LONGEAU. Bivouaced near the station.	
STEENWERCKE	22nd	8-46am	"X" and "Y" batteries entrained for STEENBECQUE. "Z" battery for BAILLEUL. Billeted at night at LE ROSSIGNOL, STEENWERKE, having come there in lorries.	"Y" battery reformed
ARMENTIERES	24th		"X" battery relieved X/18 battery in ARMENTIERES, and "Z" battery relieved Z/18 in ERQUINGHEM-LYS.	
	26th		"Y" battery took over the centre sector of Divisional front and billeted in I.1.c.1½.12.6½. All ammunition taken over from the 18th Division was in very bad condition.	
	29th		"X" battery registered hostile wire and parepet about LILLE ROAD with 5 rounds. There was considerable artillery retaliation. Weather wet.	
	30th	5.p.m.	"X" battery bombarded hostile wire and parapet about LILLE Road from "CHARD'S FARM" SALIENT with 3 guns. 28 rounds fired. Heavy rain and retaliation. Enemy blew up one Stokes detachment and ammunition, damaging a medium emplacements well. 20 D.A.C men per medium battery were attached for digging from this date.	
	31st	4.p.m.	"X" battery fired 18 rounds on the same target as before	
	SEPT 1st	2.pm	"X" battery again fired 16 rounds from CHARD'S FARM SALIENT.	
	3rd	pm	"X" battery registered, hostile wire to the left of RUE DU BOIS SALIENT, and also fired a few more founds from CHARDS FARM.	
	5th		"X" battery fired 30 rounds from CHARD'S FARM. "Z" battery damaged hostile wire and trenches about LE BRIDOUX.	
	7th		"X" battery fired 19 rounds on to hostile wire. "Y" battery fired 45 rounds on hostile wire 400 yds to the right of RUE DU BOIS SALIENT. Excellent results.	

1875 Wt. W593/826 1,000,000 4/15 J.B.C. & A. A.D.S.S./Forms/C. 2118.

Army Form C. 2118

WAR DIARY
or
INTELLIGENCE SUMMARY
(Erase heading not required.)

Instructions regarding War Diaries and Intelligence Summaries are contained in F.S. Regs., Part II. and the Staff Manual respectively. Title Pages will be prepared in manuscript.

Place	Date	Hour	Summary of Events and Information	Remarks and references to Appendices
ARMENTIERES	8th	3.p.m.	"X" battery fired 28 rounds to the left of GERMAN HOUSE. Considerable damage was done.	
	9th		"Y" battery fired on to same target as before, and cut wire. At this time "Z" battery fired occasionally to register various new positions.	
	10th		The D.A.C. digging parties left the batteries. About this time "Y" battery fired one round, which fell short into "No-man's land". "X" battery fired 23 rounds from CHARD'S F ARM, and also considerably damaged wire in front of "SNIPERS HOUSE".	
	11th		"Y" battery effectively cut wire as before.	
	12th		"X" & "Z" batteries both cut wire in right Brigade's sector.	
	13th		"X" & "Y" batteries cut wire in same places as before, and also damaged hostile parapet. All three batteries cut wire in their zones, results being especially successful. 9½ rounds fired. Heavy retaliation.	
	14th	10-30am	"Z" battery fired 49 rounds on various targets in its zone in accordance with right group scheme.	
	15th		"Z" battery fired 9 rounds.	
	16th	12-15am.	"Y" battery co-operated with left groupe R.F.A. in raid scheme. Fired 73 rounds on to hostile trenches	
			"X" battery fired 40 rounds; night wet.	
			"Z" battery fired 8 rounds during the day. No 1 emplacement smashed.	
		5-30pm	"Y" battery fired 8 rounds effectively.	
			"X" battery fired again in the evening, about 35 rounds.	
	17th.		"Z" Battery fired 24 rounds in retaliation for hostile 'minnies'	
	19th.		"Z" Battery fired three rounds Registration.	
		6-30 a.m.	"X" Battery fired on hostile wire and parapet.	
	20th.	5-20p.m.	"X" Battery fired 18 rounds, bad shooting owing to the wet.	
			"Y" Battery fired 9 rounds, -do-	
	21st.	3-55p.m.	"Y" Battery successfully fired two rounds.	
	22nd.	4 p.m.	"Y" Battery took their Guns out of the Line to form part of FRANKS' FORCE.	
	23rd.	4.5p.m.	"X" Battery successfully fired on the hostile parapet.	
			"X" Battery successfully fired on the hostile parapet.	
			"X" Battery cut wire in several places supported by Howitzer fire, "Y" Battery fired two Rounds. One fell in hostile communication Trench the other burst in the air over the hostile support Line.	
	24th.	3-30 p.m.	"Z" Battery fired 23 rounds retaliation for 'Milcans'	
			"Z" Battery fired 150 rounds completely destroying a large part of the hostile parapet.	
			"X" Battery fired 35 Rounds.	

1875 Wt. W593/826 1,000,000 4/15 J.B.C. & A. A.D.S.S./Forms/C.2118.

WAR DIARY
or
INTELLIGENCE-SUMMARY

Army Form C. 2118

Place	Date	Hour	Summary of Events and Information	Remarks and references to Appendices
ARMENTIERES.	25th.	noon	"X" Battery fired 15 rounds.	
		4 p.m.	-do-	
	26th.	4 p.m.	"Z" Battery fired 5 rounds. "Y" Battery fired 2 rounds. Both burst in hostile Front Line, considerably short of where they should have burst.	
	27th.	3-30pm.	A combined Artillery shoot in Right and Left Groups. "X" and "Z" Batteries took part successfully. 2 Casualties. 159 Rounds fired.	
	28th.		"Z" Battery fired 71 Rounds, damaging hostile parapet and wire considerably.	
	29th.		"X" Battery expended 35 rounds in wire-cutting. "Z" Battery fired 4 rounds in registration.	
	30th.	10 p.m.	"Z" Battery fired two rounds Registration. "X" Battery fired 15 rounds in support of a successful raid, during which a prisoner was captured.	

SECRET.

REPORT

IN CONNECTION WITH THE FIRING OF THE "STOKES" GUNS AND 1½" and 3.7" TRENCH HOWITZERS.

Reference 34 Div. G.S./18/42.

(1)   As pre-arranged, at 2 p.m., two Stokes guns opened rapid fire on the German Salient in the vicinity of GERMAN HOUSE.

One Gun (No.2) fired from an emplacement in I.21.3 and the other (No.1) from an emplacement in the right end of the Chord line. Positions are marked "A" and "B" respectively on attached sketch of trenches.

Targets selected for No. 2 gun were in the front line trenches in the N.E. face of the German Salient – points marked "a" on sketch. No. 1 gun fired at GERMAN HOUSE and points marked "b" on sketch.

(2)   No. 2 gun was ordered to fire 50 rounds in three minutes opening fire with 10 rounds ranging at 380 yards then lengthening 10 yards every 10 rounds to 420 yards while slowly traversing right and left of /central target, while No. 1 gun was to fire 50 rounds in three minutes starting with 10 rounds ranging at 350 yards on GERMAN HOUSE and then traversing right and left of the right edge of GERMAN HOUSE fire 40 rounds on points b, b, b, and GERMAN HOUSE.

The enemy opened fire at 1.50 with H.E., and shrapnelled No. 2 gun emplacement slightly wounding one man standing near and it was not until 1.59 that both guns were ready for action.

(3)   Observing from a point in our Salient immediately opposite GERMAN HOUSE, it was evident that enemy were unaware of the intention to shell their salient for smoke from several fires

was...

was observed at 2 p.m. when shells from both guns struck the targets almost at the same instant. For two minutes an accurate and destructive fire was poured into GERMAN HOUSE and trenches, bomb proof timbers, pieces of trench boards and sheets of corrugated iron being hurled into the air and deposited on parapet, which was breached in one place.

(4) Both guns were firing at first at the rate of 25 rounds a minute, but after firing 18 rounds and landing most of these into target, the base plate of No. 1 gun shifted and the gun went off the target the shells dropping short into the German wire.

The gun was immediately ordered out of action but before "cease fire" another 8 rounds were in the air or falling and of these 3 fell almost on to our parapet in front line trenches of Salient.

(5) The bed of No. 2 gun stood the strain better and was worked splendidly for at the expiration of one minute and fifty seconds it had fired 51 rounds although the base plate started to sink after 40 rounds and caused shorts and bursts in the air.

(6) An examination of the emplacement of No. 1 gun disclosed the fact that the base plate had been driven into the prepared bed and elevated the gun barrel abnormally. When the cap was removed from the gun barrel it was found that the striker had unscrewed and was quite loose.

(7) The base plate of No. 2 gun was in the same condition, while the thumbscrew, securing the periscope, had been broken off and the collar, into which the howitzer fits, was twisted. (This was probably due to the strain thrown on the collar after the base plate had started sinking.)

(8) <u>Construction of beds for Base plate and Gun.</u>

A hole about 2' deep and 2' square was excavated inside

of the prepared emplacement and the bottom of this covered with a small brushwood hurdle. On this hurdle were placed a layer of bags filled with rubble and on that a layer of bags filled with clay. Concrete slabs and another layer of rubble and clay completed the bed for the base plate the surface of which rested on a foundation of rubble, clay, and concrete slabs. The gun barrel was also supported by sand-bags and concrete slabs. The same method was adopted for both guns.

The guns were emplaced behind the parados and specially protected by a sandbagged wall 2' thick by 4' in height.

(9) <u>Method of working the guns, ranging, etc.</u>

The exact range of targets was worked out from aeroplane photo of March 3rd. No ranging was done before opening fire on Monday at 2 p.m.

All the ammunition to be used was prepared and placed inside the emplacement by the right hand side of the gun. On the order ~~as~~ to fire No. 1 on the right of the gun handed to No. 2 who dropped them into the muzzle. No 3 on the ~~right~~ left of the gun worked the elevating screw, between every ten rounds increasing the range (for No. 2 gun) from 380 - 420, and working the traversing gear as pre-arranged. The remainder of the detachment were kept in reserve, - in a bomb proof shelter some distance away. An officer controlled and observed for each gun. In the case of No. 1 gun the distance from Chord (where gun was firing) to Salient, where officer was observing with orderlies was too great and not at all a success. The O.C. No. 2 gun was only a few yards away from his gun.

(10) <u>Ammunition.</u>

Every shell was examined and cleaned an hour before

firing...

firing, and out of 100 rounds 3 were rejected on account of defective "passengers" - not working easy.

Only red cartridges were used range being over 270 yards.

(11) Comments.

The experience gained points to necessity for adjusting the requirements for the base plate foundation, the necessity for a retaining screw for the striker, observation ~~post~~ periscope and telephone from battery to observer. Generally speaking the result aimed at was definitely attained, i.e. rapid and accurate fire was obtained for nearly one minute from both guns and in this time more than 70% of the shells fired did material damage which could be observed without doubt.

Each gun should have at least 3 base plates, for defensive work, and these should be firmly set on definite targets. Thirty rounds rapid from beds similar to those used by us, is the maximum which should be fired. Other suggestions will follow after our investigations are complete, and some more firing is experienced, but it is certain, from the abusive remarks which the enemy shouted across a few hours after our firing, that we did a good deal of damage.

Report on the co-operation of X 34th 1½" Medium and 102/1 3.7" Light Trench Howitzer Batteries with the Stokes Guns.

3.7 Battery. The 3.7 battery was emplaced in pairs at points marked C and D in the salient and ordered to burst shrapnel at 2.03½ over front line trenches of German Salient and entrance to communication trenches marked "c" and "d" on sketch.

The object of timing this battery to open fire ½ minute after artillery commenced was that it would probably

lessen....

lessen the chances of the enemy discovering that we had been using the Stokes gun, i.e. to delude, his observers into thinking that the battery had re-opened fire from salient with shrapnel.   Each gun was instructed to fire 10 rounds rapid with shortened fuze at 80 - 100 yards. A miss fire with No. 2 gun at the 8th round reduced the number of rounds fired in about three minutes to 37.

The result was extremely good: bursting of nearly all shells being well timed and over enemy's parapet.

1½" Medium T.M. Battery.

Two howitzers only were used - one gun firing from the left and one from the right of the salient in specially prepared emplacements marked E and F on sketch.

Targets for these guns were the enemy's support line and communication trenches leading into German Salient.

These mortars opened fire at 2.05½ with 33 lb shells at extreme range (290 yards) which enabled them to just reach the enemy's S line at points "e" and "f", range being shortened after a few rounds to meet points "g".

24 rounds of 33lb shells were fired from the two guns in about 15 minutes and then 5 rounds of 18lb shells were dropped in the vicinity of head of the communication trenches marked "h" on sketch - about 340 yards.

Results appeared very good although not clearly observed from position in salient.

Rifle Grenades.

At 2.10 about 20 Newton rifle grenades were fired from several points in the salient on enemy's front line and S line in rear of the German Salient.

Lieut.
34th Divisional T.M. Officer.

15-3-16.

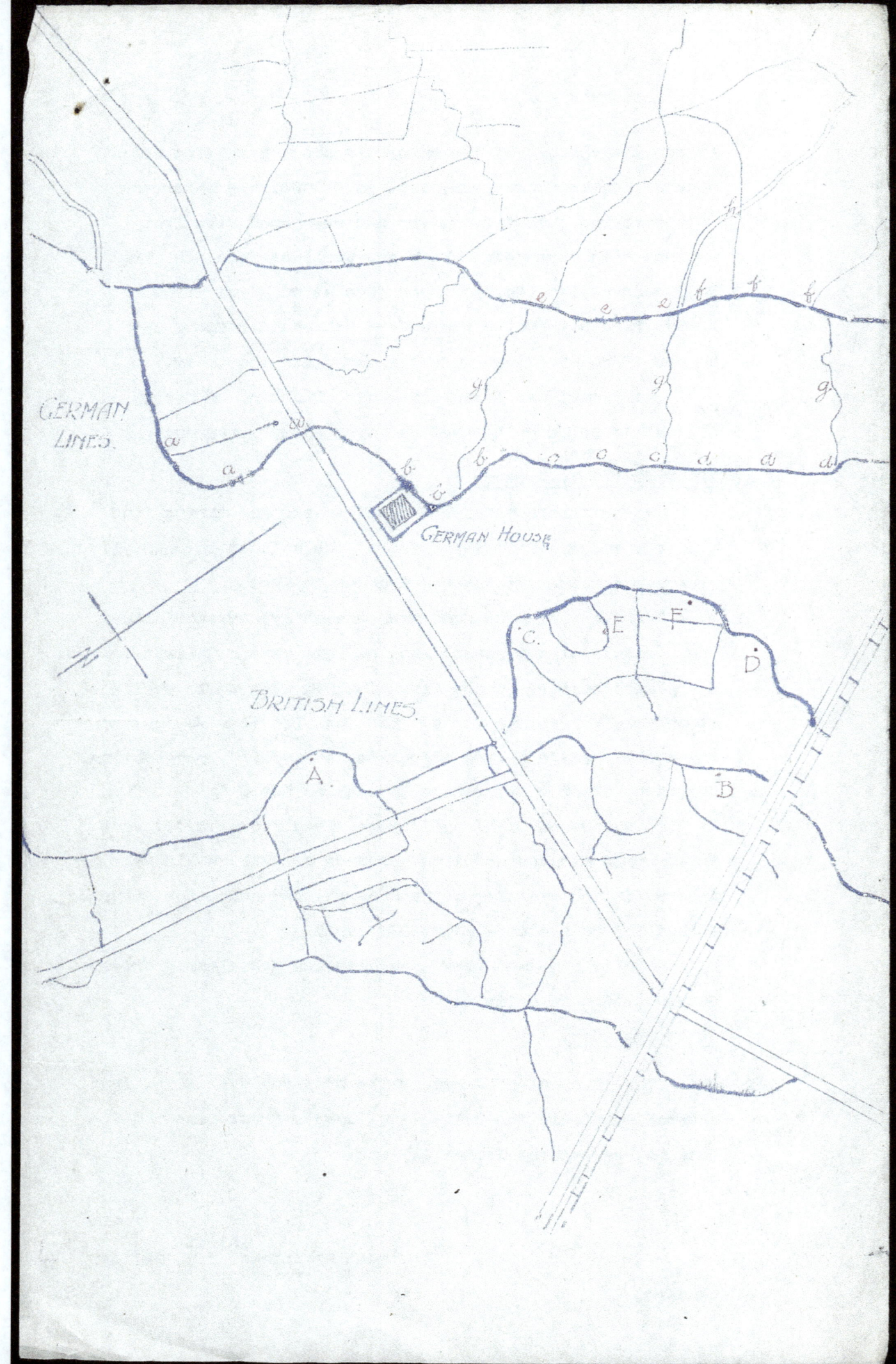

Vol 2

Confidential
War Diary
- of -
34th Division T.M. Btys.

From 1st to 31st Octr. 1916.

Army Form C. 2118

WAR DIARY
or
INTELLIGENCE SUMMARY
(Erase heading not required.)

Instructions regarding War Diaries and Intelligence Summaries are contained in F.S. Regs., Part II. and the Staff Manual respectively. Title Pages will be prepared in manuscript.

Place	Date	Hour	Summary of Events and Information	Remarks and references to Appendices
ARMENT- IERES.	Oct 1	4.0 am	"Z" battery fired 38 rounds in support of a successful raid	
		8.0 am	"Y" battery fired 2 rounds, both of which burst in the hostile communication-trench, doing considerable material damage.	
	2	12.30 pm	"X" battery fired 20 rounds, "Y" battery ("FRANK'S FORCE") 8.	
	3		"Y" battery (F.F.) fired 38 rounds, "Z" battery 23 rounds. Heavy retaliation.	
	4	11 am	"Y" battery (F.F.) fired 20 rounds. "X" battery fired 21 rounds. New heavy gun emplacement at I.15.a.0.8. completed. A second 9.45" mortar was allotted to "Y" battery.	
	5		"X" battery fired 25 rounds, "Y" battery (F.F.) 50 rounds. "Z" battery 8 rounds. Enemy shelled WHITE CITY with 5.9s.	
	6	3 pm	"Z" battery fired 206 rounds. Excellent results. Heavy retaliation. Dr Hydes wounded.	
			"X" battery fired 32 rounds.	
		3.30 pm	"Y" battery fired 2 rounds, 2D a blind, from new emplacement.	
			"Y" battery (F.F.) fired 20 rounds.	

WAR DIARY
or
INTELLIGENCE SUMMARY

(Erase heading not required.)

Army Form C. 2118

Instructions regarding War Diaries and Intelligence Summaries are contained in F.S. Regs., Part II. and the Staff Manual respectively. Title Pages will be prepared in manuscript.

Place	Date	Hour	Summary of Events and Information	Remarks and references to Appendices
ARMENTI-ERES.	Oct. 7	a.m. 1.20.	"Y" battery fired 71 rounds in support of an unsuccessful raid by FRANKS FORCE. Heavy retaliation. Lieut. BURLING-HAM and 3 O.R. wounded.	
		p.m. 4.30	"X" battery fired 18 rounds.	
	8	p.m. 2.15	"Y" battery (F.F.) fired 30 rounds. "X" battery fired 33 rounds, wire-cutting. "Z" battery fired 5 rounds.	
	9	noon	"Z" battery fired 10 rounds, wire-cutting. "Y" battery (F.F.) fired 8 rounds. "Y" battery fired 4 rounds successfully from I.15.a.08. 2nd round burst in air. "X" battery damaged wire at I.21.a.51. "X" battery fired 28 rounds, at various times during the day. "Z" battery fired 43 rounds.	
	10		"Y" battery fired 31 rounds. "Z" battery effectively fired 50 rounds. Considerable retaliation. "Y" battery fired 13 rounds.	
	11		"X" battery fired some rounds into hostile wire. Erratic owing to wind. "Y" battery fired on "German House" 5 rounds; 1 Klaxon. Wind which was gusty spoiled shooting.	
	12	p.m. 7.30	"Y" battery fired 78 rounds, "X" battery fired rounds, "V" battery fired 73 rounds in raid.	

WAR DIARY or INTELLIGENCE SUMMARY

Army Form C. 2118

(Erase heading not required.)

Place	Date	Hour	Summary of Events and Information	Remarks and references to Appendices
ARMENTIÈRES	Oct 13		"X" battery fired 25 rounds	
	14,16		"X" battery fired 45 rounds	
	16	5pm	"X" battery fired 15 rounds < "X" battery again cut wire	
			"N" battery also fired	
	17	11am	"X" battery fired 15 rounds. "Z" battery fired 30 rounds	
	18		"Y" battery fired 18 rounds. "X" battery cut wire	
	19		"V" battery fired 4 rounds into GERMAN HOUSE, but fifth (?round) went apparently short — only about 100 yards from the gun. Probably due to watch change. "X" battery cut wire at I.22.a.7½.8½ and at I.27.a.½.8½ "Z" battery registered.	
	20	11am	"X" battery fired a few rounds in the afternoon to clear up lanes in the hostile wire. "Y" battery also fired during the afternoon. An unsuccessful raid was attempted at 10.35pm. "Z" battery fired 97 rounds very successfully but "X" battery had bad luck with all 3 (?rifles) mechanism going wrong at the start. Hence only 4 rounds fired. Retaliation light. Casualties nil. "Y" battery also participated in an offensive (?scheme) in FRANKS FORCE	

Army Form C. 2118

WAR DIARY
or
INTELLIGENCE SUMMARY
(Erase heading not required.)

Instructions regarding War Diaries and Intelligence Summaries are contained in F.S. Regs., Part II. and the Staff Manual respectively. Title Pages will be prepared in manuscript.

Place	Date	Hour	Summary of Events and Information	Remarks and references to Appendices
ARMENTIERES.	Oct 21	noon	30 rounds were very effectively fired by Z battery on hostile parapet between I.26.b.7.3.6. & 7½.3.	
	22	3pm	2 rounds were experimentally fired from a truck. "Z" battery fired 20 rounds; good effect.	
		2.30 pm	"X" battery fired 22 rounds	
	23		"Y" battery (F.F.) fired 27 rounds. "X" battery fired 25 rounds. "Z" battery fired 15 rounds. Owing to a premature which killed a Bdr SMITH and wounded Cpl WINN, battery ceased fire.	
	24	pm	"X" battery did two shoots of 20 rounds each. Retaliation rather severe.	
			"V" battery fired 2 round; failure. One dropped short in our own front line; the second only 200 yards from the guns; latter a dud.	
	25	am	"X" battery fired on hostile wire and parapet.	
	26	pm	"X" battery cut wire both morning and afternoon. Hostile T.M. activity increased considerably from this date.	

WAR DIARY
or
INTELLIGENCE SUMMARY
(Erase heading not required.)

Army Form C. 2118

Place	Date	Hour	Summary of Events and Information	Remarks and references to Appendices
ARMEN-TIERES	Oct: 27	3. p.m.	"Z" battery fired 60 rounds in a successful wire-cutting programme at I.31.d.7½.5½. The parapet was also hit.	
		2.30. p.m.	"X" battery fired from I.26.c.9.1. to I.26.c.8.0. 101st L.T.M.B. cooperated. "X" battery damaged the hostile wire and parapet at I.21.c.6⅔.15.	
		3.45 p.m.	"X" battery cut wire at I.22.a.7.9.	
	28		Hostile retaliation, especially with mortars, was considerable. "X" battery cooperated with Left Group, 34th D.A. and H.A. 2nd ANZAC in bombardment of the hostile parapet from I.21.c.73.22 to 30.05.	
	29		Hostile Trench Mortars again very active. "X" battery co-operated in shoot by Left Group.	
	30	11 a.m.	"X" battery fired on wire at I.21.c.62.15. Shooting erratic, owing to wind.	
		3.15 p.m.	"X" battery fired on wire at I.22.a.75.82.	
		5.30 p.m.	"Y" battery in 'trunks' force, took part in a bombardment to the left of LILLE ROAD, and fired 52 rounds. Retaliation not extensive.	
	31	11 a.m.	"X" battery fired on wire in several places, doing considerable damage.	
		2.20 p.m.		
		3.30 p.m.	"Z" battery fired 50 rounds, doing considerable damage to hostile wire and parapet. Retaliation rather slight.	

Confidential

Vol 3

War Diary

— of —

34th Division T.M. Btys.

From 1st to 30th Novr. 1916.

Volume III

WAR DIARY
or
INTELLIGENCE SUMMARY

(Erase heading not required.)

Army Form C. 2118

3rd Div. T.M.Bn.

Place	Date	Hour	Summary of Events and Information	Remarks and references to Appendices
ARMENTIERES.	Nov 1st	4 pm	"X" battery registered hostile trenches to the left of the RUE DU BOIS SAILLENT very successfully. Guns in AVONDALE ROAD emplacement fired 41 rounds at maximum range (573°) of which one failed to explode. Guns to the right of WINE AVENUE fired three rounds left traverse. A NEWTON bed was inserted about 75° to the left of the latter in the front line. The weather was stormy.	
	2nd	12.30 pm	Right and left groups R.A. carried out a successful bombardment of hostile defences, in which "Z" and "X" batteries cooperated, the former got off 75 rounds and receiving a certain amount of retaliation. Mechanical trouble prevents the firing of more rounds. Hostile mortars were active in the right sector.	
		2.30 pm	"X" battery had an especially successful shoot firing 150 rounds with great effect on targets registered the day before. Practically no retaliation. "Y" battery in Franks' force, fired 22 rounds. Weather still wet and unsettled.	
	3rd		"X" battery fired in the morning and again in the afternoon. A Great Lane was cut at I.22.a. I.21.c.62.15, and a man hole lane at I.22.a.7.9. Ammunition expended: 60 rounds. "Y" battery fired 24 rounds in support of a raid in Franks' force. Great trouble with rifle mechanisms, otherwise more rounds would have been fired. "Z" battery continued to work on positions, and did not fire.	
	6pm			

WAR DIARY or INTELLIGENCE SUMMARY

Army Form C. 2118

3rd Div. I.M.Bty

(Erase heading not required.)

Instructions regarding War Diaries and Intelligence Summaries are contained in F.S. Regs., Part II. and the Staff Manual respectively. Title Pages will be prepared in manuscript.

Place	Date	Hour	Summary of Events and Information	Remarks and references to Appendices
ARMENTIÈRES	Nov. 4th	2.30 pm to 4 pm	"Z" battery seriously damaged hostile wire and parapet from I.31.a.80.55 to I.32.c.75.20 in a successful shoot. The shoot proved very with 3 guns. 158 rounds were fired. Very considerable retaliation with "minnies". Very good results were obtained from the use of a concrete bed.	J.Lyon Lt-Col
		3.15 pm	"Z" battery fired 13 more rounds.	
		4.10 pm to 4.25 pm	During the day "X" battery fired 24 rounds on the hostile frontline defences, and especially the wire at I.22.a.7.9.; where a good lane was cut. Considerable difficulty was experienced in obtaining ammunition for expenditure during the next few days.	
	5th "		"Z" battery fired nine rounds registering, one of which blew up a bomb-store at I.26.c.9.2. "X" battery did not fire and was mainly concerned in the relaying of beds.	
	6th "	2.25 am	"Z" battery opened fire from 3 guns on machine-gun emplacement at I.32.a.4.6.30. and I.26.c.8.0.; and drew hostile minenwerfer fire by bombarding I.26.c.8.0. – I.26.d.05.20. 48 rounds were fired; weather very wet.	
		2. pm to 2.30 pm	"Z" battery fired 67 rounds on the following targets: I.26.b.75.45. and I.26.d.2.5. for 40 or 50 yards on either side of the former the hostile parapet had been completely levelled. Retaliation on the right, severe	

WAR DIARY
or
INTELLIGENCE SUMMARY

(Erase heading not required.)

Army Form C. 2118

2nd Div. 2 M Bde

3

Place	Date	Hour	Summary of Events and Information	Remarks and references to Appendices
ARMENTIÈRES (cont)	6	am & pm	Both morning and afternoon "X" battery fired on the hostile wire to the right of the ARMENTIÈRES - WAVRIN Railway. excellent results were obtained, in spite of very wet weather and heavy retaliation.	147 rounds
		pm	"Y" battery fired 59 rounds, to which retaliation was slight.	
	7	am	"X" battery registered in left subsector with 3 rounds. An unsuccessful raid took place in the night in(to?) gate 3 which was supported by "Z" battery who fired 20 rounds. "X" battery created a diversion by firing 20 rounds, but further firing was stopped. Heavy hostile mortar and whizz-bang fire. Torrents of rain fell almost throughout the day, and most of the gun pits were flooded.	
	8	am & pm	"X" battery fired 51 rounds in two shoots in the left subsector. Retaliation light. "Z" battery fired 4 rounds.	
	9	4.30 am	"X" and "Z" batteries each fired 8 rounds in conjunction with R.A. Group scheme.	
		am & pm	"Y" battery fired 42 rounds, to which retaliation consisted almost entirely of "4.2" duds.	

WAR DIARY
or
INTELLIGENCE SUMMARY

Army Form C. 2118

3rd Div. 2 MBhy

Place	Date	Hour	Summary of Events and Information	Remarks and references to Appendices
ARMENTIERES.	Nov. 10	9am / pm	"X" battery fired 40 rounds on the hostile wire at I.22.a.79. and I.16.a.1.25. Much work was done on emplacements which had suffered considerably owing to rain, especially by "Z" battery who did not fire.	
	11		No firing all day owing to relief of the infantry. "X" battery fired 20 rounds into hostile wire at I.22.a.79.	"Y" Battery fired 24h
	12			
	13	4.30 am	"X" battery fired 88 rounds in support of a raid by the left Brigade. Raid unsuccessful. Retaliation light, except near WHITE HORSE trench.	
	14		"Z" battery fired 10 rounds.	
	15	2.30 pm	"Y" battery fired 45 rounds. No firing took place. "Y" battery fired 30 rounds. "X" battery registered with 3 rounds to the right of the railway.	
	16	3pm / pm	"X" and "Z" batteries took part in a combined artillery bombardment. Each battery fired two series during the afternoon, the former totaling 145 rounds, the latter 101. Gunner Bennett of "Z" battery wounded by shrapnel in head and neck. Weather exceptionally fine (but cold).	
		11pm	"Y" battery, in Franks' fore fired 35 rounds.	

WAR DIARY or INTELLIGENCE SUMMARY

Army Form C. 2118

2/6 Div. In. Bde.

Place	Date	Hour	Summary of Events and Information	Remarks and references to Appendices
ARMENTIERES	17	2:30 pm	Captain C. Filsbury O.C. "X" battery, and R.S.M. Lilley wounded slightly. "X" battery fired 30 rounds.	
		4 pm	"X" battery fired 30 rounds. Weather very cold.	
	18		Wet and Stormy. "X" battery fired 60 rounds on the hostile wire at I.21.d.5,14 and I.16.a.25.5. "Z" battery carried out some experiments with firing 3" Stokes ammunition with 2 tails. Good results,— but retaliation considerable. "Y" battery fired 10 rounds. "Z" battery moved billets from H.4.a.27.62 to H.23.a.05.05.	Targets:— X: I.16.a.25.5. Z: I.21.c.23.0. Z: I.26.b.8.1. I.26.b.5.75.43
	19		"Z" battery fired 50 rounds. "X" battery successfully fired 60 rounds in two series. Results good.	I.26.b.8.7 † (+ 20 NZ) *Targets:—
	20		"Y" battery fired 38 rounds. "Z" battery fired 60 rounds. "X"*battery fired 43 rounds, to which the retaliation, for firing on the right especially, was very heavy.	(X: I.21.c.5.14 I.16.a.25.5 Z: I.31.a.4.5 I.31.a.9.7
	21	12:30 am to 2:30 am	FRANKS' FORCE. "Y" battery fired 780 rounds in support of a raid in former: I.21.c.22.0. & I.16.a.25.5.; Latter: I.26.b.7.3. & I.26.a.6.75. "X" battery fired 30 rounds, "Z" battery 40 rounds. Targets for	

WAR DIARY or INTELLIGENCE SUMMARY

Army Form C. 2118

8th Div. M.Arty

(Erase heading not required.)

Place	Date	Hour	Summary of Events and Information	Remarks and references to Appendices
ARMENTIÈRES	Nov 22		"X" battery fired 44 rounds on the following targets:- I.16.a.25.5., I.21.a.5.b.4. and I.21.c.22.0. Enemy retaliates with 4.2"s and 15 pdrs heavily.	6
	23	3.30 pm	"Z" battery fired 102 rounds at I.26.84.03., I.21.c.22.0. Retaliation Moderate.	
			"X" battery fired 72 rounds, to which retaliation was heavy. Targets: I.21.c.5.14., I.21.c.22.0. and I.16.a.25.5. "Z" battery fired 68 rounds. Much trouble with rifle mechanism and sights.	
			"Y" battery fired 58 rounds.	
		8.7 pm	"X" battery fired 51 rounds in support of a particularly successful raid. Targets to the right of the railway and where railway enters hostile parapet. Retaliation very heavy.	
	24		There was no action out of "Z" battery being temporarily owing to unserviceable rifle-mechanisms. Present: and gun platforms. Work was continued on positions.	BSM. J. Nelson RFA, Bars: E. Massey "Y" E. Hull "X" H. Sharpe "Z" C. Barrett "Y" RGA Bdr Morris RGA
	25		Very wet all day. Work on a concrete emplacement was commenced on the left near WHITE HORSE trench.	
	26		No firing. Weather damp and misty. Work continued on emplacements. Presentation of award at D.H.Q. (CROIX DU BAC)	

WAR DIARY
or
INTELLIGENCE SUMMARY

(Erase heading not required.)

Army Form C. 2118

2nd Div. 2 M.B/1p

Instructions regarding War Diaries and Intelligence
Summaries are contained in F.S. Regs., Part II.
and the Staff Manual respectively. Title Pages
will be prepared in manuscript.

Place	Date	Hour	Summary of Events and Information	Remarks and references to Appendices
ARMENTIÈRES	Nov. 27		Very quiet; no firing.	
	28		A thick fog obscured all observation; but "X" battery fired 20 rounds into the hostile wire at I.22.a.15.45.	
	29	1 pm	"Z" battery fired 72 rounds from position in left sub-sector. One rifle-mechanism broke, and both beds used subsided. "X" battery fired 75 rounds on the hostile wire at I.21.b.5.27., I.21.b.6.8.18, and I.21.b.33.23, doing considerable damage.	I.26.b.8.5.
	30		"X" battery fired 70 rounds. Lane cut at I.22.a.29.56. Wire damaged at I.22.a.15.45 and I.22.a.43.75.	
	30		"Z" battery fired 58 rounds on the hostile wire at I.26.b.6.0. and I.26.b.8.5, doing considerable damage, especially at the former. The weather was cold, but dry which greatly facilitates the maintenance of good trees for firing.	

Vol 4

Confidential

War Diary

— of —

34th Division T.M. Batteries.

From 1st to 31st Decr. 1916

Volume. 4.

Army Form C. 2118

WAR DIARY
or
INTELLIGENCE SUMMARY

(Erase heading not required.)

Instructions regarding War Diaries and Intelligence Summaries are contained in F. S. Regs., Part II. and the Staff Manual respectively. Title Pages will be prepared in manuscript.

Place	Date	Hour	Summary of Events and Information	Remarks and references to Appendices
ARMENTIERES	Dec. 1st	p.m. 1, 2, & 3.	"X" battery fired 33 rounds at the following targets: I.22.a.54.82., I.16.a.25.5.8., and I.21.b.5.27. Observation, owing to the mist was very difficult, but results seemed satisfactory at the two latter places. Retaliation fairly heavy. "Z" battery fired 50 rounds at I.26.c.84.03. Observation difficult, retaliation normal. Lieut. [W.] G. Wyllie, 19th M.G., "X" battery, awarded the Military Cross.	
	2nd		"X" battery considerably damaged the hostile wire at I.21.b.68.18., I.21.b.83.23., and I.21.a.15.45. 70 rounds fired. "Z" battery fired at hostile wire I.31.a.0.3. 20 rounds fired. Hostile Mortars were active in the Right Sector.	
	3rd	2.20 p.m.	"Y" battery fired 15 rounds. "Y" battery fired 30 rounds. "Z" battery cut wire at I.26.c.84.03., 68 rounds being fired.	
		1.45 p.m.	Hostile Mortars were again very active in the right sector, but were silenced by Group Retaliation. "X" battery cut wire at I.22.a.29.56., I.22.a.43.75. and I.22.a.54.82. Rounds fired: 66.	
	4th		Weather damp, but slightly warmer. "X" battery damaged or cut wire at I.16.a.25.50., I.21.b.50.27. and I.21.b.68.18. 65 rounds were fired. "Z" battery fired 38 rounds in cutting hostile wire at I.31.a.44.5. and I.32.c.09.9. Retaliation was extremely heavy.	[signature] O/C Batt.

1875 Wt. W593/826 1,000,000 4/15 J.B.C. & A. A.D.S.S./Forms/C. 2118.

WAR DIARY
or
INTELLIGENCE SUMMARY.
(Erase heading not required.)

Army Form C. 2118.

Place	Date	Hour	Summary of Events and Information	Remarks and references to Appendices
ARMEN-TIERES	Dec. 4th		The enemy blew away our parapet with 5.9" H.E. immediately in front of "Z" battery's right gun, leaving the detachment exposed to rifle-fire. For this reason only 15 rounds were fired from this gun. Right Group retaliation failed to quell hostile mortars, which were active.	
	5th	2.30 pm	"X" battery fired 105 rounds on the hostile wire at I.27.a.05.85, I.21.b.83.23., I.22.a.15.45. and I.22.a.29.56. Lanes were cut in all these places.	
			"Z" battery fired 40 rounds, causing much damage to the hostile wire at I.26.a.18.50. Group retaliation by Right Group succeeded in silencing the hostile mortars.	
	6th	1.30 pm	"Y" battery fired 54 rounds. "X" battery fired 75 rounds, cutting wire at I.21.c.61.16., I.22.a.43.75.0., I.22.a.54.82. and I.16.Z.25.50. "Z" battery widened a lane at I.26.b.18.50. and further damaged the COURAU DE LA CHAPELLE. 28 rounds fired. Lieut. (A.S. Bell, R.F.A., "Z" battery awarded the military Cross.	G.O.Bailey B/S/O L Capt.
	7th	3.10 pm	"X" battery cut wire at I.21.b.68.18., I.22.a.15.45, I.22.a. 29.56. and I.21.b.8.23. 80 rounds were fired in all. Right Group retaliates for hostile Mortar fire.	

Army Form C. 2118.

WAR DIARY
or
INTELLIGENCE SUMMARY.
(Erase heading not required.)

Instructions regarding War Diaries and Intelligence Summaries are contained in F. S. Regs., Part II. and the Staff Manual respectively. Title pages will be prepared in manuscript.

Place	Date	Hour	Summary of Events and Information	Remarks and references to Appendices
ARMENTIÈRES	Dec 8th	P.m.	"X" battery cut wire at I.21.b.5.27., I.22.a.15.45., I.22.a.29.56. and I.16.d. 25.5. Some retaliation, especially with minenwerfer. "V" battery fired 7 rounds most successfully with new 17 03 charge at the hostile support line behind GERMAN HOUSE SALIENT. One machine enemy retaliated with 4.2" and 15 pdr. One stray shot rattled close. All rounds went full distance. "X" battery fired 80 rounds in all. A hostile mortar was active, firing from I.22.a.52.0. Group retaliation was carried out by both Groups for hostile mortar fire.	1 airburst
	9th		Weather very wet. "Y" battery fired 15 rounds. "Z" battery fired 3 rounds, all direct hits on hostile trench I.26.b.72.45 in retaliation for hostile mortars, and 2 rounds registration. "X" battery fired 66 rounds. Targets: I.22.a.29.56., I.27.a.05.85. and I.21.b. 68.18. Good results, and but little retaliation.	SyOct
	10th		"Y" battery fired 15 rounds. "Z" battery fired 5 rounds in retaliation for hostile mortars but fine, with good results. "X" battery fired 55 rounds. Targets: I.21.b.68.18., I.21.b.83.25., I.22.b. a.15.45. and I.22.a. 29.56. Retaliation rather light. Both groups carried out group retaliation for hostile mortar fire during the day.	

Army Form C. 2118.

WAR DIARY
or
INTELLIGENCE SUMMARY.
(Erase heading not required.)

Place	Date	Hour	Summary of Events and Information	Remarks and references to Appendices
ARMENTIERES	Dec 11th	1 am	"X" battery fired 45 rounds in support of a successful raid by the left brigade. 3 prisoners (unwounded) were captured, whilst our casualties were 2 killed. "Z" battery fired 26 rounds, to draw and locate a hostile mortar, weather was too foggy. Target: I.26.c.9. N.B. During the raid, "X" battery observed a hostile machine-gun firing, and silenced it.	
	12th		Very wet and gloomy; no firing. Left sector, hostile TMs active. The detachment of "V" battery at "Frank's Force" has a successful shot, but afterwards the enemy bombarded the neighbourhood of the emplacement with heavy mortar, the sixth of these rounds landed right on the emplacement, killing Sgt. Geddes M.M. and seriously wounding 2ND LT. T.S. CHEADLE R.F.A. and an R.E. officer R.A.F. "Y" battery in "Frank's Force", fired 30 rounds.	6 rounds
	13th	2.47 pm	"X" battery fired 17 rounds at the hostile were at I.26.c. 87.78. 5 of these were silent, and very irregular in flight, probably owing to badly filled shell. Hostile retaliation brisk, with 15 PDRs, 4.2 Gas mortars, the first two from 91 being especially close. "Y" battery fired 48 rounds.	[signature]

Army Form C. 2118.

WAR DIARY
or
INTELLIGENCE SUMMARY.
(Erase heading not required.)

Instructions regarding War Diaries and Intelligence Summaries are contained in F. S. Regs, Part II and the Staff Manual respectively. Title pages will be prepared in manuscript.

Place	Date	Hour	Summary of Events and Information	Remarks and references to Appendices
ARMEN-TIERES	Dec 14th		"Z" battery fired 75 rounds on some concrete works visible between I.26.c.77.45 and I.26.c.82.65. These were entirely destroyed, and the front-line trench levelled for 40 yards. "X" battery fired 25 rounds into the hostile wire at I.16.c.3.62. Very heavy retaliation from the hostile Heavy and Light Trench Mortars. The Enemy's "Rum-jars" and heavy Trench mortars were very active in the Right sector, and troop retaliation from the Divisional Artillery failed to silence them.	
	15th	am	"V" battery fired 4 rounds, of which one was blind, into the hostile support line at I.21.c.6.0. to I.21.c.9.0.5. No retaliation. Some misfires with T-tubes.	
		pm	"X" battery fired 25 rounds into the hostile wire at I.22 a.15.45. cutting a lane. Retaliation very light.	
		2.40	"Z" battery fired rounds from new concrete position, in retaliation for the enemy mortar fire at the "BULL'S EYE" position, in retaliation for the enemy mortar fire. Enemy retaliation was also allied for.	

Army Form C. 2118.

WAR DIARY
or
INTELLIGENCE SUMMARY.
(Erase heading not required.)

Instructions regarding War Diaries and Intelligence Summaries are contained in F. S. Regs., Part II. and the Staff Manual respectively. Title pages will be prepared in manuscript.

Place	Date	Hour	Summary of Events and Information	Remarks and references to Appendices
ARNEN-TIERES	Oct. 16th		"Z" battery fired 18 rounds in retaliation for hostile mortar fire from new concrete BULL'S EYE' position. "X" battery cut wire at I.22.a.3.55 and I.21.c.15.0.	Target I.26.c.9.1
	17th		"X" Target fired. "X" battery fired 20 rounds into the hostile wire at I.22.a.3.55. Wire damaged but observation difficult. "Z" battery fired 56 rounds into the hostile wire and parapet at I.32.a.45.32. Retaliation was not	
	18th	2.55 pm	heavy and stopped by fire from right group. "X" battery fired 20 rounds into the hostile wire at I.21.b.68.18.; good results. "Z" battery fired 76 rounds into the hostile wire at I.26.a.3.7 and I.26.a.2.5. Wire practically cut.	f.f.f.(af)
		2.36 pm	Left Group carried out Group retaliation for hostile mortar fire on CHARDS FARM sector.	
	19th		"Y" battery fired 94 rounds in a successful shoot. Retaliation rather light. "V" battery successfully fired 5 rounds at hostile mortar near LARGE FARM. Good shooting very close to target; mortar ceased fire; a broad lane was cut at "Z" battery fired #95 rounds. I.26.a.37.1, and a narrow	

Army Form C. 2118.

WAR DIARY
or
INTELLIGENCE SUMMARY.
(Erase heading not required.)

Instructions regarding War Diaries and Intelligence Summaries are contained in F.S. Regs., Part II and the Staff Manual respectively. Title pages will be prepared in manuscript.

Place	Date	Hour	Summary of Events and Information	Remarks and references to Appendices
ARMENTIÈRES	Dec. 19th		lane at I.26.a.2.5. Retaliation fairly light. Right group carried out group-retaliation at 1.35 pm and 3.20 pm for hostile mortar fire, "X" battery damaged the hostile wire at I.16.c.9.5 "O." firing 25 rounds.	
	20th pm		"V" battery fired 4 rounds at hostile mortar in front of LARGE FARM. Weather exceptionally bright; some aerial activity. "X" battery fired 30 rounds widening an old gap at I.21.b.45.30, and I.21.b.45.28. "X" battery fired 43 rounds into the hostile wire at I.27.a.05.85. Wire and parapet much damaged at both places.	2/Lt J.E.H. [illegible] Captain
	21st 6pm		"Z" battery fired 14 rounds in support of an un-successful raid in Right Sector. Target: I.26.b.6.55.85 Considerable retaliation. "X" battery fired 79 rounds into the hostile wire during the day. Targets: I.22.a. 28.55. and I.27.a. .05. 85. Good results; some lanes cut.	83.7
	22nd		"V" battery fired 4 rounds at hostile T.M. near LARGE FARM.	

WAR DIARY
or
INTELLIGENCE SUMMARY.

(Erase heading not required.)

Army Form C. 2118.

Place	Date	Hour	Summary of Events and Information	Remarks and references to Appendices
ARMENTIE-RES	Sept. 23rd		"Y" battery fired 37 rounds. Weather was very windy, and all T.M. shoots on 34th Divisional front were cancelled in consequence. Very quiet all day. Heavy T.M. section of "V" battery rejoined from "Franks" Force R.A.	
	24th		"X" battery fired 30 rounds; 25 at hostile wire I.22.a.54.80, and 5 to test new platform, at I.31.a.4.4. "Z" battery fired 10 rounds at hostile parapet to test new platform. Unsuccessful. Bomb broke Group retaliation carried out by both bombs. Guns and gun equipment of "Y" battery were returned, - but not personnel.	
	25th		No firing all day.	
	26th		"Z" battery fired 43 rounds at the hostile parapet at I.31.a.4.5. and I.31.a.9.6. in retaliation for hostile minenwerfer. Considerable damage was done, although 8 rounds were "duds", probably due to defective shell-filling. Right Group twice afforded group-retaliation during the day for hostile mortar fire.	

Army Form C. 2118.

WAR DIARY
or
INTELLIGENCE SUMMARY.
(Erase heading not required.)

Place	Date	Hour	Summary of Events and Information	Remarks and references to Appendices
ARMENTIERES	Dec 26th	p.m.	"X" battery fired 25 rounds into the hostile wire at I.21.c.78.28.1. and I.16.c.95.0. Results appeared good, but observation was difficult owing to mist. Left Group attempted group-retaliation for hostile mortar fire on the CHARDS FARM SALIENT once during the day.	
	27th		"Z" battery fired 80 rounds, targets:- I.31.d.53. to I.32.c.1.4. Hostile second line. Much material was thrown up. Retaliation mild. "X" battery fired 50 rounds into the hostile wire at I.22.a.15.45. and I.21.c.82.42. New wire put out since last shoot in both places not yet destroyed. Hostile mortars were fairly active during the afternoon. There was a very thick mist at night.	
	28th		"X" battery fired 35 rounds. Target: I.22.a.54.8. & I.21.c.78.28. 2 gunners wounded by heavy retaliation. Left Group carried out Group retaliation on to hostile mortars.	6/2
	29th		"X" battery fired 60 rounds into the hostile wire at I.22.a. At 75. and I.22.a.15.45. In the latter place a clear lane was cut. Left Group carried out Group retaliation for hostile mortars.	

WAR DIARY
or
INTELLIGENCE SUMMARY

Army Form C. 2118.

(Erase heading not required.)

Place	Date	Hour	Summary of Events and Information	Remarks and references to Appendices
ARMENTIERES	Dec. 29		"Z" battery did not fire owing to Brigade relief. The weather was equally foul.	
	30.		"Y" battery rejoined the 34th Division, and was billeted near by. "V" battery at H.12.c.9.3., 500 yards north of L'ARMEE. Put off action as "X" & "Z" batteries each became 6-gun batteries on the fire line. "X" battery fires 17 rounds into the hostile wire at I.21.c.6.9.30., just north-west of ARMENTIERES-WAVRIN Railway. A lane was cut but much wire still remains. "Z" battery fired 39 rounds, breaching the parapets & cutting wire at I.26.b.81. Hostile onestan on the left sector gave great trouble all day. The weather	
	31st.		"X" battery fired 40 rounds into the hostile wire at I.21.c.82b.42 & I.22.a.4.75. and practically cut clear. left lines carried out retaliation for hostile trench mortar fire, which was considerably above normal. At NEWTON elevating stands were obtained through the R.E. from II. Army Workshops.	

Confidential

Vol 5

War Diary
— of —
34th Division T. M. Btys.

From 1st Jany to 31st Jany 1917.

Volume 5.

WAR DIARY
or
INTELLIGENCE SUMMARY.
(Erase heading not required.)

Army Form C. 2118.

Place	Date	Hour	Summary of Events and Information	Remarks and references to Appendices
ARMENTIÈRES	June 1st	p.m.	"Z" Battery fired 128 rounds at the hostile wire I.31.a.8.6. and I.28.d.18.30. 3 rifle mechanisms blown out, – all of them from one gun. "X" Battery fired 50 rounds on the hostile wire at I.21. c.82.42? and I.22.a.54.80. Lanes were cut almost through in both places.	
	2nd	a.m.	"X" Battery fired 15 rounds, further damaging the hostile wire at I.21.c.79.30. [Retaliation exceptionally heavy with large mortars. Whole attachment buried, but unhurt.] "Z" battery owing to rifle-mechanism troubles, only managed to fire 8 rounds. Target I.26.a.5.7.	
		3.30 p.m.	"V" battery fired 5 rounds of which one was "dud", into enemy's trenches at I.22.a.14. Good results. This	
		3.40 p.m.	was during heavy bombardment of I.16.a. by our heavy Artillery. Enemy retaliated with whizz-bangs and heavy Minnies! At the same time "X" battery fired 4 rounds	
	3rd		"Z" battery fired 105 rounds, in spite of some difficulties with rifle mechanisms. Targets wire at I.26.a.5.7. and I.26.b.8.2. Moderate retaliation. Wire nearly cut. "X" battery obtained new gun No 538 (screws and clips)	

Army Form C. 2118.

WAR DIARY
or
INTELLIGENCE SUMMARY.
(Erase heading not required.)

Place	Date	Hour	Summary of Events and Information	Remarks and references to Appendices
ARMENTIÈRES	3rd	pm	"X" battery fired 35 rounds Targets: I.21.c.82.4.2. and I.21.c. 45.30. Wire was further damaged and cut, but retaliation was exceptionally heavy, with mortars.	
	4th		"X" battery fired 25 rounds each at I.21.c.79.3. and I.16.d.95.0. Retaliation only moderate, 3 rifle-mechanisms casualties. "Z" battery fired 53 rounds at I.26.d.5.7. and I.26. d.18.3. & 3 rifle-mechanisms casualties. "V" battery installed the heavy mortar in the new temporary position near EMMA POST	
	5th		"X" battery fired 25 rounds each into the hostile wire at I.21.d.82.4.2. and I.22.a.15.45. & at about 8pm	
	6th		"X" battery fired 43 rounds into the hostile wire at I.21.c.79.3., where 2 lanes were completed, and I.21.b.68.18, where the wire was damaged. "Y" battery still in reserve, commenced two reserve defensive emplacements in COLLEGE GREEN AVENUE.	
	7th		"Z" battery fired 85 rounds Target I.32.c.08.48. "V" battery fired 5 rounds (1 dud) on OYSTER FARM from new temporary emplacement near EMMA POST. Good shooting, but had damaged.	

A 5834 Wt W4973/M687 750,000 8/16 D. D. & L. Ltd. Forms/C.2118/13.

Army Form C. 2118.

WAR DIARY
or
INTELLIGENCE SUMMARY.
(Erase heading not required.)

Instructions regarding War Diaries and Intelligence Summaries are contained in F.S. Regs., Part II. and the Staff Manual respectively. Title pages will be prepared in manuscript.

Place	Date	Hour	Summary of Events and Information	Remarks and references to Appendices
ARMENTIERES	Jan 7th	am	"X" battery fired 34 rounds into the hostile wire at I.21. c.84.42 and I.21.&.84.2. Lane cut in former case, wire damaged in latter.	
	8th	am 11.45	"Z" battery fired 37 rounds. Target: I.26.a.2.5. Heavy retaliation, 3 rifle-mechanisms blew out. Some retaliation.	
		pm 12.30	"X" battery fired 32 rounds. Targets: 20 rounds on I.22.a.2.9.5 where old gap had been completely filled with new wire. 12 rounds on I.22.a.4.75. Wire was considerably damaged in both places. Observation was particularly good.	
		pm 1.30	about midday "Z" battery fired 91 rounds, of which ten were fired at OYSTER FARM and the remainder at the hostile wire and parapet at I.31.a.73.6 – I.32.c.0.7, cutting lanes (i) at the former and (ii) at I.31.a.87.62. "Y" battery fired 5 rounds at LE BRIDOUX – two good bursts, two inferior, and one blind.	
	9th		"X" battery fired 45 rounds into the hostile wire at I.16.b.83.3 and I.22.a.54.8. Wire was damaged at the former, and nearly cut at the latter. "X" battery fired 69 rounds nearly completing a lane in the hostile wire at I.22.a.67.81.	
	10th			

WAR DIARY or INTELLIGENCE SUMMARY

Army Form C. 2118.

Place	Date	Hour	Summary of Events and Information	Remarks and references to Appendices
ARMENTIÈRES	Jan 10th 11th		"Y" battery relieves "X" battery in the left sector, both batteries retaining their billets. "Y" battery fires 21 rounds into the hostile were at I.22.a.14.43 and I.21.c.79.3. Wire damaged in both places. Right Group carried out Group retaliation for hostile Mortar fire.	
	12		"Y" Battery fired 6 rounds on OYSTER FARM all good bursts numbly good "Y" Battery fired 36 rounds on hostile wire and were I.21.c, 82, 43 and I.22.a 28,56 "Z" Battery fired 103 rounds on hostile wire and were I.26.d 80,85 and I.26.d 95,10 at I.2.c.6,0 no wire or parapet left for 15 yards.	
	13		"Y" Battery fired 14 rounds on wire I.1.d 85,13 and I.22.a 68,41 were damaged. Retgroup fired retaliation over for enemy TMs. Heavy TM brought fire of Y. D—— today and fired onto Parasine S4 pgedoon on 14# 34 × TM Batteries met on return today	
	14		Enemy TM Batteries on Right very active damage was done to 2 OG positions. Right Group artillery carried out Zone front retaliations.	
	15		Captain James Lury Talley late of Y.34 struck off along th on being evacuated sick to England. Y.34 fired 36 rounds were mil and alarm at I.1.d 85,13 and I.22.a 68,81 Z.35 fired 7 and 4 on enemy trench Oyster Farm I.31.d. 95, 38 one hit on Farm and much French material thrown up.	

Army Form C. 2118.

WAR DIARY
or
INTELLIGENCE SUMMARY
(Erase heading not required.)

Instructions regarding War Diaries and Intelligence Summaries are contained in F.S. Regs., Part II. and the Staff Manual respectively. Title Pages will be prepared in manuscript.

Place	Date	Hour	Summary of Events and Information	Remarks and references to Appendices
ARMENTIERES	15		Y 3.4 fired 18 rounds, 4 on Trenches O.I. & 35.95 – O.I.B. 42.68 Buildings at O.I.B. 42.68 and 9 rounds at Trench I.22.a. 20,15. Observed trench material thrown up. These shoots which formed part of Silly scheme when enemy fire which was retaliated to by Field Battery. To 37582 Gr Werbin L.B.I.Y.25. To T.M. operation very near and must.	
	16			
	17		Y 3.4 fired 10 rounds on Communication Trench I.22.a. 20,30 – 15,45 (one (blind) round damage atone.	
	18		Y 3.4 fired 32 rounds at wire at I.22.a. 28,56 line out and I.21.d.84,25 wire damaged. Z " " " 64 " . I.26.d.18,30 considerable number of knights and dark heads thrown up.	
	19		Y B.4 fired 23 rounds onto enemy wire I.21.c.79,38 line out and I.21.c.82,42 old line re-opened Right front retaliated out three front retaliation for T.M. fire.	
	20		Y B.4 fired 22 rounds at wire at I.22.a.14,43 line out and I.22.a.49,75 were damaged. Z " . 45 " at Parapet I.32.c.2,9 parapet knocked in two places. Z " 5 " at I.31.d.5,3 one shed remain good result. V . Retaliation heavy immediate and accurate.	
	21		Z B.4 fired 42 rounds at Trench I.26.6.0 much wire and material thrown up. Enemy T.M. active at I.26.d.78,28 silenced by 18 pdr Battery.	

2449 Wt. W14957/M90 750,000 1/16 J.B.C. & A. Forms/C.2118/12.

Army Form C. 2118.

WAR DIARY
or
INTELLIGENCE SUMMARY
(Erase heading not required.)

Place	Date	Hour	Summary of Events and Information	Remarks and references to Appendices
ARMENTIERES	22		"Y" By fired 39 rounds on to enemy wire and trench and wire at I.22.a.65.91, I.22.a.28.56 and I.21.b.84.25.	
	23		"Y" Battery fired 15 rounds at the hostile wire at I.21.c.80.32, I.21.c.44.15,	
	23		"Y" Battery fired 5 rounds on C.T. at O.16.30.75.	
	24		"Z" Battery fired 20 rounds at wire at I.31.d.40.55. Lieut H.S. Bell M.G. & "Y" Battery fired 6 rounds at trench in O.16.65.85. 2nd Lieut H.Thomas wounded	
	25		"Y" Battery fired 30 rounds at wire at I.22.a.28.56 & I.22.a.40.90.	
	26		"Y" battery further damaged the hostile wire at I.16.a.28.57., I.22.a.28.56. and I.22.a.68.81. 40 rounds were fired.	
	27		All batteries were withdrawn from the line, including guns, W. Heavy Mortars were handed over. 3rd Australian Division took over left sector and New Zealand Division right sector in old billets. Batteries remained in old billets.	
	30		"X" battery returned to the line and took over left sector of left sector for special	

Army Form C. 2118.

WAR DIARY
or
INTELLIGENCE SUMMARY

(Erase heading not required.)

Instructions regarding War Diaries and Intelligence Summaries are contained in F.S. Regs., Part II. and the Staff Manual respectively. Title Pages will be prepared in manuscript.

Place	Date	Hour	Summary of Events and Information	Remarks and references to Appendices
ARMENTIÈRES	Jan 30th	3.15	Wire-cutting operation; "Y" battery took over left sub-sector of Right sector; "X" battery fired 45 rounds into the hostile wire at I.22.a. 45.45 3.58. 4.7. 68.8. Considerable retaliation. "Y" battery arrived in position.	

Trench Mortars.

VOL VI

WAR DIARY
or
INTELLIGENCE SUMMARY

(Erase heading not required.)

Army Form C. 2118.

Place	Date	Hour	Summary of Events and Information	Remarks and references to Appendices
ARMENTI-ERES.	1917 Feb. 1st		"X" battery again cut wire for the raid in Square I.22.a. Slight retaliation. the weather remained fine, but very cold. 2nd Lt P. Banks, R.F.A. joined "Z" battery at H.3.d.1.3.	
	2nd		"X" battery again fired 40 rounds into the same targets	
	3rd 4th		"X" battery did not fire, but the enemy put out some new wires into the newly-cut gaps each night.	
	5th		"X" battery fired 40 rounds, but the shooting was somewhat erratic.	
	6th		"X" battery only fired 6 rounds, as a premature occurred which killed Bombardier Moran.	
	7th		At this period "Y" battery in the left sub-sector of the Right sector, (i.e. between PARK ROW AVENUE and WEST PRINCESS STREET,) were firing most days a diversion shoot into the hostile wire and parapet S.W. of P.88, to draw off some fire from the NZ battery, which was wire-cutting for a raid in the extreme Right sector.	
	8th		"X" battery fired 40 rounds.	
	9th		"X" battery fired 50 rounds. Prospective raiders expressed satisfaction at the gaps cut.	

WAR DIARY or INTELLIGENCE SUMMARY

Army Form C. 2118.

(*Erase heading not required.*)

Instructions regarding War Diaries and Intelligence Summaries, are contained in F. S. Regs., Part II. and the Staff Manual respectively. Title Pages will be prepared in manuscript.

Place	Date	Hour	Summary of Events and Information	Remarks and references to Appendices
ARMENTIÈRES	1917 Feb. 10th		"Z" battery were still in reserve, but at the Disposal of the N.Z. Division, and liable to be called on at any time. Eventually 2 guns and teams were dispatched for a shoot in or near WYE FARM SALIENT, but no personnel was required.	
			"X" battery fired 40 rounds into the gaps to clear up the new wire put out during the night. This was successfully accomplished.	
	11th	noon	"X" battery fired 30 rounds as a trial shot into the gaps. 3 L.E.R.M's were blown out.	
		5:30 pm	"X" battery fired 15 more rounds to the night of the ARMENTIÈRES – WAVRIN RAILWAY in darkness.	
		10:30 pm	A raid consisting of 12 officers and about 250 O.R. of the 23rd N.F.'s under Lt. Col. PORCH took place. "X" battery fired 126 rounds to cover the flanks. These were got off without mishap, but retaliation was heavy. Only 5 prisoners were captured, but several officers (enemy) were killed. Casualties amongst the raiders were heavy – nearly 75 in all.	

Army Form C. 2118.

WAR DIARY
or
INTELLIGENCE SUMMARY
(Erase heading not required.)

Instructions regarding War Diaries and Intelligence Summaries are contained in F. S. Regs., Part II. and the Staff Manual respectively. Title Pages will be prepared in manuscript.

Place	Date	Hour	Summary of Events and Information	Remarks and references to Appendices
ARMENTIERES	1917 Feb 12th	pm	"X" battery fired 30 rounds, without very satisfactory results. Retaliation on the right was heavy. "Y" battery	
	13th		"Z.3.A.T.M.B." relieves "X" battery. [Xray went South. Kit "B" Feb 34th D.A.C. Preparations were made for 1st move at an early	
	14th		date.	
	16th	8pm	Bombardment in Right Sector, but no raiders of 101st Bde went over. A stray shell (small) hit "X" battery's billet, doing no damage. "Y" battery did not participate.	
	17th		"Y" battery finally came out of action. An advanced billeting party was sent on to STEENBECQUE.	"Y" battery reached ARRAS
	18th	noon	After much argument and changing concerning our transport, only 4 G.S. Wagons were allotted to us for the move. 2 of them took all the guns, & one stores to the D.A.C. at LE KIRLEM, and nearly broke down on the way. The other two just managed to take our kits off, and the batteries marched to NEUF BERQUIN, which was reached between 6 & 7 p.m. Capt J.W.G. Wylie came over from 2nd Army to see us off. Billets satisfactorily	

Army Form C. 2118.

WAR DIARY
or
INTELLIGENCE SUMMARY

(Erase heading not required.)

Instructions regarding War Diaries and Intelligence Summaries are contained in F.S. Regs., Part II. and the Staff Manual respectively. Title Pages will be prepared in manuscript.

Place	Date	Hour	Summary of Events and Information	Remarks and references to Appendices
NEUF BERQUIN	1917 Feb 19	9.30 am	We packed up and marched off to STEEN BECQUE, via MERVILLE, HAVERSKERQUE. Weather was damp, turning to thaw, but distinct. We billeted in STEEN BECQUE.	
STEEN-BECQUE	20	11.30 am	The weather was wet all day, but otherwise the march was satisfactory. Proceeded to FONTES, via BOESEGHEM and AIRE. We reached billets at 4 pm.	
FONTES	21	9.30 am	The weather was better, and we marched off to CAUCHY-A-LA-TOUR via ST HILAIRE, LIÈRES, AMES and FERFAY. Billets were reached at 12.30 pm. Rations were drawn, but no forage.	
CAUCHY-A-LA-TOUR.	22.	10.30 am	The weather again became wet, but fortunately there was only a short march to do. Marched off to MAREST, via FLORINGHEM. Reached billets at noon. Weather damp and billets dirty	
MAREST	23		Marched by almost non-existent roads to entrain at BRYAS STN at 1.20 pm. We missed the train at ST POL for AUBIGNY, and so proceeded on to FRÉVENT, where we reached AUBIGNY by light railway at 7 pm. Rations at this time were unspeakably bad. To-day deficient.	
FRÉVENT CAPELLE	24	12.30	to FRÉVENT-CAPELLE.	

Army Form C. 2118.

WAR DIARY
or
INTELLIGENCE SUMMARY

(Erase heading not required.)

Instructions regarding War Diaries and Intelligence Summaries are contained in F. S. Regs., Part II. and the Staff Manual respectively. Title Pages will be prepared in manuscript.

Place	Date	Hour	Summary of Events and Information	Remarks and references to Appendices
FRÉVENT-CAPELLE	24TH	2:30 PM	Marched into ARRAS, where the batteries were billeted in the RUE DE LILLE. There was no food on arrival, and the boots of many of the men were quite worn out. Since their arrival in ARRAS, "V" battery were employed exclusively on camouflaging for that XVIIth Corps.	
ARRAS	25TH		The day was spent settling into and cleaning out the billets. Some of the officers were conducted round the line by Lt RAINE, "Y" battery, who had been sent on in advance to see to the preparation of positions. The weather at this time was fair, though generally dull.	
	26TH		Work was begun by the batteries on positions, in conjunction with the R.E. and infantry. The line was fairly quiet, except for some hostile T.M. activity and a little desultory shelling.	
	27TH		Regular working-parties were organised at this time and shifts of 3 N.C.Os. & 34 Gnrs. inspected the horse lines in the line.	
		9pm	The enemy dropped some shell into the RUE DE LILLE, wounding a few infantry, the batteries R.A.M.C. orderly and Y battery remained resistance. Arrangements were made to retire with the infantry from 1st Avre inclusive.	

Army Form C. 2118.

WAR DIARY
or
INTELLIGENCE SUMMARY

(Erase heading not required.)

Instructions regarding War Diaries and Intelligence Summaries are contained in F. S. Regs., Part II. and the Staff Manual respectively. Title Pages will be prepared in manuscript.

Place	Date	Hour	Summary of Events and Information	Remarks and references to Appendices
ARRAS.	Feb: 28th		Took up position in "K" sector. was carried on as usual. Nothing of importance occurred during the day.	

Army Form C. 2118.

WAR DIARY
or
INTELLIGENCE SUMMARY
(Erase heading not required.)

34 Div T.M. Bttn...

Vol 1

Place	Date 1917	Hour	Summary of Events and Information	Remarks and references to Appendices
ARRAS	March 1st 2nd 3rd		Work was continued on both Medium and Heavy emplacements. The weather was on the whole fine. "X" battery prepared to take over the line from 2/9 T.M.B. "X" battery took over and fired 49 rounds with rather unsatisfactory results. There were several short rounds and 1st Charge was not efficient or reliable. Target: A.30.c.4.7.03.	
	4th		"X" battery fired 30 rounds. Results again not satisfactory. Same target. "Y" battery reported for duty from Comontafing. Some shows during the previous night, which melted during the day. Owing to an infantry carrying-party failing us, "X" battery only fired 22 rounds. Target: G.6.e.6.3. Results better. Retaliation practically nil. "X" battery went into the line to line. Very misty all day.	
	5th			
	6th		"X" battery fired 35 rounds on hostile wire from KIT ST and FALKLAND positions, — with good results. Work was at this time and onwards carried out on as many positions as possible and each battery fired almost daily onto the hostile wire. Difficulties concerning R.E. material and ammunition supply were great, and time was known to be pressing.	

WAR DIARY or INTELLIGENCE SUMMARY

Army Form C. 2118.

(Erase heading not required.)

Instructions regarding War Diaries and Intelligence Summaries are contained in F.S. Regs., Part II. and the Staff Manual respectively. Title Pages will be prepared in manuscript.

Place	Date	Hour	Summary of Events and Information	Remarks and references to Appendices
ARRAS	March 7th, 8th, 9th		Work on positions continues.	
	12th		"Y" battery took over from "X", for purpose of firing in the line. Work as usual. 3 O.R. attended medal-ribbon presentations by M.O.C. XVII Corps. About this date 2/2 Jones 34th Div.(TM.Bs.) for evening offensive operations.	
	13th		Lt. C.G. Lodrick R.F.A. transfers from "X" to "Z" battery to command as from 25/1/19[?]. 2/Lt H.M. Nicholls R.F.A. proceeds on special and indefinite leave. Gunners Smith and Rogers "Z" battery were killed in action near WEEK END TRENCH by a direct hit from a 4.2".	
	14th		"X" battery fired 30 rounds from KIT ST. emplacement. Some personnel from 34th D.A.C. (brains) was attached for duty. Corpl. T. White, R.G.A. "Z" battery was mortally wounded by a premature caused by hostile shell splinter hitting No.187 MkI fuze immediately before firing. He dies the following day and was buried at AUBIGNY-EN-ARTOIS.	
	15th		"X" battery fired 50 rounds on the left. Ammunition, as often, failed to turn up, though warned.	

Army Form C. 2118.

WAR DIARY
or
INTELLIGENCE SUMMARY
(Erase heading not required.)

Place	Date	Hour	Summary of Events and Information	Remarks and references to Appendices
ARRAS	March 16th		Work continued, and hastened, — although R.E. material was hard to obtain.	
	17th		Some infantry personnel, trained, was attached to the batteries from this date. 11th Suffolks, including 2nd Lt. J.M.R. Hunt, to "X" battery; 15th Royal Scots to "Y" battery, including 2nd Lt. L.O. Heughi; to "Z" battery, including 2nd Lt. L. Crosse, both att. 15th R.S., were attached to "Y" battery.	
	18th		Infantry carrying-parties on a large scale, for battle ammunition continued daily henceforward.	
	19th		At this time it was found very difficult to fit in the firing, ammunition supply and little work on positions. Capt. l. Vick, R.F.A. transferred from "X" to "Z" battery, in exchange for Bomb. BROWNE, R.G.A. 2nd Lt. W. Cock, R.F.A. B/152? Bde.	
	20th			
	21st		"X" battery fired 60 rounds. Other batteries also fired, -Z/2 without much success, although assisted by 2/34. After several days a lane was cut at G.12a.1.52.97. about 30 yards wide.	2=2. H.E. Drawn from St.? D.A.P.C. to "X" Batty.
	22nd		"Y" battery again fired 60 rounds (on left) "Y" battery also cut -Z/34 and Z/2 on left, -Z/34 and Z/2 on right.	

Army Form C. 2118.

WAR DIARY
or
INTELLIGENCE SUMMARY
(Erase heading not required.)

Instructions regarding War Diaries and Intelligence Summaries are contained in F. S. Regs., Part II. and the Staff Manual respectively. Title Pages will be prepared in manuscript.

Place	Date	Hour	Summary of Events and Information	Remarks and references to Appendices
ARRAS	March 23rd	2.pm.	"X" battery fired 30 rounds each on A.30.c.55.65 and A.30.c.55.70. Slight results.	
			"Y" battery fired 30 rounds on A.30.c.6.5. and 17 rounds on A.30.c.6.3. Also good results.	
			"Z" battery and "Z/2" also fired, 35 rounds and 17 respectively.	
	24th	1.30 pm	"X" battery fired 30 rounds each on A.30.c.55.60. & A.30.c.55.65	
		1.30 pm	"Y" battery fired 30 rounds on A.30.c.6.5. and 7 rounds on A.30.c.6.6.25. Results were satisfactory, hit "Y" battery blew out 2 rifle-mechanisms.	
		3.30 pm	"Z" battery satisfactorily damaged wire on Targets 2.2 & 2.3 with 35 rounds each.	
			"Z/2" damaged the hostile wire at L.12.a.51.98 with 41 rds.	
	25th	2pm	"X" battery fired 35 rounds each on Targets 7 & 8, widening over gaps.	
			"Y" battery fired 30 rounds on Target 9, cutting a gap 20yds broad, and 20 rounds on Target 11.	
			"Z" battery fired 20 rounds onto Target 23, cutting a narrow lane.	
		3.15 pm	"Z/2" fired 54 rounds on L.6.c.5.0, cutting 2 narrow lanes.	

Army Form C. 2118

WAR DIARY
or
INTELLIGENCE SUMMARY
(Erase heading not required.)

Instructions regarding War Diaries and Intelligence Summaries are contained in F.S. Regs., Part II. and the Staff Manual respectively. Title Pages will be prepared in manuscript.

Place	Date	Hour	Summary of Events and Information	Remarks and references to Appendices
ARRAS	March 26th	12pm	"X" battery fired 35 rounds each on targets 3 & 4: Wire damaged. "Y" battery fired 15 rounds on target 11, and 27 rounds on target 13. 9 rifle-mechanisms blown out. "Z" battery fired 72 rounds on target 24: some damage done. Z/2" battery fired 60 rounds on 4,12,a, 52.9.4, cutting two lanes 30' & 10 yards wide. Shooting was erratic as a whole, owing to a gusty wind.	
	27th	1.15 pm	"X" battery fired 35 rounds each on targets 3 & 4. The wire was badly damaged at both places. "Y" battery fired 30 rounds each on targets 11, 8, 18. A new lane was cut at the latter place. "Z" battery fired 70 rounds on target 24, causing considerable damage to the wire. Z/2 fired 6 rounds registration. X/2" and Y/2" fired the division about this date.	
	28th	3 pm	"X" battery fired 35 rounds each on targets 2 and 3. A lane was cut at the latter place. "Y" battery fired 30 rounds each on targets 11 and 13. Some damage was done. "Z" battery fired 35 rounds each on targets 2,3 and 2,4. A lane was cut in the latter place. Z/2 fired 53 rounds at 4,6, 0.5.0, where wire was damaged.	

WAR DIARY or INTELLIGENCE SUMMARY

Army Form C. 2118

Place	Date	Hour	Summary of Events and Information	Remarks and references to Appendices
ARRAS	March 29th	1.15 pm	Weather was exceedingly wet, causing a very high % of duds. "X" battery fired 70 rounds as usual. Shooting spoilt by duds. "Y" battery fired (?) 57 rounds. "Z" battery fired 28 rounds on target 22, cutting a lane. "Z/2" fired 144 rounds on L.6.c.5.0. About 50 more duds! "X" battery fired 35 rounds each on targets 1 and 2. Really no more suitable targets. "Y" battery fired 30 rounds on target 11, damaging the wire. "Z" battery fired 33 rounds on target 21. Many trifling newcomers were blown out.	
	30th	1.30 pm	"Z/2" fired 44 rounds at L.6.0.5.0, causing two small explosions in hostile front line.	
	31st	1 pm	"X" battery fired 26 rounds on target 1. A premature occurred, line to the tail driving through. No casualties. "X" battery fired 35 rounds on target 4, wire being damaged. "Y" battery fired 14 rounds on target 12. More trouble with rifle mechanism. "Z" battery fired 6 rounds on target 25. Direct hit from hostile minenwerfer blew up round in bore and 10 ozen no. Casualties. "Z/2" fired 71 rounds on L.6.c.50. Results not satisfactory.	

WAR DIARY or INTELLIGENCE SUMMARY

Army Form C. 2118

34 D TM Bty
Vol 10

Place	Date	Hour	Summary of Events and Information	Remarks and references to Appendices
ARRAS	April 1st		37th Bty T.M.B. were attached for (?) this day only "1/2" gri- not from 51st Div.	
		5 pm	"X" battery fired 35 rounds each on Targets 2 and 4, also widening existing lanes. "Y" battery fired 36 rounds each on Targets 8 and 12, attacking the wire considerably. 17th A.W. T.M.C.Bs joined. All wire aid preparations were hastened, as zero day was arranged to be expected any day.	
	2nd	1 pm	"Y" battery fired 30 rounds each on targets 8 and 12, widening existing lanes.	
		3 pm	"X" battery fired 35 rounds each on targets 2 and 4. A high cross-wind prevented accurate shooting. Many duds also occurred. "Y" battery registered.	
	3rd		All batteries did small shoots and completed regis- tration. By the end of the day, all preparations for the forth- coming attack was complete. Order of battle was as follows:- Rt. Flank: 34th Divn. under Lt. Raine R.F.A. Y V/2" 10 2" 8 3 9.45 Centre: Z/17 Y X/17 X V/17 8 2" 8 3 9.45 Right: 2nd Divn under Lt McNaghten, X/2 V/2, V V/34 10 2" 8 3 9.45 Ammunition carrying parties continued:- unsatisfactorily because the infantry were at-	6/4/17

Army Form C. 2118

WAR DIARY
or
INTELLIGENCE SUMMARY
(Erase heading not required.)

Instructions regarding War Diaries and Intelligence Summaries are contained in F.S. Regs., Part II. and the Staff Manual respectively. Title Pages will be prepared in manuscript.

Place	Date	Hour	Summary of Events and Information	Remarks and references to Appendices
ARRAS	April 4th	6.15 am	General bombardment commenced. Shooting on to the wire continued every day. Weather was extremely wet.	
" day	5th		Wire-cutting continued. Heavy rain and storm in the late afternoon. Btte.	
" "	6th		Pte. Cope R.A.M.C. was wounded. Lost carrying parties at night.	
" "	7th		Gunner Walker, R.G.A. 'X' battery, mortally wounded. Lt. Davis, R.G.A.	
" "	8th		'X' battery admitted to hospital with shell-shock.	
"Z"	9th	5.30 am	General assault took place at dawn. Great success. Advance of about 3000 y⁰⁵ to BROWN LINE achieved. Lt Walker killed. The batteries (personnel) came out of the line in the evening.	S/Lt Goodyll E/C/Cap Keen D-Wire
	10th		The next few days were spent shifting according to the inevitable orders and counter-orders! Ammunition salving.	
	11th		It was proposed to send us forward to BROWN LINE &	
	12th		more men up much, but the order was cancelled in time it could be put into effect. Guns were put back into old gun-pits and ammunition taken there also. It was very wet as usual.	
	13th		A fine day,— spent cleaning up everything in billets. All infantry personnel were returned to infantry.	

1875 Wt. W593/826 1,000,000 4/15 J.B.C. & A. A.D.S.S./Forms/C. 2118.

Army Form C. 2118

WAR DIARY
or
INTELLIGENCE SUMMARY
(Erase heading not required.)

Instructions regarding War Diaries and Intelligence Summaries are contained in F.S. Regs., Part II. and the Staff Manual respectively. Title Pages will be prepared in manuscript.

Place	Date	Hour	Summary of Events and Information	Remarks and references to Appendices
ARRAS	April 14th		Another fine day. Orders were received to commence salving of gun ammunition for D.A.C., but too late for anything to be done that day.	
	15th	7 am	Parade of all available men under Capt. Sikes, C.F.A., & battery for ammunition salving in the ROCLINCOURT valley. 34th C.F.A. were left in support of 63rd Div. Infantry, and transferred to XIII Corps. The weather was very wet again.	First Army
	16th	7 am	Parade for ammunition-salving fatigues under Lt. Laila. The morning was fine, but it rained later in the day.	Third Army
	17th	7 am	Ammunition salving fatigues under Lt. Raine. Very wet. As usual, 24 surplus attached D.A.C. men were returned to 34th D.A.C. in the morning.	[signature] [signature]
	18th	7 am	Fatigue parties under Lt. Zwicki, Walton. Weather was exceptionally bad. Rained all day.	[signature] [signature]
	19th	7 am	Fatigues under Captain Wilkin.	
	20th	7 am	Fatigues under Lieut. Lanhan. Weather very dry.	
	21st	7 am	Fatigues under 2nd Lieut. Watt. Weather fine.	
	22nd	7 am	Fatigues under 2nd Lieut. Heather.	
	23rd	7 am	Fatigues under 2nd Lieut. Banks. Started on Howitzer ammn.	
	24th	7 am	Fatigues under Lieut. Raine.	

Army Form C. 2118.

Vol X
3rd Div. T.M. Battery

WAR DIARY
or
INTELLIGENCE SUMMARY.
(Erase heading not required.)

Instructions regarding War Diaries and Intelligence Summaries are contained in F.S. Regs., Part II. and the Staff Manual respectively. Title pages will be prepared in manuscript.

Place	Date	Hour	Summary of Events and Information	Remarks and references to Appendices
ARRAS	1917 May 1st	7am	Fatigues under Captain Filkins; salved 4.5" How⁰ charges. The weather remained continuously fine.	
	2nd	7am	Fatigues, as usual.	
	3rd	5pm	Orders were received for the personnel of the Battery to be attached to the Divisional Artillery to relieve some of the R.F.A. for a rest. Personnel attached to the D.A.C. was withdrawn. "V" battery, plus 2nd Lieuts. Banks and Watt to 152nd Brigade, R.F.A., "X", "Y" & "Z" to 152nd Brigade. Details were left behind, to guard gun-stores, &c.	
	4th	2pm	Corp¹ Barham, "Y" battery, was wounded by the accidental explosion of a dud fuze.	
		7.45 pm	Large ammunition dump about 4.22 c. 7.9. set on fire accidentally. There were one or two very violent explosions, and the blaze did not subside before midnight.	
	5th		Occasional shells continued to explode throughout the day. Sergt. Green, "Y" battery was posted to the 111th Heavy Battery, R.G.A., 12th H.A.G.	

Army Form C. 2118.

WAR DIARY
or
INTELLIGENCE SUMMARY.
(Erase heading not required.)

34th Div TM Bttn

Place	Date	Hour	Summary of Events and Information	Remarks and references to Appendices
ARRAS	May 6th to 15th 1917		Nothing of importance occurred, and the weather was very fine.	
	16th		Corpl. BARROWCLIFFE killed in action, & Gunr. HARROD N/34 att. mortally wounded by shell-fire.	(D)/160
	17th to 29th		Nothing of importance occurred.	
	29th		Batteries were reconnoitres in ARRAS, and a reconnaissance was made of the whole divisional front - GAVRELLE to GREENLAND HILL. All batteries were much under strength, especially in officers.	
	30th & 31st		There was a heavy rain storm which smartly flooded the trenches.	

Army Form C. 2118.

WAR DIARY
or
INTELLIGENCE SUMMARY.

(Erase heading not required.)

Instructions regarding War Diaries and Intelligence Summaries are contained in F. S. Regs., Part II. and the Staff Manual respectively. Title pages will be prepared in manuscript.

Place	Date	Hour	Summary of Events and Information	Remarks and references to Appendices
ARRAS	April 25th		Fatigues as usual in ROCLINCOURT VALLEY. Weather was continuously fine	
	26th		Fatigues as usual	
	27th		Ditto	
	28th		"	
	29th		"	
	30th		By Order of the Town Commandant, billets were removed to 10, RUE ONZE MILLE VIERGE for "X","Y" and "Z" T.M.Bs. H.Q. removed to J, RUE DU CROISSANT. "V" battery remained at 17 RUE D'AMIENS, consequently Fatigue party was consequently smaller than usual.	

Army Form C. 2118.

WAR DIARY
or
INTELLIGENCE SUMMARY.

(Erase heading not required.)

31st Div T.M. Battery

Vol 12

Place	Date	Hour	Summary of Events and Information	Remarks and references to Appendices
ARRAS	June 1st 1917		Headquarters was now at No. 9, RUE DU CROISSANT, other billets being: 4 & 3, RUE DES AUGUSTINES (officers) and 10 & 12, RUE DU CRINCHON.	
		1 am	A party paraded for the trenches under LIEUT: J.A. RAINE and 2nd LIEUT: W. HEATHER. Work was continued by shifts on the shaft of the dug-out in CURSE TRENCH. The dugouts, belonging to captured hostile 13 cm gun-pits near the aid-post at H.5.a.11. were occupied as Trench H.Q." There was desultory and erratic shell-fire all day. The weather remained fine and hot.	
	2nd "		The shaft in CURSE TRENCH was further deepened, with a view to cover for the detachments to fire in forthcoming operations. The trenches were still extremely muddy. Hostile air-raid on ARRAS and the wagon lines.	
		11 pm	Rations and water at this time went up to trench H.Q. nightly at 11 pm by a L.G.S. Wagon from the D.A.C.	
	3rd "		Work in the trenches as usual.	
		6 pm	Reinforcements from the D.A.C. arrived in the evening to complete establishment in O.R.	

Army Form C. 2118.

WAR DIARY
or
INTELLIGENCE SUMMARY.
(Erase heading not required.)

Instructions regarding War Diaries and Intelligence Summaries are contained in F. S. Regs., Part II. and the Staff Manual respectively. Title pages will be prepared in manuscript.

Place	Date	Hour	Summary of Events and Information	Remarks and references to Appendices
ARRAS	June 1917 3rd/4th	11 p.m.	Hostile air raid as before. LIEUT: RAINE came out of the trenches. The work on the shaft in CURSE TRENCH progressed as usual.	
		10.30 p.m.	The usual air-raid took place.	
	5th	1 a.m.	CAPT: FILKINS and 2ND LIEUT: ANDERSON relieved 2ND LIEUT: HEATHER in the line, and LIEUT: RAINE with 2 detachments of "Y" battery went into the line for the operations. The afternoon was quiet and very hot. Considerable progress was made on the dugout in CURSE TRENCH.	
		8 p.m.	Assault on GREENLAND HILL, CHARLIE CHAPLIN and CUTHBERT trenches, by 102ND INF: B'DE in conjunction with J" Div: 39 rounds were fired successfully from the emplacements in CURSE TRENCH. Hostile shell-fire started before Zero, and was very heavy about our guns. No casualties, and fire was effective. firing personnel of "Y" battery came out of the line as soon as shelling permitted.	

WAR DIARY
or
INTELLIGENCE SUMMARY.
(Erase heading not required.)

Army Form C. 2118.

Place	Date	Hour	Summary of Events and Information	Remarks and references to Appendices
ARRAS	June 1917 5th	11 p.m.	Hostile air-raid on wagon-lines, and shelling most of the night. Several counter-attacks on extreme right.	
	6th		Work on a new position behind sunken road near junction of CLIVE with the front line on the extreme left of the divisional front, (and of 3rd Army) began. There was a thunderstorm late in the afternoon, which made the trenches knee-deep in mud. Enemy counter-attacks near CURLY.	
	7th	11 a.m. 1 p.m.	The relief, consisting of LIEUTS. L.E. LANHAM and C.E. Lo-VICK and 12 O.R., went up the line. There was another counter attack just beyond the right of the divisional front early in the morning. LIEUTS. J.A. RAINE and L.E. LANHAM awarded the military cross, dated 3/6/1917.	
	8th		Some work was done on the new position in CLIVE. New dug-out at captured gun-pits was opened out. CLIVE position continued. "Chinese attacks" at 8.30 pm. and 11.45 pm.	

WAR DIARY
or
INTELLIGENCE SUMMARY.
(Erase heading not required.)

Army Form C. 2118.

Place	Date 1917	Hour	Summary of Events and Information	Remarks and references to Appendices
ARRAS	June 9th	1am	60 rounds T.M.B. were brought up to the GAV- RELLE - FAMPOUX line, and 19 of these were taken right up to CURSE trench. Most of the infantry carrying-party got lost, owing to the hostile barrage.	
		10am	A single stray shell (4.2" How?: [?]) landed right in the old gun-pits at H.5.a.1.1. wounding 4 O.R. Bomb: Markham, Pte Saundooks (V), Sgt Thomas, (Z) Pte Pearce, M), and an infantryman, - the last severely. The two guns in CURSE trench were cleaned & the pieces deposited in the shaft. Some more work was done on the CLIVE emplacement.	
	10th	1am	LIEUT: J.A. RAINE, M.C., 2ND LT ANDERSON, and 160.R. relieves the party in the trenches. Work was continued at CURSE and CLIVE. The weather was very fine.	
	11th	3am	There was a heavy thunderstorm, and it was not throughout the day. Work was however continued, and guns were kept in readiness for shooting, in case orders should be received.	

A 5834 Wt. W4973 M687 750,000 8/16 D.D. & L. Ltd. Forms/C.2118/13.

WAR DIARY
or
INTELLIGENCE SUMMARY.
(Erase heading not required.)

Army Form C. 2118.

Place	Date	Hour	Summary of Events and Information	Remarks and references to Appendices
ARRAS	1917 June 12th	012⁴	4 L.L. Wagons from the D.A.C. arrived to move the batteries to a camping-ground in the park at SAINT-LAURENT-BLANGY, H.13.a.3.2. We were allotted six large bivouacs. Enemy shelled ARRAS with 38.cm H.V. The emplacement at CLIVE was practically finished, and a start was made on a shaft for a dugout. The dug-out at CURSE was now about 8' x 5' x 5', but lined with timber. Several new trenches had been dug in the neighbourhood of CURSE, which was now no longer in "No-Man's Land".	6/6/Return 6.P. Capt
	13th	1230 am	CAPT. FILKINS, LIEUT: LOVICK, and 18 O.R. relieved those in the line, and a reconnaissance was made with a view to finding any wire to cut on GREENLAND HILL. None was visible. Work was continued on both CURSE and CLIVE. The previous day 2nd Lieuts. P. BANKS and J. WILLIAMSON reported for duty. The former was posted to "Y" battery, and the latter to "Z".	

Army Form C. 2118.

WAR DIARY
or
INTELLIGENCE SUMMARY.
(Erase heading not required.)

Instructions regarding War Diaries and Intelligence Summaries are contained in F.S. Regs., Part II. and the Staff Manual respectively. Title pages will be prepared in manuscript.

Place	Date 1917.	Hour	Summary of Events and Information	Remarks and references to Appendices
ARRAS	June 14th		Work in the line proceeded as usual, and was considerably facilitated by the condition of the trenches which was improving.	
	15th		From now onwards there was a nightly fatigue-party of 1 officer and 50 O.R. for the 184th Tunnelling Company, R.E., to carry dugout material from ATHIES to the trenches.	
	16th	1 a.m.	LIEUT. L.E. LANHAM, M.C. and 2ND LIEUT. P. BANKS relieved the party in the trenches.	
		8.45 p.m.	The day was fairly quiet, but in the evening the enemy shelled our trench Headquarters with 5.9" How. He obtained one direct hit on one of the gun-pits, mortally wounding BOMBR. CULLY (X) (who died 1 hour later,) and wounding GUNR. WINGFIELD (V).	6/6 Cat.
	17th		Progress was made on the shaft of the CLIVE position. The enemy shelled the road near trench Headquarters and TOWY trench (C.T.) in the afternoon. LIEUT: W. HOLDEN, R.F.A. reported for duty as 2nd Lieutant.	
	18th	11.45 a.m.	BOMBR. CULLY was buried in the cemetery at R.15.b. 71.31.	
			The weather was extremely hot. Work in the line as usual.	

Army Form C. 2118.

WAR DIARY
or
INTELLIGENCE SUMMARY.
(Erase heading not required.)

Place	Date	Hour	Summary of Events and Information	Remarks and references to Appendices
ARRAS	June 18th 1917.	11:30 pm	3 mules of the team bringing up rations to the line were hit by shell-fire whilst unloading at trench Headquarters.	
	19th		There were several thunderstorms during the day, and the weather was generally wet and sultry.	
		12:30 am	LIEUT. J.A. RAINE, M.C. and 2ND LIEUT. J. WILLIAMSON relieved in the line.	
			Billets in the rest area were arranged at TILLOY-LES-HERMAVILLE with the 18TH D.S.C.	
			All guns, except those in the line, were sent back to the D.A.C. for care.	
		10pm	The enemy put a few shells into BLANGY TANK beyond our camp during the early part of the night.	
			Trench - Headquarters was very heavily shelled during most of the night.	
	20th		The day was fairly quiet, but stormy. Work was commenced on a new emplacement just off CORK trench, about 20 yards behind the front line, and 100 yards to the right of CLIVE. Work on the two other positions	

Army Form C. 2118.

WAR DIARY
or
INTELLIGENCE SUMMARY.
(Erase heading not required.)

Instructions regarding War Diaries and Intelligence Summaries are contained in F. S. Regs., Part II. and the Staff Manual respectively. Title pages will be prepared in manuscript.

Place	Date	Hour	Summary of Events and Information	Remarks and references to Appendices
ARRAS	June 20th 1917	11.45 pm	Whilst on the carrying fatigue for the 184th Tunnelling Company, R.E., Gunner Roebuck was wounded by shellfire.	
	21st	6.10 pm	The weather was again stormy, but great ended the evening when the enemy commenced to shell Battery Headquarters very heavily with 21 cm Howitzers. This was maintained for 3 hours and the entrances to almost all the dugouts were blown in. Although no casualties were sustained, it became necessary to evacuate the Headquarters permanently. During the night the 17th Divisional Trench-Mortar Batteries relieved us, the Infantry having relieved the previous day.	
	22nd	10 am	The camp at H.13.a.3.2. BLANGY handed over to the 17th Division, and during the morning the personnel and horse to the D.A.C. 2 days previous.) Proceeded in 2 lorries and 1 maintenance to	

A 5834 Wt.W4973 M687 750,000 8/16 D. D. & L. Ltd. Forms/C.2118/13.

Army Form C. 2118.

WAR DIARY
or
INTELLIGENCE SUMMARY.

(Erase heading not required.)

Instructions regarding War Diaries and Intelligence Summaries are contained in F.S. Regs., Part II. and the Staff Manual respectively. Title pages will be prepared in manuscript.

Place	Date 1917	Hour	Summary of Events and Information	Remarks and references to Appendices
TILLOY-LEZ-HERMAVILLE	June 22nd	2.30 pm	TILLOY-LEZ-HERMAVILLE. The move was completed by 2.30 pm. The weather during the morning was again wet, we were billeted next to 9th and 18th D.S.C's and the 34th M.V.S.	
HERMAVILLE	23rd		There were parades under battery arrangements, chiefly for inspection, cleaning up &c. The weather was fine, but cooler.	
	24th	am 9.15	Batteries paraded for Church (C. of E.) under Lieut. L.E. LANHAM, M.C. and marched to D.H.Q. service at HERMAVILLE. Application was made to R.A.H.Q. for reinforcements to complete establishment.	
	25th	11am	The G.O.C. R.A., 34th Division, BRIGDR-GENL E.C.W.D. WAL-THALL, D.S.O, inspected the billets &c.	
		9.15 am 5pm	Route march under 2nd Lt. W.J. WATT. Returned 10.45 am. Billets were inspected by A.A. & Q.M.G., 34th Division Lieut-Col: R.M. TYLER, D.S.O.	
	26th	9 am 2 pm	Parades for marching and gas drill.	

Army Form C. 2118.

WAR DIARY
or
INTELLIGENCE SUMMARY.
(Erase heading not required.)

Instructions regarding War Diaries and Intelligence Summaries are contained in F. S. Regs., Part II. and the Staff Manual respectively. Title pages will be prepared in manuscript.

Place	Date 1917	Hour	Summary of Events and Information	Remarks and references to Appendices
TILLOY-LES-HERMAVILLE	June 27th	9 a.m. & 2 p.m.	Early parade, physical exercises, as usual. Parades for marching drill &c. Weather fine, but cool.	
	28th.	9.30 a.m. & 2 p.m.	Parades for drill &c, as before.	
	29th.	9.30 a.m. & 2 p.m.	Parades for drill, &c., as usual. Weather fine.	
	30th.	9 a.m. 1 p.m. to 5 p.m.	Parade. Weather wet all day. All batteries bathed at IZEL-LES-HAMEAU.	

Army Form C. 2118.

WAR DIARY
or
INTELLIGENCE SUMMARY.

34ᵈ Div T.M.Bty

(Erase heading not required.)

Instructions regarding War Diaries and Intelligence Summaries are contained in F. S. Regs., Part II. and the Staff Manual respectively. Title pages will be prepared in manuscript.

Place	Date	Hour	Summary of Events and Information	Remarks and references to Appendices
TILLOY-LES-HERMAVILLE.	July 1917 1st	10.30 a.m.	Church parade. Service conducted by the S.C.F. (C. of E.)	
	2nd	3.pm	Football	
		9.30 am to 11.30 am	Route-march under Lieut: LOVICK, R.F.A. Sergt Greig and N.C.C's Cormack joined for duty.	
		2.pm	Parade (drill.)	
	3rd	9.30 am	Parade (drill.) All guns, stores, &c's were overhauled in the afternoon.	
	4th 5th		The usual parades took place.	
			As before, but everything was packed up by 7pm., when 3 lorries from the 18th D.A.S.P. arrived, and, making two journeys, took all personnel, excepting officers and batmen, as ⋀ baggage, to the entraining station at LIGNY-ST-FLOCHEL. One lorry from the 9th D.S.C. took the remainder to the station. 50 O.R. sent in an earlier train, but the	

A5834 Wt.W4973/M687. 750,000 8/16 D. D. & L. Ltd. Forms/C.2118/13.

Army Form C. 2118.

WAR DIARY
or
INTELLIGENCE SUMMARY.
(Erase heading not required.)

Instructions regarding War Diaries and Intelligence Summaries are contained in F. S. Regs., Part II. and the Staff Manual respectively. Title pages will be prepared in manuscript.

Place	Date 1917	Hour	Summary of Events and Information	Remarks and references to Appendices
LIGNY-SAINT-FLOCHEL. PÉRONNE.	July 6th	8.30 am	Rest left by No. 21 (the last) train, for PÉRONNE, viâ SAINT-POL, FRÉVENT, DOULLENS, AMIENS and CHAULNES. Our destination was reached late in the afternoon, and the batteries were billeted near the CITADEL. Weather was very fine.	H.Q. at N° 8, Ave de la République.
	7th	4.30 pm	The day was spent in cleaning up and settling into	
		6 pm	billets. Most of the men attended the divisional theatre in the town, where a collapse of the floor took place, causing some casualties, but not in any of the batteries.	
	8th	12.30 am	There was a thunderstorm and a heavy downpour of rain. There were heavy showers throughout the day, and church parade had to be abandoned. However the evening was finer. "Y" Battery was sent to be attached to D/168 un- til further orders, to build gun-positions.	
	9th	8.15 am	A party of officers went forward to see the D.T.M.O. 59th Div. (attd. 4th Cav.y Div.) concerning taking over in the line, at TEMPLEUX-LE-GUÉRARD. However their had orders not to hand over to us, so a reconnaissance of the line was not made. The weather was stormy.	
	10th		Nothing of importance occurred during the day, but preparations were made for moving.	

WAR DIARY
or
INTELLIGENCE SUMMARY.
(Erase heading not required.)

Army Form C. 2118.

Place	Date 1917	Hour	Summary of Events and Information	Remarks and references to Appendices
PÉRONNE - HERVILLY.	July 11th	8 a.m.	3 lorries arrived from the 18th Div: Amm: S.P., and, making two journeys, took "X", "Z" & "V" batteries and the guns of "J" to HERVILLY, where we were billetted next to 102nd Inf. Bde. and 160th Bde. R.F.A. D.T.M.O. and O.C. "V" battery took over from the 59th D.T.M.B's. Most unsatisfactory; not a single good position, and almost all nearly derelict. There was not a bit of shell-proof cover, & the enemy maintained a continuous, but erratic, shell-fire all the evening. A gun was left in trench H.Q., HARGICOURT, from "V" battery and another from "Z" battery in advanced billets, TEMPLEUX-LE-GUÉRARD. We took over altogether one H.T.M in a very bad position, {288 rounds Boche lethal gas T.M. shell for light mortars, & 6 rounds H.E.} T.M.B. The weather was fine. The O.C. "V", "X", "XZ" batteries made reconnaissances. As a result, it was decided to put in two positions on the left of the "slag-heap" east of HARGICOURT. In the evening the right section of "V" bat. went into the line to trench HQ. and the gun position at L.5.d. 65.00. Weather fine and warmer.	[signatures]
	12th			

Army Form C. 2118.

WAR DIARY
or
INTELLIGENCE SUMMARY.

(Erase heading not required.)

Instructions regarding War Diaries and Intelligence Summaries are contained in F.S. Regs., Part II. and the Staff Manual respectively. Title pages will be prepared in manuscript.

Place	Date 1917.	Hour	Summary of Events and Information	Remarks and references to Appendices
HERVILLY.	July 13th	a.m.	The O.C. "V" battery laid out a new line of fire for the gun, and work was commenced on building some shell-proof cover for both the detachment and ammunition. A reconnaissance was made of the neighbourhood of VILLERET, but no suitable position was found, as our posts were found to be much further back than those marked on the maps. Several suitable O.P's were found in square L.10.d, sheet 62C. Weather was fine and very warm. The enemy's artillery was very active against the north-eastern portion of HARGI-COURT and the left of the slag-heap, two medium for L.5.c.8.1. & L.5.c.2.8.7 sitions were definitely selected about L.5.c.8.1. & L.5.c.2.8.7 and another possible position next to the heavy mortar was noted. All positions, however, require much	Capt. [signature] O.C. [signature]
		p.m.	work, especially as regards cover for the detachments. In the evening 2 L.G.S. Wagons with 4 mules each and two riding horses reported for permanent at- tachment to the batteries. These were attached to the 160th Bde., R.F.A. Communication to	

Army Form C. 2118.

WAR DIARY
or
INTELLIGENCE SUMMARY.
(Erase heading not required.)

Place	Date	Hour	Summary of Events and Information	Remarks and references to Appendices
HERVILLY.	July 14th 1917	about 2.a.m.	H.Q: Wagon lines. 10 tents were drawn from ROISEL. During the night the enemy raided the neighbourhood of "unnamed" farm, N.E. of the slag-heaps. "X" and "Z" batteries moved forward to take over the billets in TEMPLEUX-LE-GUÉRARD. Weather was much cooler. The disposition and organisation of the batteries was now as follows: 1. Owing to the width of "no-man's" land on the centre and right of the divisional front, trench-mortar activity was restricted to an area represented by the 1100 yards on the extreme left of the divisional front. Accordingly, all trench mortars came tactically under the Left Group R.A. (Lieut: Col: W.M. WARBURTON, D.S.O., R.F.A.) 160th Bde. 2.(a) T.M.B. H.Q: (D.T.M.O. & Adj:) at K.23.b.97.87., next to Group & Infantry Brigade H.Q:s (b) Medium Batteries H.Q: (X"&"Z") at L.2.c.6.6., working in the line daily. (c) "Y" battery, attached to D/160, at L.9.d.., for digging. (d) "V" battery, forward section L.5.c.0.4.; rear section K.23.d.7.1. 8.3. (e) Transport at K.23.d...	[signatures]

Army Form C. 2118.

WAR DIARY
or
INTELLIGENCE SUMMARY.
(Erase heading not required.)

Instructions regarding War Diaries and Intelligence Summaries are contained in F. S. Regs., Part II. and the Staff Manual respectively. Title pages will be prepared in manuscript.

Place	Date	Hour	Summary of Events and Information	Remarks and references to Appendices
HERVILLY.	1917 July 14th		The day was very quiet, and the afternoon was fine. Progress was made on the two medium emplacements on the left, and on the heavy position. Cellar in HARGICOURT was cleaned out, disinfected, and set in order as accommodation for two officers. There was heavy rain during the night. At this time there was a marked increase in the leave allotment. 2ND LIEUT: L. HARKNETT, R.F.A. reported for duty from D/152; attached to "X" battery, to complete establishment.	
	15th "		Another quiet day: work in the line was steadily continued. Section relief in "V" battery, at night. 8 rounds T.M.F. were sent forward. 2ND LIEUT: E.D.COX, R.F.A. joined for duty from C/160; attached to "V" battery. There were again several showers during the night. The G.O.C. R.A. 34th Division inspected H.T.M positions and trench H.Q. The day was quiet on the whole, but there was slight mortar activity by the enemy. Work on Lewis H.Q. was begun, shafts being sunk with the help of 3 sappers from	
	16th "	5.30 am		

Army Form C. 2118.

WAR DIARY
or
INTELLIGENCE SUMMARY.
(Erase heading not required.)

Instructions regarding War Diaries and Intelligence Summaries are contained in F. S. Regs., Part II. and the Staff Manual respectively. Title pages will be prepared in manuscript.

Place	Date	Hour	Summary of Events and Information	Remarks and references to Appendices
HERVILLY	1917 July 16th 17th	9.25 am 12.30 pm	the 208th Field Coy, R.E. The night was very wet. The enemy was very active with medium and heavy trench-mortars, especially about the slag-heaps and "X" and "V" battery positions. There was one man slightly wounded in "V" battery. 8 more rounds T.M.F. were taken up overnight to "V" battery position, and 2 more possible positions were selected. In the evening a retaliation scheme was drawn up for the H.T.M. in conjunction with O.C. left shells into the enemy but a few damage. The night was fairly quiet.	
	18th		TEMPLEUX: doing practically no damage. The day was fairly quiet. Work again very wet. The day commenced by "V" battery on two derelict positions in the sand-pit about N.5.d.3.5. Work on other positions was continued. As usual, there was considerable rain in the night. Work on all positions, and on trench HQ was continued	
	19th	11 am	In the morning the enemy	

Army Form C. 2118.

WAR DIARY
or
INTELLIGENCE SUMMARY.
(Erase heading not required.)

Instructions regarding War Diaries and Intelligence Summaries are contained in F.S. Regs., Part II. and the Staff Manual respectively. Title pages will be prepared in manuscript.

Place	Date	Hour	Summary of Events and Information	Remarks and references to Appendices
HERVILLY.	July 19th 1917	11 a.m.	was again active with mortars, especially against the quarry. "V" battery on receipt of its Sunday of the left Group, R.F.A, fired 4 rounds in retaliation at the hostile mortar group near POND COPSE. The enemy was more or less	
		6 p.m.	quiet for the rest of the day. About 6 p.m. he put a few small shells along the road about half a mile west of TEMPLEUX. The weather was still somewhat unsettled. The day was on the whole fairly quiet. CAPT. KENNEDY, M.C., R.F.A, 4th Army School of Mortars, inspected the positions in the line. Work on the SAND-PIT Heavy position and the two medium positions in front of	
	20th			
	21st	10 a.m.	INDIAN TRENCH was continued. In the morning the enemy became active against the neighbourhood of the 'slag-heaps', with medium mortar. "V" battery fired 7 rounds (2 duds, 1 direct hit) on the supposed Company	

Army Form C. 2118.

WAR DIARY
or
INTELLIGENCE SUMMARY.
(Erase heading not required.)

Place	Date	Hour	Summary of Events and Information	Remarks and references to Appendices
HERVILLY.	July 21st		about L.1.a.0.55. (POND COPSE). The enemy retaliated with 3 rounds 4.2" Hows; but the mortars stopped firing. The rest of the day was fairly quiet. The weather was very fine. In the evening, after a quiet day, the enemy became troublesome with mortars. "V" battery fired 4 rounds in retaliation on a hostile mortar at L.1.a.7.28, with good effect, although one round was "dud". A reconnaissance was made of VILLERET and a position for light German 75 m/m mortar was found at about L.18.b.1.4. to engage the northern end of FARM TRENCH. During the night one of these mortars was put in about L.11.b.56.86. to engage the same target. In the morning the enemy fired a few long-range H.V. shell into HESBÉCOURT and ROISEL. Weather continued to be fine.	
	22nd 5.30 pm			
	23rd 10 am		"V" battery fired 4 rounds on suspected enemy Comdr. H.Qrs. L.7.a.0.55, obtaining 2 direct hits on earthworks. Two rounds were also fired at hostile T.M. at L.1.a.7.28. Both shots in retaliation	

WAR DIARY
or
INTELLIGENCE SUMMARY.

(Erase heading not required.)

Army Form C. 2118.

Place	Date	Hour	Summary of Events and Information	Remarks and references to Appendices
HERVILLY.	July 1917 23rd	4.30 P.M.	4 rounds were effectively fired in retaliation on the hostile T.M. position at Q.1.2.7.28., by "V" battery. "Z" battery registered the hostile T.M. Lynors at the north end of FARM TRENCH, Q.7.d. with light mortar firing from Q.11.2.6.8. 11 rounds 75m were fired. Whizz-bang retaliation captured 75m light gas T.M. shell. Z battery at night the enemy fired gas T.M. shell. Z bat-	Belgian 62 (Chilian)
	24th		tery moved the 75m L.T.M. to trench behind hedge at L.11.2.6.8. Enemy was very quiet all day, and "V" battery did not fire. Further re- connaissances were made of VILLERET. There was to have been a gas shoot at night but wind was unfavourable. Enemy was active with H.T.M. during the night, and there was considerable shell-fire on both sides. Weather continued fine but rather sultry. The day was very quiet.	
	25th		Another L.T.M. was put in by "X" battery at L.11.6.4.6.	

Army Form C. 2118.

WAR DIARY
or
INTELLIGENCE SUMMARY.
(Erase heading not required.)

Instructions regarding War Diaries and Intelligence Summaries are contained in F. S. Regs. Part II. and the Staff Manual respectively. Title pages will be prepared in manuscript.

Place	Date 1917	Hour	Summary of Events and Information	Remarks and references to Appendices
HERVILLY	July 25	5.15 p.m	"V" battery fired 3 rounds in retaliation for a few hostile light trench-mortars. The enemy was quiet throughout the night, and 101st Bde. relieved 102D.	
	26		The enemy registered all our posts from right to left with 7.7 cm and 10.5 cm how. Otherwise he was quiet. "X" battery registered the POND with 6 rds 75 m/m, R.M.L., H.E. Lost 2 rounds were direct hits.	
		4.30 p.m	"Z" battery silenced hostile mortar fire from 24.7.d. [illegible]	
		5.30 p.m	0.6. with 8 rounds. The last six rounds were direct hits on this mortar group. 4 rounds were also fired onto mortars at 24.7.d.83.36. Some sheets of corrugated iron were thrown up. The night again passed quietly and the weather remained fine.	
	27	9.15 a.m	The enemy fired a few medium T.M's at our posts in front of VILLERET, to which "Z" battery replied with 2 rounds 75 m/m ; after this the enemy was quiet for the rest of the day. In the evening	
		7 p.m	"Z" battery registered a gun at L.11.d.9.5.15 successfully.	

A 5834 Wt. W4973/M687 750,000 8/16 D. D. & L. Ltd. Forms/C.2118/13.

WAR DIARY
or
INTELLIGENCE SUMMARY.

Army Form C. 2118.

Place	Date	Hour	Summary of Events and Information	Remarks and references to Appendices
HERVILLY	July 1917 28.	3.15 am	The enemy put over several heavy "minenwerfer" rounds, the heavy gun position and the slagheaps. "X" battery's detachment on the 75th R.M.L. fires with two rounds, but the firing-pin broke and the gun was out of action. The enemy was quiet throughout the day. The weather was very hot. "X" battery fired one more round in attempts to get the gun into action again. "Z" battery fired	
		5.45 pm	6 rounds onto hostile mortar group in Q.7.d. Sergt. L. Moss, R.J.A., "X" battery, was posted to 160th Bde. R.G.A. The enemy was very active during the night, both with shells and mortars, especially	
	29.	10.40 pm	against HARGICOURT and the slag-heaps. "X" battery 1. am retaliates on the POND locality 3 times during the 3rd night, each with 6 rounds 75m/m R.M.L. The enemy also fires a few T.M.'s into VILLERET posts, for which "Z" battery retaliates with 10 rounds 75m/m R.M.L. The enemy continues to be active with mortars during the morning and "V" battery	

Army Form C. 2118.

WAR DIARY
or
INTELLIGENCE SUMMARY

(Erase heading not required.)

Instructions regarding War Diaries and Intelligence Summaries are contained in F. S. Regs., Part II. and the Staff Manual respectively. Title Pages will be prepared in manuscript.

Place	Date 1917	Hour	Summary of Events and Information	Remarks and references to Appendices
HERVILLY	July 29.	9.30 a.m.	fired 3 rounds on hostile T.M at 21.1.a.27.32., one of which was an air-burst. As this did not quench	[signature] /D/ Captain B.H.A.
		9.50 am	the hostile fire, "V" battery fires 3 more rounds at 21.1.a.5.2.; one of which was again an air-burst.	
		10 am	"X" battery again fires 6 rounds 75 y/m R.M.L on the Rd. The enemy was quiet for the next 2½ hours,	
		12.45 pm	but after that "V" battery once more fires 3 rounds on 21.1.a.27.32. This was very effective. The day was	
	30.	3am to 4am	stormy and wet. The night past quietly, but at dawn the enemy became active with mortars a-gainst the slag-heaps. "X" battery twice retaliates with 6 rounds. "Z" battery fires one round registra-tion. The day passed uneventfully. During the night,	
		10 pm	however, HARGICOURT was shelled, and the enemy T.Ms sent over a few T.Ms at our posts. "Z" battery re-	
		10.30 pm to	taliated with 8 rounds 75 y/m R.M.L and "X" battery with 5	
	31.	midnight 3 am	"X" battery again fired 5 rounds at dawn in re-taliation for hostile T.M's. "V" battery retaliates for	
		11 pm	hostile T.M's about midday with 5	

Army Form C. 2118.

WAR DIARY
or
INTELLIGENCE SUMMARY

(Erase heading not required.)

Instructions regarding War Diaries and Intelligence Summaries are contained in F.S. Regs., Part II. and the Staff Manual respectively. Title Pages will be prepared in manuscript.

Place	Date 1917	Hour	Summary of Events and Information	Remarks and references to Appendices
HERVILLY.	July 31st	1pm	Rounds on 21.1.R. 1055. The day was stormy and wet. There was no further mortar activity, and it rained heavily all night. Expenditure of ammunition for the month :— L.T.M.B. — 42 rounds T.M.G. & 107 rounds 75m R.M.L. T.M.B. :- nil	G/c Captain 6/c R.M.L. B.M.a.

Army Form C. 2118.

WAR DIARY
or
INTELLIGENCE SUMMARY

(Erase heading not required.)

34 D T M Bty 3

Vol 14

Place	Date	Hour	Summary of Events and Information	Remarks and references to Appendices
HERVILLY	1917 Aug 1		The day was wet and dull. There was practically no activity on either side all day. Lieut Lenham sent over to SAULCY-SAILLISEL to examine dump of salved ammunition in search of 75m/m R.M.L. 7/m Ammunition. Only a few rounds were found & the dump was very wet and sticky and fuzes unexactly	
	2		A new system of relief of O.C. left chargt was introduced under the order of lancts-ft always manned by an officer the night was very wet & another wet and uneventful day. H.T.M. were brought to H.P.Rgt Howitzer the H.T.M. were taken over from COURT at night. They had been permanently with the 35th Bn a day previously with a sec at F.23 & 62. B.M.R.A. reports the positions were shelled in the night on	El Offoundy (up PMA)
	3		Fine and no activity on our side. about 10 rd were fired from the enemy from 10 n.m. to 2" TENLOUX No 629 we threw retaliated for Emery at 3 rds	
	4	10.30		

WAR DIARY or INTELLIGENCE SUMMARY

Army Form C. 2118.

Place	Date 1917	Hour	Summary of Events and Information	Remarks and references to Appendices
HERVILLY	Aug 5	6.30 am	Enemy put 3 L.T.M.'s into VIBERET post. 'Z' retaliated with 3 rounds. The day was fairly quiet. Y battery received from 160 Bde R.F.A. 9 billets in TEMPLEUX. The work on HQ's was allotted to Y as a task. The day has	
	6		sect. uneventfully. About 11 pm the enemy became extremely active with LMG and more tars "X" battery retaliated on L.T.M. with 10	
	7	12.45 am	rounds .75 m/m. During the more activity in the early morning, Z battery fired 10 .75 m/m rounds T.M.T. on the same target in retaliation. Batteries were dull during the day and enemy was inactive. In the evening he shelled the slag-heaps and the valley in L.H.L. with	
		10.30 pm	17 m/m and 4.2" HOW and put some H.T.M.S into the neighbourhood of the (younger) battalion. tion 's (but not including mortars) restored calm for the rest of the night.	

Army Form C. 2118.

WAR DIARY
or
INTELLIGENCE SUMMARY.
(Erase heading not required.)

Instructions regarding War Diaries and Intelligence Summaries are contained in F. S. Regs., Part II. and the Staff Manual respectively. Title pages will be prepared in manuscript.

Place	Date 1917	Hour	Summary of Events and Information	Remarks and references to Appendices
HERVILLY.	Aug 8	11 a.m.	The weather was fine but rather misty. Y bat- tery did a destructive shoot on L.6.a.38.59. an important hostile strong point. The new gun in the sandpits' position was used, and the results were not satisfactory. After the first shot, which was several degrees to the left of the target, the lea began to shift and the next three rounds were very erratic. The 5th round was just about a direct hit. Out of the next five rounds were high- air-bursts, but fairly good line shots after the 10 rounds had been fired, the L.O. was taken out and carefully relaid. About one repeated with more successful results; there were only two air-bursts, and one. And the remaining 9 rounds all fell about the target, but more light in it. Although the enemy was occasionally active with mortars, there were	
	9	3 p.m.		

Army Form C. 2118.

WAR DIARY
or
INTELLIGENCE SUMMARY.
(Erase heading not required.)

Place	Date	Hour	Summary of Events and Information	Remarks and references to Appendices
Huvilly	Aug 1917 10"	2.30 p.m.	retaliation about this time. Heavy rain in the evening. V battery did a successful destructive shoot on POND COPSE, 12 rounds were fired, of which 8 were effective. There were 2 duds and 2 low air bursts. The day was fine. Considerable progress was made with Trench Headquarters. Some new team ammunition "T.M.K." with fuzes percussion - M.P. 110, for new long range 9.45" A.M. arrived. The day	
	11"	4.20 a.m.	was uneventful. V battery did a very successful shoot on POND COPSE with new percussion fuzes, which detonate, but there were 2 duds and with the aid of time fuzes. "Z" battery, covered by "Q" R.H.A.	
		5 a.m.	firing on Sugar Trench, fired one gun from the sandpits (L.S.A.40 37.) on to the trench junction of ENFILADE and NEW TRENCHES. 20 rounds T.M.8 were fired at maximum range; soft ground, 6 duds. One hand was witnessed 2 yards of the target, others ore close and all round it just before fire was opened the enemy. But 3 4.2 H.v. shell very close.	

A5834 Wt.W4973/M687 750,000 8/16 D.D. & L.Ltd. Forms/C.2118/13.

WAR DIARY
or
INTELLIGENCE SUMMARY

Army Form C. 2118.

Place	Date	Hour	Summary of Events and Information	Remarks and references to Appendices
HERVILLY	Aug 12th 1917		The enemy became slightly active with T.M.'s and 13 rounds German L.T.M.'s were fired into BETTY post and 12 Andes. The British & the German St. E. on L.H.S., and detachments were withdrawn from the two guns. Run in the evening.	
	13th	8 am	Lieut. Jakeman M.C., "Y" battery, proceeded on DTMO course to 3rd Army School of Mortars.	6/1 Cap'n O
		noon	Shelled ROISEL with 12 rounds 24 cm naval. The day was stormy. "X" battery fired 15	
		3 pm	rounds T.M.B. from temporary position in the sandpit onto the trench-junction ENFILADE and NEW trenches "Q" R.H.A. Covered the shoot with M.M.X.	
			There was rain in the evening but otherwise the weather was fine. "V" battery fired 10 rounds on trench-junction POND KNIP trenches. One dud & some some good shots. On the previous afternoon our new 9 4.5" M.K. VII 1/2 ff" (long-range) arrived & a new 9 4.5 M.K. I commenced at HERVILLY	
	14th	5.30 pm		

WAR DIARY or INTELLIGENCE SUMMARY

Army Form C. 2118.

Place	Date 1917	Hour	Summary of Events and Information	Remarks and references to Appendices
HERVILLY	Aug 15	1.45 am	"V" battery fired on round on to hostile T M group R.i.d. central in conjunction with Left group R.F.A. There was no further firing throughout the day & great difficulty was experienced (as usual) with ammunition supply; especially as regards T M B & T M K. The weather continued to be showery, and there was a heavy thunderstorm in the afternoon. It was ascertained that the enemy had definitely withdrawn his front line somewhat, and his attitude became more defensive. In the night he fired St QUENTIN Cathedral.	
	16th	11.15 am	V/62 H.T.M.B. arrived from "VII" Corps for attachment to the Division. Work on the shafts at F.23.d.6.2. was continued by V battery.	
		4 to 4.30 pm	V battery put 10 rounds into the SUGAR FAC^y and "x" battery put 20 bo pdr's into the junction of ENFILADE and NEW TRENCHES & (was arranged that V/62 should take over the Left sector) (F.23.d and thereabouts.)	

WAR DIARY
or
INTELLIGENCE SUMMARY

(Erase heading not required.)

Army Form C. 2118.

Place	Date	Hour	Summary of Events and Information	Remarks and references to Appendices
HERVILLY "A" day.	Aug. 17th 1917		Weather was very fine all day, and 18 pdrs cut wire. Enemy was very quiet, but early in the	
		1.45 to 3.15 pm	afternoon he suddenly shelled the area immediately west of the slag-heaps with 4.2" duds not a round exploded although about 100 rounds were fired	
		12.30 pm	V battery fired 10 rounds on southern portion of SUGAR TRENCH. The O.P. was lightly shelled once during the day. V/62 started work on the emplacements at F.23.d.6.2. There was some signal	
"B" day. 18th			activity on our front at night. Weather was catastrophically fine until about 4.30 pm, when heavy rain came on for about 2 hours. V battery fired 10 rounds on POND COPSE and trench with	E.B. Bradley Capt. D.M.O
		2.3- pm	No.1 gun. 31B fuzes were used successfully shooting good. The long range MK III gun was fine and carefully on to north end of FARM TRENCH. He had to be relaid after the shoot. It was in front of NEW TRENCH that the enemy	
			a reconnaissance was made of the area in front	

WAR DIARY or INTELLIGENCE SUMMARY

Army Form C. 2118.

Place	Date 1917	Hour	Summary of Events and Information	Remarks and references to Appendices
HERVILLY	Aug 18th	4.30 pm	Fired some T.M's on to the SLAG HEAPS after our shot. The night was fine and ammunition was sent up to F.23.a.6.2.	
	Aug 19th	4 am	Left Bn. III. Corps. (35th) attacked GILLEMONT FARM successfully. The day was fairly quiet and fine.	V/162 h.2 3 rounds
		4 pm to 5.30 pm	V battery fired 5 rounds on Rifle Trench-Mortar experienced at Q.7.b.85.85. with observation by No 29 K.Balloon section. Owing to no communication no further rounds were fired on this target. No O.K. was obtained. Hostile mortar-emplacement at Q.8.c.17 was engaged with 11 rounds from the Mk III gun, with good result. 13 rounds were also fired into POND COPSE, many hits being obtained on the trenches in the neighbourhood. V/162 fired 24 rounds on the position of MALAKOFF and MALAKOFF-SUPPORT trenches, being direct hits were obtained on the latter two of them close to the track junction with 12 hourly were also fired into the road –	

Army Form C. 2118.

WAR DIARY
or
INTELLIGENCE SUMMARY

(Erase heading not required.)

Instructions regarding War Diaries and Intelligence Summaries are contained in F. S. Regs., Part II. and the Staff Manual respectively. Title Pages will be prepared in manuscript.

Place	Date	Hour	Summary of Events and Information	Remarks and references to Appendices
HERVILLY	Aug 1917 19	about 8pm	Ametie at RUBY FARM. Several hits were obtained on the farm and the roads. The enemy staring a direct hit on one of our aeroplanes with A.A. fire and brought it down almost on top of V/162 battery gun placements at F.23 & 6.2. Both Pilot and observer were killed. The enemy shelled shortly afterwards, obtaining several direct hits on the road and one on the dug-out left, doing some damage. Weather continues to be fine.	E.Duffy (Captain) 2/L.O.
"D" day	20th	11.15 to 12.15 pm	V battery fired 40 rounds on POND COPSE and POND TRENCH, doing extensive damage to the earthworks in this neighbourhood V/162 repeated the previous days programme, 36 rounds being fired in all.	
		4 pm	The enemy unsuccessfully counterattacked the de-vision on our left at dawn. V & Y battery fired 15 rounds on the junction of FARM & RAILWAY trenches	

Army Form C. 2118.

WAR DIARY
or
INTELLIGENCE SUMMARY

(Erase heading not required.)

Instructions regarding War Diaries and Intelligence Summaries are contained in F. S. Regs., Part II. and the Staff Manual respectively. Title Pages will be prepared in manuscript.

Place	Date	Hour	Summary of Events and Information	Remarks and references to Appendices
HERVILLY	Aug 20th 1917	4 pm	3 rounds were fired. One direct hit was obtained in the wire at this front, and one in RAILWAY trench. The weather continued to be fine.	
"	21st	1.30 pm to 3.30 pm	"V" battery fired as follows:- 10 rounds on the junction ENFILADE and NEW trenches. 2 rounds were fired and one fell considerably short. Wrong in this area was further cut up. 10 rounds on RUBY FARM road junction — direct hit on the junction, and another on the road. There were 3 duds and 2 rounds fell much short of the target. 1 round fell in the wire about L.6.a.85. 11 rounds (TMK) were fired on branch trench at L.1.d.95.50. Two hits obtained on the trench. 10 rounds from right gun on branch junction L.1.d.62 with good results. Then fire was opened fire on the 2 mortars at L.1.b.85.85 SLAGHEAPS	[initials] 6/2 (a/fm) D.H.H.D

Army Form C. 2118.

WAR DIARY
or
INTELLIGENCE SUMMARY

(Erase heading not required.)

Instructions regarding War Diaries and Intelligence Summaries are contained in F. S. Regs., Part II. and the Staff Manual respectively. Title Pages will be prepared in manuscript.

Place	Date	Hour	Summary of Events and Information	Remarks and references to Appendices
HERVILLY	Aug 2/9	From	12 rounds were fired in retaliation in this neighbourhood and the enemy ceased fire. 1 dud & 1 airburst. V/62 fired 50 rounds from 3 guns on the trench junction MALAKOFF and MALAKOFF support. Hit struck on both trenches and MALAKOFF farm buildings. 7 rounds were blind, no one shot and 1 airburst.	
"day.		3pm to 4pm	The enemy opened fire with a section of 13cm guns first on L.S.C.S.E and then on the SLAG-HEAPS. Simultaneously a 15 cm Howitzer shelled the neighbourhood of UNNAMED FARM, and hostile mortars were active against the slag-heap. As a raid was expected in this area at night, night action of V/62 was laid on for S.O.S on SUGAR TRENCH and POND COPSE	Lt. F. F. [signature] B.Co (afterw) 2/Lt Woo	

Army Form C. 2118.

WAR DIARY
or
INTELLIGENCE SUMMARY

(Erase heading not required.)

Instructions regarding War Diaries and Intelligence Summaries are contained in F.S. Regs., Part II. and the Staff Manual respectively. Title Pages will be prepared in manuscript.

Place	Date 1917	Hour	Summary of Events and Information	Remarks and references to Appendices
HERVILLY	Aug 22nd	10 am	The enemy heavily bombarded SLAG-HEAPS area evidently preparatory to a raid 6 minutes later S.O.S. went up and V/62 shelled the pre-arranged targets with 10 rounds. The enemy were however not seen, but some casualties were caused to the infantry by the bombardment. Weather continued to be fine.	
Friday		1.6 am		
		from 9 am to 1 pm	V battery fired a very successful series of 28 rounds on the enemy's company headquarters near POND COPSE. Among other things the same farm was hit M. III gun fired 9 rounds, some with instantaneous fuzes on G.2.d.Q.5. Two direct hits were obtained on FARM trench. much material was thrown up, and some gaps in the wire cut. At the moment the silent Hun gun blew up not a shell in the line twenty hours did to it next. Cpl Horn a Lance Cpl W.N. Shell, Sgt Holland Rev Cpl & Gunner Shaw	6/2 Cpl Shaw 7th.

Army Form C. 2118.

WAR DIARY
or
INTELLIGENCE SUMMARY

(Erase heading not required.)

Instructions regarding War Diaries and Intelligence Summaries are contained in F.S. Regs., Part II. and the Staff Manual respectively. Title Pages will be prepared in manuscript.

Place	Date 1917	Hour	Summary of Events and Information	Remarks and references to Appendices
HERVILLY	Aug 22nd	2.25 pm	killed or died of wounds shortly after. Two other gunners suffered from shock, but were not admitted to hospital.	E(O)(Capture) Dunno
		3pm to 11pm	V/62 fired 24 hours on the junction of MALA-KOFF and MALAKOFF support trenches, also 16 rounds on POND COPSE from night gun. There were 2 air-bursts, 1 dud and 4 unsafe amongst these, as well as several abnormal short rounds. It was found that No. 1 gun position had been blown in overnight but the gun was uninjured. "X.Y. and Z" batteries were withdrawn to HER-VILLY, with the exception of the detachments for firing.	
	23rd	9.25 am to 11 am	V battery fired 60 rounds on hostile TM's in No. 1 A.52 and between SUGAR FACTORY and RUBY FARM. The enemy dropped several T.M's in entrenchments temporarily away the north	

Army Form C. 2118.

WAR DIARY
or
INTELLIGENCE SUMMARY
(Erase heading not required.)

Instructions regarding War Diaries and Intelligence Summaries are contained in F. S. Regs., Part II. and the Staff Manual respectively. Title Pages will be prepared in manuscript.

Place	Date	Hour	Summary of Events and Information	Remarks and references to Appendices
HERVILLY	Aug 23rd 1917	6pm to 7pm	shell-fire. "V"/62 fired 19 rounds on MALAKOFF FARM, causing the enemy to retaliate vigorously, but not effectively. Weather still remains very fine	
	24th	2am	"V"/62 fires 20 rounds into MALAKOFF FARM	
		8am to 9am	During the morning bombardment commenced. Wire-cutting as follows by 60 Pdrs. "Z" battery — 8 + 25 rounds on wire about L.6.a central (NEW TRENCH) 2 gaps being cut	
		9am to 12pm	25 rounds on wire about L.6.c. 74 (SUGAR TRENCH)	
		12pm to 3pm	25 rounds on same target. Shooting was erratic owing to wind but wire was much damaged and several narrow lanes cut	
		Noon to 12.30 pm	"X" battery — 25 rounds on wire about L.6.c. 60.05, L.6.c. 6.2, 6.35. Exact results not visible owing to the contour of the ground but several direct hits were	

Army Form C. 2118.

WAR DIARY
or
INTELLIGENCE SUMMARY
(Erase heading not required.)

Instructions regarding War Diaries and Intelligence Summaries are contained in F.S. Regs., Part II. and the Staff Manual respectively. Title Pages will be prepared in manuscript.

Place	Date 1917	Hour	Summary of Events and Information	Remarks and references to Appendices
HERVILLY	Aug 24th	3.45 pm	25 rounds were fired on the wire about L6	
		4.15	C. 70 35., where damage was done,	
		5.45	25 rounds on the wire near the junction of	
		6.15	ENFILADE and NEW TRENCHES.	
		11 pm	A new 9.45" Mr III T. How? arrived from ORDNANCE.	
	25th	5.25	A Chinese attack by our R.R. 35th Div. Enemy shelled TEMPLEUX and HARGICOURT, GILLEMONT FARM from	
		2 pm	Bombardment continued all day, 1/2 battery with 33 mins, cut two lanes in the enemy's wire at L.6.a.68.36 and L.6.a.72.42. and further damage. It in after place.	
		6.40 pm	"V" battery fired 24 rounds on SUGAR FACTORY and trench junction in cooperation with 33rd Bty. Many of the enemy could be seen running away. The open as a result of the intense concentrated fire at L/6.2. hailed out at night, and were	Capt Rutland wounded 4/1/34

WAR DIARY
or
INTELLIGENCE SUMMARY

Army Form C. 2118.

Place	Date	Hour	Summary of Events and Information	Remarks and references to Appendices
HERVILLY	Aug 26th 1917	4:30 am	handed over to 35th Division the division successfully assaulted COLOGNE FARM HILL. Several hundred prisoners were captured the two Pioneer fight mortars were in position to All RUBY WOOD but [illegible] not [illegible] Enemy shelled HARGICOURT all day. There was a heavy shower in the evening.	
	27th		The day was much more quiet. A and 2" L.T.M. nearly Batteries each had one L.T.M. laid to cover RUBY WOOD, but the infantry did not return it. The enemy made several tried counter-attacks during the night but were unsuccessful. It was very wet all day & de Latto from early	E/[illegible] Captain DTMO
	28th		morning pursuant throughout the day. The evening No. 1 gun of V. battery was taken over to K.F.33.d.6.2. when left section	
	29th		At 1/V/62 went to his work on a new S.P. to lower QUENNET COPSE and	

Army Form C. 2118.

WAR DIARY
or
INTELLIGENCE SUMMARY
(Erase heading not required.)

Instructions regarding War Diaries and Intelligence Summaries are contained in F. S. Regs., Part II. and the Staff Manual respectively. Title Pages will be prepared in manuscript.

Place	Date	Hour	Summary of Events and Information	Remarks and references to Appendices
HERVILLY	Aug 29th 30th		TRIANGLE TRENCH was started. There was no firing all day. Weather stormy. Left emplacement completed. Enemy shelled TEMPLEUX at night. Weather still cold and unsettled.	
	31st	11.45 am to 12.30 pm	Y. Battery fired 25 rounds on the southern end of QUENNET COPSE with excellent results. Several men were seen to run, and the last round was consequently fired to be a few air burst. There were no adds.	
			Total expenditure for August, 1917.	
			Germans 75% (R.M.L) H.E. 39 rounds	
			T.M.B. 28 "	
			T.M.F. 518 "	
			T.M.K. 66 "	

c/o B.[?]
c/o C.[?]
D.T.M.O

Army Form C. 2118.

WAR DIARY
or
INTELLIGENCE SUMMARY.
(Erase heading not required.)

34th Bde 7 RFA

7/6/15

Place	Date	Hour	Summary of Events and Information	Remarks and references to Appendices
HERNU	1st Aug		No shooting throughout the day. Weather very unsettled. Preparing for new mortar defence scheme reconnoitred.	
	2nd Aug	2pm	2nd Lieut L. Hartnett posted to 6/1133 from "A"/34 M.M. Battery. Twenty rounds were fired on QUESNET COPSE in retaliation by A/34 Heavy T.M. Battery. Weather very fine all day.	
	3rd Aug		Weather continues very fine & warm. There was no shooting throughout the day. The 235 & 5 Bombs L.W. Lough was attd by Field General Court Martial. Further reliefs to the numbers & in arrear 56 ag. 5.9 no 1. The 58 ag. & 9 no 1 was promoted to the E.O. Engag. — 2nd Lieut L. Blythe posted to A/34 M.M. Battery from 6/1133 39c RFA.	
	4th Aug		Capt. E.O. Baddeley 12w/t A.S. Anderson proceeded on leave to England. The weather was very fine — There was no shooting throughout the day owing to the balloon observation work was commenced on four new positions in connection with a defensive scheme for trench mortars.	

Army Form C. 2118.

WAR DIARY
or
INTELLIGENCE SUMMARY.
(Erase heading not required.)

Instructions regarding War Diaries and Intelligence Summaries are contained in F.S. Regs., Part II. and the Staff Manual respectively. Title pages will be prepared in manuscript.

Place	Date	Hour	Summary of Events and Information	Remarks and references to Appendices
HERVILLY	5/6		Captain P. Filkins 1/34 assumed duties of I.M.O. during the absence of Capt. Peddeley. Commenced new pooling of Heavy I.M. s to engage FARM TRENCH's o/9.13 & 9/.75 and communication trenches. Weather was very fine and enabled Balloon observation successful shooting — X Y Z Batteries vacated Billets at TEMPLEUX — Detachments remaining with Guns in light coy in action — Remaining RCOs & men were billeted at HERVILLY.	
	6/6		No shooting throughout the day. Weather good. A new Mk III Long 9.45 Heavy I.M. received from Ordnance.	
	7/6		Shooting was carried out today & 30 rounds of I.M. "K" were fired by "N"/34 Heavy I.M. Battery on FARM TRENCH and communication trenches from G.16. a 29.68 — Ten of these rounds were fired by the new Mk III Long H.T.M. & excellent results were obtained — The range 9.45 I.M. was withdrawn from the line & returned to I.O.M. work on defensive positions continued by "J"/34 M. I.M. Batty.	

A5834 Wt.W4973 M687 750,000 8/16 D.D.&L.Ltd. Forms/C.2118/13.

WAR DIARY or INTELLIGENCE SUMMARY

Army Form C. 2118.

(Erase heading not required.)

Place	Date	Hour	Summary of Events and Information	Remarks and references to Appendices
ERVILLY	8		Four new defensive positions completed for M.I.M's – Hostile shelling continued considerably with out T.M. activity – Issue of 75 rounds of gas shells by V/34 T.I.M. Battery on QUEEN'S COPSE – G.7.b.65.00 and G.13.d.95.75. VILLERET was heavily shelled throughout the day – weather was warm & fine – LIEUT AT RAINE returned from D.I.M. & course.	
	9		Weather continued very warm – there was no firing all day. Enemy very active around VILLERET.	
	10		Orders received to select a medium Battery to undergo a course of training in 6" stokes mortar. No T.M. activity – weather fine.	
	11		The weather continues fine – 2/34 Motor Battery continues work on medium defences headquarters – Y/34 reported in A.25 m.ab. 60/50 Y/34 M.I.M. withdrawn from line having been selected to undergo course in T.M. instead in 6" stokes mortar.	
	12	2.30 am	Y/34 M.I.M. fired 20 rounds of German H.E. on RUBY WOOD in retaliation & Heavy hostile T.M. were very active from direction of RUBY WOOD actply 3 rounds. LIEUT LANHAM reported in from leave. Corpl R BARHAM reported from leave.	

Army Form C. 2118.

WAR DIARY
or
INTELLIGENCE SUMMARY
(Erase heading not required.)

Place	Date	Hour	Summary of Events and Information	Remarks and references to Appendices
HERVILLY	13	10am	LIEUT J.A. RAINE 2nd LIEUT P. BANKS and 2.O.R proceeds to III Army I.M. School for course in 6" Stokes mortars — LIEUT W.L. BLYTHE & J.M. Reports to R.F.A. for course to R.F.A Depot. — 2nd LIEUT. C.E. LOVICK proceeds to J.M. Battery. — 2nd LIEUT J. WILLIAMSON assumes command of Z/34 m.J.M. Battery — tested new mortar defensive position exchanged by J.M. T/34 & Z/34 M.J.M. Batteries — march to new position for Heavy J.M. commenced. — A Party of men from Z/34 the R.T.A. Heavy J.M. took over the fire-power Bourne fields & 2.O.R members reported proceeding to T/Battery position in reserve.	
"	14	—	Weather fair & dry. LIEUT. W. HOLDEN proceeds on leave. T/& Z Batteries continued work on defensive positions. 43 R.O.R. men H.E. on RUBY WOOD in retaliation — at 10.30 p.m	
"	15	—	2nd LIEUT K.J. FRANKLIN proceeds Z/34 M.J.M. Battery from 13/160 Bde. 10 R.O.R men H.E on RUBY WOOD in retaliation on RUBY WOOD weather showery & rough —	
"	16	10am	Enemy J.M. very active — his own Barrage H.E. on RUBY WOOD were fired by our M.J.M's between 10.40 p.m. and 1 a.m. — Newberry Party of 8 men from D.A.C. for engaging mortars in line. The Commander in Chief congratulates the troops on repeated repulses of enemy in several attempts in this sector — weather fair —	

WAR DIARY
or
INTELLIGENCE SUMMARY

Army Form C. 2118.

Place	Date	Hour	Summary of Events and Information	Remarks and references to Appendices
HERVILLY	Sept 17th		Two Sappers Joined from R.E. to assist in construction of dug-outs. 33 Rds of German H.E. fired on RUBY WOOD in retaliation - at 10.30 pm - 2 Rds of J.M.K were fired in registration on QUENNET COPSE G.2.87.0.50 weather fine.	
	18th		Weather continued fine. 42 Rds German H.E. were fired on RUBY WOOD - 9 Rds J.M.K. were fired on DIAMOND COPSE at 11.15 am + 3.30 pm in retaliation for heavy T.M. activity. "X+Z" Batteries continued work on positions in rear.	
	19th		Bombardment of Football tournament commences - In retaliation for hostile mortars 4/34 fired 14 Rds of J.M.K. on DIAMOND COPSE 12.30 am, 3.0 am + 3.30 pm on QUEANSMONT TRENCH - 12 Rds of German H.E. were fired on RUBY WOOD at 7 pm.	
	20th		Heavy T.M² fired 10 Rds on QUENNEMONT TRENCH four of which were on registration 6 Rounds German H.E. fired on Dugouts about G.2.C.1.3 and RUBY WOOD	

Army Form C. 2118.

WAR DIARY
or
INTELLIGENCE SUMMARY
(Erase heading not required.)

Instructions regarding War Diaries and Intelligence Summaries are contained in F. S. Regs., Part II. and the Staff Manual respectively. Title Pages will be prepared in manuscript.

Place	Date	Hour	Summary of Events and Information	Remarks and references to Appendices
HERVILLY	21	4pm	Capt. Baddeley returned from leave — 13 Res of 2m.R. were fired about QUENNEMONT TRENCH and DIAMOND COPSE Nf 5:30 pm. where Res Bomer 1.8 on DIAMOND COPSE 6 pm. A successful attack was made on DIAMOND COPSE and all objectives taken at 6.7 pm.	
	22		Our Heavy Trench Mortars fired on RUBY WOOD and by 2nd 92.0.10.30. N.E. wire fired on RUBY WOOD and by 2nd 92.0.10.30. There was fired in retaliation & our S.O.S. cent —	
	23		The enemy launched a counter attack between 6.76 pm which was a complete failure — our Artillery fire prevented them from coming our trenches — 10th an intense Defensive fire was put up. 1 & 2 mon. positions engaged at Frampden – 25 Rds Bomer 1.8 west fires on RUBY WOOD & G 2.c 16.30 Our Heavy Tr. Mor. fires 15 Rds on G 3.0.1.2 on DIAMOND COPSE. Enemy activity – Weather continues very fine — sniping on both sides. 2.9.17. 7.B. Cox Lieut	

Army Form C. 2118.

WAR DIARY
or
INTELLIGENCE SUMMARY
(Erase heading not required.)

Place	Date	Hour	Summary of Events and Information	Remarks and references to Appendices
MERVILLE	24		2nd Lieut N.G. Andrews return from leave. Two more machine guns [?] were pulled on - 11 Rounds of T.M. was fired on DIAMOND COPSE and QUESNES MONT TRENCH. The Cap T.M. officer (Capt. Beard) went with the Btle.	
	25th		Three more Rounds of T.M. [?] [?] complete 1 gun fired in our heavy Trench Mortars 126 Rds on QUESNEMONT TRENCH at 12 [?] and Otherwise suff. Two [?] several Batterys of 2"S.T.M. firing at HERVILLE - 2nd Lt. N.G. Andrew gave to Details H.M.G. for attachment on one months course.	
	26th		Lt. S 1 M.O. & Batty Comdr. 24 S.Trench M? arrived at HERVILLE they were currently crossing the line. and heavy trench mortars 3 Rds on QUESNEMONT TRENCH at 7 pm	
	27th		Y Battery return from III Army. I.M. In charge of completion of course m C. [?] - No T.M. activity throughout the day. Lt. McO [?] the T.M. in Section - Eleven medium difference pontoons were being completed 8 Stores put in - The handing over of stores & heavy T.M.s commenced by the S.M.O. of 34 & 24 T.M. Btrys.	

2449 Wt. W14957/Mg0 750,000 1/16 J.B.C. & A. Forms/C.2118/12.

Army Form C. 2118.

WAR DIARY
or
INTELLIGENCE SUMMARY
(Erase heading not required.)

Place	Date	Hour	Summary of Events and Information	Remarks and references to Appendices
MERVILLE	28		The working parties of 293 Bee - R.E¹ - 4.6. A.6. return to their units. One heavy trench mortar is removed on B6⁰/CCORT ROAD on reparation. Handing over of provisions & stores to 24 S.J.M? continues.	
	29		The personnel Guns & stores of 24 S.J.M? arrive at MERVILLE. The personnel of 34 S.J.M? then withdrawn from line. Handing over of Guns, provisions, stored stores etc now relief completed at midnight. Weather fine & warm - Capt Beckerley proceeds on expended Course to the Army School of mortars. The three Greman L.T.M. fired by the unit since ARRAS are handed over to 24 S.J.M? Receipts for mortars & amb. handed over or forwarded to Staff Offr R.A. - The handing over to the 24 S.J.M? has been a very satisfactory one.	

WAR DIARY
or
INTELLIGENCE SUMMARY

Army Form C. 2118.

Place	Date	Hour	Summary of Events and Information	Remarks and references to Appendices
HERVILLY	Sept 30		All personnel Guns Tripods prepared to DOINGT in 6 motor lorries from 18th Supply Column. The units were concentrated in main trenches at DOINGT which was reached at 12 noon - No enemy was fire however - The Total Amounts fires during the month - = 3 m.g. Z = 100 Rds = 3 m.g. R = 146 " = M 8 = 252 " 9 m.g'3 = 3 " R.Holden Lt to 2m.D. for 34th Bron'l M.G. Coy 34th Bron'l M.G. Coy	

Army Form C. 2118.

Vol 76

WAR DIARY
or
INTELLIGENCE SUMMARY. D.T.M.O.
54 Division
Vol XIV
(Erase heading not required.)

Place	Date	Hour	Summary of Events and Information	Remarks and references to Appendices
DOINGT	Sept 1/17	9 am	T.C.O's men settling in Billets. Training commenced — Gas Drill, Signalling, Kit Inspection & setting up Rifle — Musketry Drill carried out under review/supervision of B'M'S Hay	
		2 pm		
	2	9 am	As above — Weather very dull & foggy — Three C/Pts recruits motors received from S.T. Army — weather turned now to hot sunny day	
		2 pm		
	3	9 am	Training continuing — Route march 11 to 1 pm — remainder Orderly Officer — Inter Battery football match at 2 pm.	
		2 pm		
	4	"	Gas trial etc as for 1st — particulars atchd — given to instruction in Gas — Lieut L. E. Lanham returned from leave	
	5	9 am	As above	
	6	"		
	7	2 pm		

Army Form C. 2118.

WAR DIARY
or
INTELLIGENCE SUMMARY.
(Erase heading not required.)

Instructions regarding War Diaries and Intelligence Summaries are contained in F. S. Regs., Part II. and the Staff Manual respectively. Title pages will be prepared in manuscript.

Place	Date	Hour	Summary of Events and Information	Remarks and references to Appendices
DOINGT	8/11/17	9 a.m.	Preparations for move to POPERINGHE -	
		11 "	V, X & Y Batteries proceed to PERONNE - FLAMICOURT STATION	
		4.30 p.m	Z Battery to CHAPELETTE STATION, leaving these stations in trains nos 12, 13, 14 & 15. - four F.J trains were used for transport of stores from DOINGT to stations & 2 journeys each had to be made - weather was very wet all the afternoon & evening.-	
POPERINGHE	9th	6 p.m	Arrived at POPERINGHE and units marched to Camps at F.4.A.4.2. independently - All units were in Camp at 11.30 p.m.	
	10th			
	11th		Improving accommodation for horses, man - ordnance of stores, kits etc & bow studs - weather very wet all morning -	
	12th			

WAR DIARY or INTELLIGENCE SUMMARY

Army Form C. 2118.

Place	Date	Hour	Summary of Events and Information	Remarks and references to Appendices
POPERINGHE	Oct/17 13	6am	Left Camp for forward area — 1/34 North Hd 3 sheets, 2/34 with No 2 Coy Hq, 3/34 with "H" sheets, 4/Z/34 with Headquarters A.S.C. Arriving about 3-30 pm as GAY FARM & JOYOUS FARM. Weather was showery all day...	
GAY FARM	14th	7am	Improvements for accommodation for men commenced.	
		12noon	Enemy Aircraft active — Bombs dropped in and around camp.	
"	15th	9am	Lec. Dreis & General instruction for N.C.O.s men. Lect's referable to charge of pumps, Gate Bands, fire-steamers, deliveries a station, mealies at wounded & Country stations respectively. Preparations for crews of these Pumps commenced — Lieut. H.S. Lanham announced a party of 50 men to 160/Bde for work in the line...	
		7pm 10pm	Enemy Aircraft active & a number of bombs dropped in County one man injured. One officer & twelve men returned to Billets. Camp shelled throughout the night.	

Army Form C. 2118.

WAR DIARY
or
INTELLIGENCE SUMMARY.
(Erase heading not required.)

Instructions regarding War Diaries and Intelligence Summaries are contained in F.S. Regs., Part II. and the Staff Manual respectively. Title pages will be prepared in manuscript.

Place	Date	Hour	Summary of Events and Information	Remarks and references to Appendices
GAY FARM.	October 16th	8 a.m.	The Camp was shelled during the day. The weather fine and dry.	
"	17th	9 a.m.	Gunner Forrest was tried by Field General Court Martial for overstaying leave. Lieut Colvin went to 34th Divisional Ammunition Column for Adjutant. Weather fine.	
"	18	2 p.m.	E. Eng Swept dropped Bombs on the Camp – no casualties – weather continued to be fine.	
"	19	2 P.M. till 8 P.M.	1 C Gunner detailed for duty with No 3 Section D.A.C.	
		4 P.M.	52 N.C.O.'s & men detached for duty with 152 Siege R.G.A. for carrying on work at Gun Positions. Weather was stormy.	
		8 P.M.	110265 Gunner Foote. H.S. (R.G.A.) of Y Battery killed by shell, while temporarily employed on Gun Positions at 160th Brigade.	

Army Form C. 2118.

WAR DIARY
or
INTELLIGENCE SUMMARY.

(Erase heading not required.)

Place	Date	Hour	Summary of Events and Information	Remarks and references to Appendices
GAYTARM.	20	2p.m.	3/C N.C.O. & Men from T.M Batteries, detailed to assist at 1st D.A.C. in carrying ammunition to positions.	
		3.p.m.	No. 25296. Gunner Winter M. proceeds on 26 days Course at 5th Army School of Instruction at ARNEKE.	
		6.p.m.	No. 5112. Pte Lalemie H.G. slightly shell whacked, while taking ammunition up to the Guns.	6.L C.B.7.N2. 51
		6.p.m.	All N.C.O. & Men temporarily attached for fatigues with 152nd Brigade returned to their Units. Weather fine.	
"	21	8.a.m.	6.n.c.o.& 22. Men temporarily attached for duty with No 2 Section, D.A.C. Weather fine.	

Army Form C.2118/13.

WAR DIARY
or
INTELLIGENCE SUMMARY

(Erase heading not required.)

Army Form C. 2118.

Place	Date	Hour	Summary of Events and Information	Remarks and references to Appendices
GAY FARM	October 22	1 a.m.	5 N.C.O.'s & 26 Men temporarily attached to No 1 Sec. D.A.C.	
			2 " " " 20 " " " " " " " "	
			2 " " " 16 " " " " " " " "	
			Those of No 1 Section remained there on full duty. Those of No 2 & 3 Sections were relieved there & accommodated during temporary attachment.	
			Weather dull.	
"	23		ditto Weather wet.	
"	24	11 a.m.	All Batteries (L.M.) moved from GAY FARM and proceeded to Camp near WOESTEN & G.S. Wagons from the D.A.C. were sent here for the purpose.	
			All N.C.O. & Men at the Column returned to their units and the following restated:	
			1 " N.C.O & 9 Men to No 1 Section	
			1 " " " 16 " " " 2 "	
			1 " " " 14 " " " 3 "	

WAR DIARY
or
INTELLIGENCE SUMMARY

(Erase heading not required.)

Army Form C. 2118.

Place	Date	Hour	Summary of Events and Information	Remarks and references to Appendices
WOESTEN	October (continued)			
	24th	1-4 pm	Arrived at WOESTEN Camp.	
		2 pm	2 N.C.O's & 9 men detailed for Guard at the Pol.6 New Camp. Finding their arrival.	
	25	a.m.	Orderly Sergt. Sergt. O'Donnell U.I. Parade of all N.C.O's men on camp, sandbagging and improving the conditions of the Camp.	
			The 21. 16 O.1 men at No 1.12 Section went to Linville Dump for duty and a further 32 N.C.O's men went to their Dump from the Camp. Weather clear.	
	26	a.m.	Parade - Orderly Sergeant. Sgt Green at. Fatigues continued on as on previous day. Weather very wet.	
	27	a.m.	Parade & Fatigues, same as on the 26th. Orderly Sgt. J. Griggs. 7 Men from No 2 Section B.A.C. proceed to Linville Dump for duty.	

Army Form C. 2118.

WAR DIARY
or
INTELLIGENCE SUMMARY
(Erase heading not required.)

Instructions regarding War Diaries and Intelligence Summaries are contained in F. S. Regs., Part II. and the Staff Manual respectively. Title Pages will be prepared in manuscript.

Place	Date	Hour	Summary of Events and Information	Remarks and references to Appendices
WOESTEN	October 27	5 P.M.	5. Men posted from No 293rd A.B.R.S.A. No 34 K.S.M.F.A. reported here.	Weather fine.
"	28.	8 a.m.	Parade. Lt Blore Ordly Sergt. Fatigues as yesterday. Captain E.L.O. Badeley redeployed on Course at 3rd Army School of Mortars. Gunner Winter 2/6, returned from Sanitary Course at 5th Army School of Sanitation.	Weather fine.
"	29th	6 am to 1 pm	1. N.C.O. & 10 men detailed for duty at No 2 Section D.A.C.	
		8 a.m.	Parade. 1 N.C.O. & Men remaining in Camp. Ordly Sgt Long. Lt Copper O.O. Fatigues continued	Weather dull.
	30	8 am	2. N.C.Os & 15 Men detailed to proceed to BOISINGHE DUMP.	
		8 am	Parade — Ordly Sgt. Sgt O'Donnell.	Weather dull.

2449 Wt. W14957/M90 750,000 1/16 J.B.C.&A. Forms/C.2118/12.

Army Form C. 2118.

WAR DIARY
or
INTELLIGENCE SUMMARY

(Erase heading not required.)

Instructions regarding War Diaries and Intelligence Summaries are contained in F.S. Regs., Part II. and the Staff Manual respectively. Title Pages will be prepared in manuscript.

Place	Date	Hour	Summary of Events and Information	Remarks and references to Appendices
WOESTEN.	October 31.	9 am.	Parade - Orderly Sergt: Sgt Gurwin W. all N.C.O.'s not on Camp or General Fatigue. Capt D. F. Burns proceeds on leave.	

Army Form C. 2118.

34th Div. TRENCH MORTARS

WAR DIARY
or
INTELLIGENCE SUMMARY
(Erase heading not required.)

Instructions regarding War Diaries and Intelligence Summaries are contained in F. S. Regs., Part II. and the Staff Manual respectively. Title Pages will be prepared in manuscript.

Place	Date	Hour	Summary of Events and Information	Remarks and references to Appendices
WOESTEN	1. November 1917	9 a.m.	Parade for N.C.O. and Men remaining in Camp. Fatigues and generally improving the Camp. Orderly Sergt. Sergt. Gregory J.B. Weather fine and dry.	
"	2.	8 am	Parade &c as on the 1st inst. Orderly Sergt. Sergt. Blow L.A. Lieut S. Raine and Lanham return to Camp from the advanced stations.	
		6 pm	2/Lt. W. Heather, & N.C.Os. + men gone Linesville Dump, TURK DUMP, & BOESINGHE DUMP, return to their Units.	
3.		6- am	9 E.S. Wagons were attached to T.M. Batteries, for the forthcoming move, 3 N.C.O.s and men commenced loading up.	
		11 am	Left Band with WOESTEN and proceeded to SARAWAK CAMP, arrived there at 2-50 p.m. 9 men were detailed for duty at Number 5 detentn. Bn.	

Army Form C. 2118.

WAR DIARY
or
INTELLIGENCE SUMMARY
(Erase heading not required.)

Place	Date	Hour	Summary of Events and Information	Remarks and references to Appendices
SARAWAK CAMP	3	6 p.m.	40 N.C.O's and men attached for duty with 160 Brigade.	
	4	9 a.m.	Parade. Orderly Sergeant Sgt O'Donnell T. All men on fatigues. Cleaning Wagons & harness to the Wagons were inspected, also preparations made for the following move.	
		4 p.m.	1 Sgt Cave returns from 152 Brigade. The N.O. N.C.O. and men returned to Units. Numbers known 160 Bde. 1 N.C.O & 5 men unallotted for duty with the 18th Supply Column during the march. Waiting fire.	
	5	6 a.m.	21 N.C.O's & men detailed for duty with N.3 Section A.S.C. during the move.	
		11.	Started on the first day's march to near of N.3. October, B.E.F. and Mortar Batteries	

WAR DIARY
or
INTELLIGENCE SUMMARY

Army Form C. 2118.

Place	Date	Hour	Summary of Events and Information	Remarks and references to Appendices
	November			
	5	5 p.m.	Arrived at STEENVOORDE: The route taken was via POPERINGHE - ABEELE - STEENVOORDE. The French Motor Batteries were billeted at STEENVOORDE, no billets were available at EECKE.	
	6	11 a.m.	The destination for the day was CALONNE-SUR-LYS, the route taken was via CAESTRE - STRAZEELE - MERVILLE, and arrived at destination about 4 p.m.	
	7	9 a.m.	March continued, the destination for the day was LABEUVRIERE. Route was via ROBECQUE - GONNEHEM - and CHOCQUES. Arrived at destination about 1 p.m. In the afternoon all the Sergeants were instructed, the 16 animals cleaned, in preparation for next day's journey.	
	8	9 a.m.	March continued, destination for the day being BETHONSART via BRUAY - HOUDAIN - REBREQUE - HERMIN, and CAUCOURT. As no billets were available at BETHONSART the French Motor Batteries billeted at CAUCOURT for the night.	

WAR DIARY
or
INTELLIGENCE SUMMARY

Army Form C. 2118.

Place	Date	Hour	Summary of Events and Information	Remarks and references to Appendices
	November			
	9	9 a.m.	The destination for the day was to BOIRY-ST-MARTIN, route taken was VIA CAMBLIGNEUL - CAMBLAIN-L'ABBE MONT-ST-ELOI - ANZIN - ST AUBIN. ARRAS. FAUBOURG, RONVILLE, returned at destination about 4 p.m. and went detached in the accommodation for the night.	
		5 p.m.	2/Lt Franklin and 2/25 B4TH Bn. returned to Unit from 152 Bde R.F.A.	
	10	10 a.m.	The French Mortar batteries left BOIRY-ST-MARTIN and took up billets at BOIRY-BECQUERELLE. Officers and N.C.O's left the Camp to take over the line given the 2nd Division.	
		1-30 pm	Personnel of the 34th French Montain succeeded to the line, and relieved those of the 51st Division.	
	11		4 - Lewis Guns were sent to Lynol to the 20th Divisional S. S. Battery + Stag and 1 Lewis remained at Camp for transport outfits.	

WAR DIARY
or
INTELLIGENCE SUMMARY
(Erase heading not required.)

Army Form C. 2118.

Place	Date	Hour	Summary of Events and Information	Remarks and references to Appendices
BOIRY BECQUERELLE	Nov. 11	12 noon	The 51st Divnl Trench Mortar Battery, of X Corps, and the British Expeditionary Force was to be in civil condition. In the line the trenches were found to have very bad condition & waterlogged much work. One 6 inch and one 2 inch gun were found wrecked up, & others incomplete owing to lack of pits to mount off the ammunition taken over was also found to be in a bad condition.	
		6	The Heavy Trench Mortars fired 4 Rounds for Registration (1 Dud)	
		6 p.m.	2" Medium Mortars fired 12 Rounds on Wire between O.26.a.60.08. and O.26.a.98.25. Weather fine.	
	12		During the day all N.C.O.s & men were employed in cleaning and in proving the demolitions of the Enemy.	

WAR DIARY or INTELLIGENCE SUMMARY

Army Form C. 2118.

(Erase heading not required.)

Place	Date	Hour	Summary of Events and Information	Remarks and references to Appendices
BOIRY BECQUEREL.S.	November 13		Z. Bty fired 30 Rounds from the 2" Mortar on Wire and Front line trench from, O.26.a.6.1. to O.25.a.95.30. Enemy retaliation was slight.	
		3-30 to 4- pm	X. Bty. fired 20 rounds of 2 inch on Front line and wire at O.32.a.15.50. to O.25.a.22.25. Prematures occurred on the 20th round, & No. 67021 Bdr Marshall E. was wounded rather badly. Weather very fine.	
	14-	12 noon to 1. p.m.	9.45" Long Mortar registered ST RONART QUARRY - 2 direct hits obtained.	
		1-15 to 2 pm	9.45" Flat Mortar fired 10 Rounds on road junction at O.32. Central, 1 short, & one short of short fell in German Front line.	
			The Count Newton fired 7 Rounds between OTTO LANE and SUNKEN ROAD. Lieut E. Owen attached to Trench Mortars as o/Adjt from 160 Bde	

Army Form C. 2118.

WAR DIARY
or
INTELLIGENCE SUMMARY
(Erase heading not required.)

Place	Date	Hour	Summary of Events and Information	Remarks and references to Appendices
BOIRY BECQUERELLE	Nov-Dec 15th	11.4 am	6 inch Newton Mortars fired 10 Rounds on O.32.a.35.70. 1 dud, remainder on target, and also 30 Rounds at Communication Trench O.32.c.2.5. to O.32.c.4.0.45.	
		5 pm	2 inch fired 10 Rounds on U.I.b.35.70. Enemy retaliated quiet but with only one T.M.	
		9.45 pm	9.4 inch (short) M.I. Gun obtained direct hits on O.32.b.50. Destroyed 6 Rounds on O.32. Central.	
			The 2 inch Gun position was completely repaired and the Gun put in action. The 6 inch position at CAVALRY FARM was also completed, and a new position for the long Heavy mortar set in order, at about N.30.d. 2 Lt. W.L. Boyle proceeded on leave.	
	16	11 am	6 inch Gun fired 30 Rounds on Communication Trench at O.32.c.2.5. to O.32.c.4.0.45.	
			2 inch fired 6 Rounds on O.26.a.98.18. *	
		2 pm	Heavy (long) Mortars fired 7 Rds on ST. ROHART QUARRY 5 direct hits were obtained and no retaliation. 4 Rounds were also fired on VIS-EN-ARTOIS. Enemy heavily retaliated.	

Army Form C. 2118.

WAR DIARY
or
INTELLIGENCE SUMMARY
(Erase heading not required.)

Instructions regarding War Diaries and Intelligence Summaries are contained in F.S. Regs., Part II. and the Staff Manual respectively. Title Pages will be prepared in manuscript.

Place	Date	Hour	Summary of Events and Information	Remarks and references to Appendices
BOIRY BECQUERELLE	Nov. 16		One 2inch Medium Mortar fired ten rounds each direction at about O.14.a.80.14, 10 cut gaps about the Cambrai road, O.14.b.58.03 and O.14.d.72.97. 6inch Newton Mortar position was also being prepared for wire cutting south of COJEUL River.	
	17.	1.P.M.	6inch Newton Mortar fired 30 Rounds on O.32.a.90.75. 9.45"(Shot) fired 16 Rounds on O.32.b.45 and 4.7. The Enemy retaliated with 2 rounds from the Flying Pig emplacement.	
		3pm	2inch Medium Mortars fired 26 Rounds an Enemy Wire and Trenches from O.26.a.61. to O.26.a.95.30. Enemy sent over 2 rounds 9.45int, but both burst in air doing no damage. Captain P. Filkins returned from leave.	
	18.	11 am	Heavy (Shot) Mortar fired 3 rounds on "Flying Pig emplacement" vis- Enl ARTOIS. 6inch Stoggs fired ROTTEN TRENCH with 5 Rounds.	

WAR DIARY or INTELLIGENCE SUMMARY

Army Form C. 2118.

Place	Date	Hour	Summary of Events and Information	Remarks and references to Appendices
BOIRY BECQUERELLE	18 Nov	11 a.m.	2nd Newton Mortar fired 12 Rounds U.1.6.8.9. and registered Wire east of Loan Sap with 2 rounds. Weather continued fine.	
	19	11 a.m.	2nd Newton Mortar 15 Rds and cut 2 gaps in wire at O.32.a.2.4. and fired 10 Rds on O.26.c.10.38.46. O.26.c.15.16.	
			* This gun had afterwards on the 15th Novemr. The Gun fired 30 Rds on SUNKEN ROADS at O.32.a. and 5 at Corner of FONTAINE WOOD — Enemy retaliated on WOODLANE.	
		9.45	(Short) Mortar fired 5 Rds on Hostile emcement near CHERISY CHURCH. Weather was fine & dry. 2/Lt Kg. Franklin proceeded on leave.	
	20	11.30 am	6 inch Newton Mortar fired 30 Rds on O.32.a. 90.9 P. Shooting was fair on shoot & accurate and which should have proved effective. 2nd Gun fired 36 Rounds Hostile Wire on AKKAS — CAMBRAI — ROAD, about O.14.6.7.0.	

Army Form C. 2118.

WAR DIARY
or
INTELLIGENCE SUMMARY
(Erase heading not required.)

Instructions regarding War Diaries and Intelligence Summaries are contained in F. S. Regs., Part II. and the Staff Manual respectively. Title Pages will be prepared in manuscript.

Place	Date	Hour	Summary of Events and Information	Remarks and references to Appendices
BORRY BECQUERELLE	Nov 20	6.20 to 7.20 a.m.	Heavy (Short) Mortar fired 9 Rounds on 0.32. d. 0. 9. (an "enemy" M.G. material thrown up from one slit) No retaliation.	
			In accordance with instructions out 2 Stokes Mortars reached SUNKEN ROADS at 0.26.c. 75.06. 0.32.a. 85.70 and 0.32.a.25.70. each 60 Rounds 6 mil Mortars also fired 214 Rounds on the Salbury Points. V.2.c. 60.95. V.2.c.2.2. V.1.b.90.55. V.1.d.95.60. 2 med Mortars fired 18 Robin V.1.6.93.75. 9. 4.5" (Short) fired 12 Robs on Enemy Minnie or CHERIDY with good results. 9. 45" (Lop) obtained direct hit on KOHART QUARRY and ST ROHART FACTORY. 2 med fired 60 Robs on Enemy trenches & supports between 0.26.b.10.36. and 0.26.a.65.10 and at 0.26.c.50.67.	

WAR DIARY or INTELLIGENCE SUMMARY

Army Form C. 2118.

Place	Date	Hour	Summary of Events and Information	Remarks and references to Appendices
BOIRY BECQUERELLE	Nov 21	2 pm	Trench Mortars continued to be very active and the Heavy Mortars fired 15 Rounds on CHERISY and an Enemy Ammunition Dump was set on fire, this gun also fired 4 Rds on VIS-EN-ARTOIS, and obtained direct hits. The following parties that were carrying T.M. ammunition were observed from the Railway Embankment & Infantry Brigade.	
			10 carriers and 5 Officers (or N.C.O's) to carry from OUTRE FONTEZ DUMP.	
			30 " " " " " " " " " " " TAKE DUMP.	
			21 " " " " " " " " " " " PELICAN DUMP.	
	22	7·30 am	The Trench Mortars fired on O.26.b.85.60 and 12 Rds on FONTAINE - les - CROISILLES.	
			Level fired 130 Rounds on enemy wire between O.26.c.35.68 and O.26.b.20.15 and 5 Rds on Front trenches containing right of Division Front. Enemy put up 2 Green Flights which were answered by 9 more but no apparent action followed.	

Army Form C. 2118.

WAR DIARY
or
INTELLIGENCE SUMMARY
(Erase heading not required.)

Army Form C. 2118.

Place	Date	Hour	Summary of Events and Information	Remarks and references to Appendices
BOIRY BECQUERELLE	23.	2 pm	The 6 inch Mortars fired 40 Rounds on Hostile Wire about O.32.a.1.y.5. Shooting was unsatisfactory so trouble with Gun Bed. Hence there was only slight damage. The following carrying parties were available for carrying T.M. ammunitions from the Reserve Infantry Brigade; 45 Carriers and 1 Officer or N.C.O. to carry from PELICAN DUMP 50 " " 1 " " " " " CUCKOO FOSTER DUMP 30 " " 1 " " " " " KAKE DUMP.	
"	24		No 7927. Bt Walker G, from No 1 Section DAC posted to Y 34 M. T.M. Bty. 2 inch Mortars fired 25 Rds on Wire at O.32.a.10.48. were severely damaged, and 8 Rds on O.14.b.55.05. 6 inch cut Wire in places about V.20.b.10.65. with 9 Rds, and cut a lane 7 to 10 yds wide at night opposite U.1.b.61. Enemy retaliated in neighbourhood of WOOD LANE with T.M.	

WAR DIARY
or
INTELLIGENCE SUMMARY

(Erase heading not required.)

Army Form C. 2118.

Place	Date	Hour	Summary of Events and Information	Remarks and references to Appendices
BOIRY BECQUERELLE	24 November	1-30 to 2 pm.	Heavy Mortar fired 10 Rds on TRIANGLE WOOD, and ANGLE LANE. O.21.c.80.90. with good results.	
	25	2 am	2 in.L. fired 5 rds attempting to cut wire at U.1.6.5.6. Trench mortars put up a small stunt on enemy front line at about U.1.6.7.7. also 25 Rds onwire at O.26.a.5.0 to O.26.a.8.3. 6 and fired 65 Rds on wire O.25.d.6.3 to O.20.d.1.6 O.32.a.35.55. and O.20.6.7.7. Heavy Mortars fired 25 Rds on MILLSIDE WORKS and CHERISY. Starting to play very enemy owing to high wind.	
		5 pm.	6 - 6 and 2 Newton Mortars received from the 55th Div M.O. to be handed over to Batteries and 4, to be kept at Corps Reserve. The 2 inch medium mortar flashes which have prematured and not in order.	

Express digital copy service | Order details

Digital Express copy service

Order number: 17983 / 21929
Document reference: WO 95/2448   Order Date: 15 May 2008 13:55
Copy supplied subject to Terms and Conditions at www.nationalarchives.gov.uk/legal/digitalexpress.htm

WAR DIARY
or
INTELLIGENCE SUMMARY

Army Form C. 2118.

Place	Date	Hour	Summary of Events and Information	Remarks and references to Appendices
BOIRY BECQUERELLE	November 25.		Lt. J.Y. RAINE., appointed D.T.M.O. 34th Div; vice Capt E.L.O. Baddeley attached to the 22nd N.F.s	
			2/Lt. L. MACDUFF from 6/152 Bde. was posted to Y 34 H. T.M.B. with effect from to day. vice Lt JA.RAINE appointed D.T.M.O.	
	26		The fire to day is as follows. 2nd firing 70 Rounds on targets U.1.b.6.2. - U.1.b.6.5 - O.32.a.15.10 - O.26.a.7.2 and O.26.e.2.5. & md fired 50 Rounds on targets O.32.a.40.50 and O.20.d.6.5. Heavy mortars fired 35 Rounds on HILL SIDE WORKS and VIS- EN- ARTOIS. Many hits were obtained in the village. Capt E.L.O. Baddeley proceeded to join 22nd N.F.s Carrying parties for T.M. ammunition were as follows. 55 Carriers and 1 Officer on N.C.O. from CUCKOO FOSTER DUMP. 45 " " " " " " RAKE DUMP. 25 " " " " " " PELICAN "	
	27		The firing by T.M. to day. as follows. 2nd 47 Rds on targets O.32.a.15.20 and O.26.c.20.35. and ammunition right of CAMBRAI ROAD. 6inch fired 54 Rounds on targets, Dugouts at O.32.c.08.50. 4 direct hits obtained, also	

2449 Wt. W14957/M90 750,000 1/16 J.B.C. & A. Forms/C.2118/12.

Army Form C. 2118.

WAR DIARY
or
INTELLIGENCE SUMMARY
(Erase heading not required.)

Place	Date	Hour	Summary of Events and Information	Remarks and references to Appendices
BOIRY BECQUERELLE	November 27	12-30 No	3 direct hits were obtained on the H.T.M. position.	
		1-30 pm	14 rounds damaged wire at O.26.b.15.60 and 20 Rounds damaged wire at O.20.b.45.60. to O.20.b.80.90. The Long (9.45") Mortar fired 15 Rounds on HILL SIDE WORKS and VIS-EN-ARTOIS with good results. The (Short) 9.45" fired on dugouts at O.32.d.0.9. Retaliation was heavy on SWIFT SUPPORT. CURTAIN SUPPORT and WREN ALLEY. Weather was rather unsettled	
"	28	3 pm	The firing for the day was as follows 2 inch 50 Rds on wire at V.1.b.7.8. at O.26.a.5.5 to O.26.a.90.35. wire was badly damaged at V.1.b.7.8. 20 Rounds of 6 inch cut a good gap in wire at O.20.b.85.80.	
		4-30 pm	9.45" (Long) Mortar damaged buildings in VIS-EN-ARTOIS. 9.45" (Short) fired 15 Rds on CHERISY - O.32.b.35.99. with good results. Retaliation was slight. The weather was fine.	

Army Form C. 2118.

WAR DIARY
or
INTELLIGENCE SUMMARY
(Erase heading not required.)

Instructions regarding War Diaries and Intelligence Summaries are contained in F. S. Regs., Part II. and the Staff Manual respectively. Title Pages will be prepared in manuscript.

Place	Date	Hour	Summary of Events and Information	Remarks and references to Appendices
BOIRY BECQUERELLE	Nov 29	9. a.m.	The firing for the day was as follows. 2nd fired 70 Rounds on targets. V.1.6.8.9. at O.32.a. 15.35. O.26.a.50.15. and O.26.a.90.35. Wire was badly damaged and a small gap cut at V.1.6.8.9. 6 inch fired 71 Rounds on trenches at V.1.6.8.9. Road & trenches at O.32.b.05.55. and new wire between O.20.d.60.35. to O.20.d.80.70. Further damage at all points. The enemy put down a heavy barrage at 5-30 am. The Heavy Mortars fired 25 Rounds on VIS-EN-ARTOIS at O.32.b.25.30 and O.26.d.35.00 with good results. (316 fuzes were rather erratic, (2 duds & 3 air bursts) Retaliation very heavy on position.	
	30		2/Lt W. Blyth returned from Leave. 2nd continued wire cutting & 20 Rounds cut up at 25 yds at V.1.6.8.9. 6 inch shot considerably damaged trenches at V.1.6.62. and O.32.a.8.5	

Army Form C. 2118.

WAR DIARY
or
INTELLIGENCE SUMMARY
(Erase heading not required.)

Place	Date	Hour	Summary of Events and Information	Remarks and references to Appendices
BOIRY BECQUERELLE	30 Nov.		6 inch stand direct hits on Trenches at O.32.c.5.8. and on Dugout at O.32.a.5.7. 6 inch set g pits on wire at O.20.b.75.80. and O.20.b.70.75. Several Rounds fell in trenches at approx. O.20.b.80.90. Heavy Mortars fired 17 Rounds on targets O.26.d.35.00. O.32.b.40.60. O.32.b.35.40. O.32.e.95.80. Much woodwork thrown in air and several bursts observed presumably in dugouts. The total rounds fired from the 11th to 30th inclusive, 1100. T.M.G. 706. T.M.B. 228. T.M.F. 115. T.M.K.	[illegible signature]

Army Form C. 2118.

WAR DIARY or INTELLIGENCE SUMMARY

(Erase heading not required.)

34 DTMO Vol 18

Place	Date	Hour	Summary of Events and Information	Remarks and references to Appendices
BOIRY. BECQUERELLE	1.		Trench Mortars fired as follows. 6 and 9 46 Rounds on Targets, Road at O.20.d.80.15. Tracks and dugouts at O.32.b.05.55. (Harassing fire) and on Trench at O.32.a.39.82. Direct hits obtained and parapet blown in in several places at the last point. 9.45" (Short) Gun fired 12 Rounds into CHERISY about O.26.d.20.00. One house completely demolished. The Heavy Long Mortar was moved from O.14.a.66.06 to a position at O.25.a.00.75 and a bomb mortar put in the old position.	
	2.		Firing for the day was as follows. 6 inch fired 40 Rounds on Road junction at O.32.b.10.10 & crossing of road and trench at O.32.a.40.65 and on Fosse between O.20.b.55.80 to O.20.d.90.60. Shooting very accurate, & several gaps made. 9 inch fired 46 Rounds on Target, French trench junction at O.32.a.43.30. Sunk at O.26.a.48.10. at junction of NIGHT and NARROW TRENCHES.	

Army Form C. 2118.

WAR DIARY
or
INTELLIGENCE SUMMARY
(Erase heading not required.)

Instructions regarding War Diaries and Intelligence Summaries are contained in F. S. Regs., Part II. and the Staff Manual respectively. Title Pages will be prepared in manuscript.

Place	Date	Hour	Summary of Events and Information	Remarks and references to Appendices
BOIRY BECQUERELLE	Dec. 2		2 inch obtained direct hits on O.26.b.12.20. and standard at O.26.c.55.90. & O.26.c.60.55. Heavy Mortars fired 5 Rounds on CHERISY at O.32.b.55.80. (1 air burst) good results obtained.	
	3		All Personnel, Animals & Wagons attached for transport purposes returned to No 3 Station R.H.G. and were replaced by another detachment. Firing to day was as follows. 6 inch 90 Rounds on Targets, Trench Junction at O.20.b.90.60. O.20.d.95.20. Wire between O.20.d.60.26. to O.20.d.60.00. on Trench Junction O.32.a.45.30. O.32.b.60.45. Trench & road at O.32.a. to O.32.a.11.78. and 10 Rds for Registration. 2 inch fired 60 Rounds on Wire between O.26.c.25.55. to O.20.30. Wire was damaged at O.32.c.20.25. and reorganising was carried out at U.1.b.7.8. Front Line to support a further 2 Rounds Registered U.2.b.8.8. Heavy Mortars fired 19 Rds on Hostile Minnie in action at O.32.b.26.38. and silenced it. Retaliation heavy. Weather Fine, very cold.	

2449 Wt. W14957/M90 750,000 1/16 J.B.C. & A. Forms/C.2118/12.

Army Form C. 2118.

WAR DIARY
or
INTELLIGENCE SUMMARY
(Erase heading not required.)

Place	Date	Hour	Summary of Events and Information	Remarks and references to Appendices
BOIRY BECQUERELLE	Dec 14		Trench Mortars were very active, and firing took place as follows: Heavy Mortars fired 25 rounds on Targets: Minnie Emplacement, O.26.d.2.0.+ O.32.b.30.25. Dugouts at O.33.a.1.0. and Trenches in CHERISY and OTTO LANE. (1 round abnormally short) + 1. dud) 6 inch fired 97 Rounds on Wire at O.32.a.2.5 to 1.6. O.26.a.60.26 to 60.00 where large gap was cut. Trenches damaged at V.1.b.65 to O.32. T.T. not registered O.1.b.8.3 2 inch fired 40 Rounds on Wire at O.32.a. 15.30 to 1.5. O.26.c.80.25 to O.26.c.25.35. Wire was considerably damaged and gaps cut at both places. 2/Lt. O.R.P. Franklin returns from Leave 1/2. O.R. join V/34.1k H.T.M.B. from R.G.A. Batteries 4. O.R. " Z/34th L.M.B. " 3rd Batt 16 Weather fine and very cold.	

Army Form C. 2118.

WAR DIARY
or
INTELLIGENCE SUMMARY

(Erase heading not required.)

Instructions regarding War Diaries and Intelligence Summaries are contained in F. S. Regs., Part II. and the Staff Manual respectively. Title Pages will be prepared in manuscript.

Place	Date	Hour	Summary of Events and Information	Remarks and references to Appendices
BOIRY BECQUERELLE	Dec. 5.		The Heavy Long Mortars put in action at new Location 0.25.a.00.15. The Enemy Ret today was as follows	
		1.45 pm	9.45" (Short) fired 11 Rds on 0.32.c.02.60. with good results.	
			" " (Long) " 10 " Suspected Battalion Hd Qrs	
			at 0.32.d.60.93. (Very successful shoot) (done).	
		2.45 to 3.15 pm	6 inch fired 20 Rounds wire 0.32.a.15.50. Shooting was erratic.	
			" " 15 Rounds registration.	
			Weather continued to be very cold, foggy.	
	6.		In conjunction with the bombing raid in the early morning, 177 Rounds of 6" were fired on selected targets.	
			2 inch fired 12 Rounds on Wire at 0.32.a.15.40.	
			6 " " 52 " " " 0.32.a.15.50 — 0.20.d.60.26.	
		3.10 to 3.30 pm	to 0.20.d.60.00. & cut two fresh gaps at 0.20.d.60.20. and also fired on HILLSIDE WORKS.	
			The short Range Mortar fired 10 Rds on Suspected Minnie Pocken at 0.32.c.22.38, and 10 Rounds on Building at 0.26.a.32.00. Long Mortar fired 20 Rds on Suspected Bn Hd Qrs at 0.32.d.60.95. Shooting was very consistent	0.26.a.32.00 0.32.d.60.95

WAR DIARY
or
INTELLIGENCE SUMMARY
(Erase heading not required.)

Army Form C. 2118.

Place	Date	Hour	Summary of Events and Information	Remarks and references to Appendices
BOIRY BECQUERELLE	7.	2.30 to 3 pm	6" fired 10 Rds on ROTTEN TRENCH and 51 Rounds on S.W. Front the following points:- Junction of trench O.20.d.60.25. - O.32.a.10.30, and at 6.20.d.60.26. 2 inch fired 12 Rds on wire at O.32.a.15.40. The (Short) heavy mortar fired 14 Rounds on O.32.b.20.25. " (Long) " " 14 " " CHERISY at O.32.b.50.90. The Weather was fine but very cold.	
	8.		The (Short) heavy Mortar fired 2 Rounds on CHERISY at O.32.b.40.90. had to cease firing to Butterfly not shaking. The (Long) heavy Mortar fired 10 Rds on CHERISY and O.32.b.60.90. and 10 Rds on targets as per concentration scheme. 6 inch fired 72 Rds " " " " 2 inch fired 10 Rds on wire at O.32.a.15.90. 6 inch fired 26 " " O.20.d.60.15. to 60.25. shot at and on trenches line at O.26.d.8.2 to O.26.d.96.45, O.20.d.6.0. Observation was difficult owing to light. Weather fine and cold.	

WAR DIARY
or
INTELLIGENCE SUMMARY

Army Form C. 2118.

Place	Date	Hour	Summary of Events and Information	Remarks and references to Appendices
BOIRY BECQUERELLE	Dec 9.	12 noon	The 9.45" (Long) Mortar fired 9 Rounds on CHERISY at O.32.b.50.90. Fired field Trenches on Trug b of Trenches round O.26.b.05.20. - And fired 32 rounds on dugouts at V.2.a.8.2. Trench-mortars at O.26.b.20. on dugouts at O.26.b.98.76.	
		5pm	2 O.R. (R.F.A.) from 299th Siege Bty joined V/34 W/M/B. These making a total of 14. O.R. of R.G.A. + 6 on this battery. The Gun position at O.25.b.35.00. now completed and gun being placed in position. The 18th (N.F.) Pioneers recommenced work on R.A. forward positions and transport lost to be found daily from this Camp. For taking forward the material. The 9.45" (Short) Mortar being now out of action, the position was being taxed and the bed moved so as to get more elevation on the gun. Weather rather cold.	

2449 Wt. W14957/M90 750,000 1/16 J.B.C. & A. Forms/C.2118/12.

Army Form C. 2118.

WAR DIARY
or
INTELLIGENCE SUMMARY
(Erase heading not required.)

Instructions regarding War Diaries and Intelligence Summaries are contained in F.S. Regs., Part II. and the Staff Manual respectively. Title Pages will be prepared in manuscript.

Place	Date	Hour	Summary of Events and Information	Remarks and references to Appendices
BOIRY BECQUERELLE	Sept 10	7.30 a.m.	6 inch fired 94 Rounds – Enfilading Communication Trenches from U.31.b. at O.32.a. and at O.26.b.4.7.	
		12 noon and 4.15 p.m.	2 inch fired 16 Rds – Enfilading C.T's. in O.32.a. & O.26.b.0.1. The above were fired in conjunction with the concentration scheme.	
		12 noon	9.45 (Log) Mortar fired 9 Rds on O.32.b.45.90.	
			Enemy active on night with L.M. & heavy Minnies.	
	11		In conjunction with the concentration scheme the heavy Trench Mortars fired as follows: 6 inch fired 101 Rds – Lineal 20 Rounds – the heavy Mortar fired 12 Rds – on O.32.a.12.15. and O.32.a. central, on a suspected group of light Trench Mortars.	
			The weather was fine.	

Army Form C. 2118.

WAR DIARY
or
INTELLIGENCE SUMMARY.
(Erase heading not required.)

Place	Date	Hour	Summary of Events and Information	Remarks and references to Appendices
BOIRY BECQUERELLE	Dec 12		Heavy Mortar fired 20 Rounds on the following targets:- O.32.c.55.40. - 65.20. O.32.c.75.10. and O.33.a.1.1. One shot burst blamed, and much much material thrown up. 2 inch fired 8 Rds on O.26.b.O.1. 6 " " " O.26.b.15.10. - Registered Wire with the new 6" gun at O.20.d.7.0. on dugouts at O.26.b.90.28 and V.2.a.9.1, and on Trench at O.32.c.15.25. to 15.20. A red flag has been put up alongside dugout at O.32.d.15.15. and white flags from here to left edge of FONTAINE WOOD. Trench Mortar barrashed machine firing in the line with their BOX RESPIRATORS on.	
	13.		Heavy Mortar fired 15 Rounds on O.32.d. central and on Lockhi H.T.M. at O.32.d.38.58 close hit obtained which silenced it. 2 inch fired 15 Rds on junction of C.T. from O.32.a.2.2. to 15.70. 6 " " " " " " " " O.32.a.4.2. to 35.55. and on O.32.c.15.25. to O.32.c.40.15. and V.1.b.85.55. and on HILL FIRE WORKS at O.21.a. on Lockhi T.M. at O.26.b.6.7. Machine Guns fired at O.26.b.36.95. Dug outs at O.26.b.60.05. to 92.95. and on Trench junctions at O.26.b.39.60 to O.26.b.0.2. Weather very cold.	

Army Form C. 2118.

WAR DIARY
or
INTELLIGENCE SUMMARY.
(Erase heading not required.)

Instructions regarding War Diaries and Intelligence Summaries are contained in F.S. Regs., Part II. and the Staff Manual respectively. Title pages will be prepared in manuscript.

Place	Date	Hour	Summary of Events and Information	Remarks and references to Appendices
BOIRY BECQUERELLE	11th	11.45 a.m.	Heavy Mortar fired 12 Rounds on H.T.M. at O.32.b.30.50. in retaliation on hostile mortar firing in FOSTER AVENUE, and delivered at 6" fired 16 Rds. on targets as per Concentration scheme.	
	12.		Heavy Mortar fired 15 rounds on hostile H.T.M. at O.32.b.30.50. Good hits obtained. Medium Minnie retaliated from O.32.b.25.45. 6 inch fired 25 Rds on O.32.a. 80.25.	
		11 am	13. O.R. reported here for duty from Wk Sh R.G.A. to take over the guns in the Stores, while 2 battery were away at the school.	
		10.15 pm	2 Officers and 23 O.R. of L 5th H.T.M. B. proceeded to 3rd Army school opt. Montcavy, SIGNY ST FROCHEZ on a 6 inch Newton T.M. Course.	

Weather fine but very cold.

WAR DIARY or INTELLIGENCE SUMMARY

Army Form C. 2118.

(Erase heading not required.)

Place	Date	Hour	Summary of Events and Information	Remarks and references to Appendices
BOIRY BECQUERELLE	Dec 16		Heavy Mortars fired 14 Rds on O.32.b.30.50. - much material thrown up. In accordance with Bombardment programme fired 55 Rds on targets U.2.a.9.1. O.32.a.4.6. & U.1.b.6.2. and obtained direct hits on trench system at O.26.c.45.05. 2nd Lieut ____ 10 Rds on O.32.a.5.4. Say all three being made at O.31.c.2.9. and O.31.c.5.20.	
	17		In accordance with Bombardment programme fired 57 Rds on trenches between enemy front and support lines. The Heavy Mortars fired 15 Rds at O.32.b.30.50. 4th W. Heathers returned from Leave. Weather cold & frosty. Heavy (Stoke) Mortar fired 15 Rds on active trench H.T.M. Enemy and several hits were observed on building near _____.	
	18		Fired 20 Rds onto Wire at O.32.a.15.40. and blowing a _____ experience blown up. 6" fired 57 Rds on Support Lines at O.32.a.5.3. to 5.6. with good results, and on Trenches between M Fork & Castellation Shape O.26.c.6.3.	

2nd O Burley (Wounded) A5834 Wt.W4973/M687 750,000 8/16 D.D. & L. Ltd. Forms/C.2118/13. Returning on Leave. O.26.a.7.0.90.

Army Form C. 2118.

WAR DIARY
or
INTELLIGENCE SUMMARY.
(Erase heading not required.)

Place	Date	Hour	Summary of Events and Information	Remarks and references to Appendices
BOIRY BECQUERELLE	19	2-to 3-15 pm	Heavy (long) fired 4 Rds on O. 32. b. " " " 6 " (short) " One round fell short at about O. 26. c-5.1. (NABPAN SUPPORT). Enemy retaliated with 5 Rds on O. 31. b. & d. 6 and fired 56 Rds on targets — Dugouts in O. 26 & 99 Left today fire on trench at O. 32. a. 9. 3 to O. 32 a. 55. Trench junction at V. 1. b. 95. 70. and front line at O. 20 b. 9. 5. 60. and of the round for Registration. Enemy retaliated with 3 rds on O. 31. b. & O. 31. d. Weather — very cold, & stark frost.	
	20		1" in accordance with Special Bombardment; 2 M. fired out following 2 rds, 5 rounds on Enemy Front line 6 " " " Selected Targets, O. 26. d. O. 32. a. O. 20. b. & V. 1. b. Observation very poor all day owing to haze. Weather — very cold.	

Army Form C. 2118.

WAR DIARY
or
INTELLIGENCE SUMMARY.
(Erase heading not required.)

Place	Date	Hour	Summary of Events and Information	Remarks and references to Appendices
BOIRY BECQUERELLE	Dec 21.	2 p.m.	6 inch fired 32 rounds on Dugouts at O.32.c.65.65. and on NARROW SUPPORT.	
			Heavy M.R. fired 10 Rds on Kockle Mörser emplacement in CHERISY about O.32.b.30.50.	
	22.	11.30 a.m.	Heavy Long Mortar fired 5 rounds on O.32.b.3.4. 6" fired 24 rounds on NIGHT TRENCH (Enfiladin Fire) about O.26.b.5.8. to O.26.b.75.99. Dugouts O.32.a.8.2. and on O.20.b.9.6.	
			2 inch fired 23 rounds on SUPPORT LINES about U.1.b.95.75. 4 Gunners from Y.Battery were posted in the O.P.C. being employed to establish aim and watch for T.M. work.	
	23	10½ a.m. 11.30 a.m.	Heavy Mortar fired 20 Rds on CHERISY. 6 inch fired 11 Rds on Supportline O.32.c.36.45 to O.32.c.50.30. and on dugout at U.2.a.10.80. Supportline O.32.c.6.5. to O.32.a.45.20. Dugout at O.26.c.55.30. 2 inch fired 5 Rounds on dug-out O.26.a.8.2. Enemy retaliated to all the shoots. Observation was poor. Weather very cold.	

WAR DIARY
or
INTELLIGENCE SUMMARY.

(Erase heading not required.)

Army Form C. 2118.

Place	Date	Hour	Summary of Events and Information	Remarks and references to Appendices
BOILY BECQUERELLE	24		The largest 6" position at O.25.b.35.00 completed and gun put in action. Commenced a new position for the M.L.III Mortar at O.13.d.	
		8.15 am	The short mortar fired 19 Rds on Occupied Building at O.26.c.50.15 and on dugouts at O.26.a.36.00	
		8.50 am		
		11.30 am	Hostile H.T.M. retaliated	
		12 noon		
		2 pm	6 inch fired 108 rounds on selected targets and Lihons fired 20 Rds on Front Line Trench at O.32.c.2.3	
		3.15 pm	Direct hit obtained and men seen to be blown away. No shoot was according to programme. Weather very cold.	
	25		Heavy M.R.T Mortar fired 10 Rds on Hostile H.T.M. at O.32.b.5.8. 6 inch fired 120 Rds on selected targets. 2" fired 10 Rds on M.G. at O.I.c.85-95 and 10 Rds cut wire at O.32.a.15.20 Weather very cold & snow fell during afternoon.	

Army Form C. 2118.

WAR DIARY
or
INTELLIGENCE SUMMARY.
(Erase heading not required.)

Instructions regarding War Diaries and Intelligence Summaries are contained in F. S. Regs., Part II. and the Staff Manual respectively. Title pages will be prepared in manuscript.

Place	Date	Hour	Summary of Events and Information	Remarks and references to Appendices
BOIRY BECQUERELLE	26		The Heavy Mortar (M.T.) fired 3 rounds on O.32.6.50.80. Firing 1 gas and material. 6 md. fired 49 Rds on trenches & track at O.32 a. 28.8. They aim at U.2.a. 20.15, & T.M. position at U.2.a.4.4 and on O.20.6.95.60. Capt. J. K. Ramo proceeds on leave, and Capt. J.G. McKins discharged duties as D.H.M.O. during his absence. Weather very cold.	
	27		Heavy Mortar fired 24 Rds on O.32.6.50.95, & O.12.6.05.00. 21 B. types learned arms hooking. 6 md. fired 50 Rds on road at O.32.6.30.99, trenches at O.26. a.52.34, & O.26.c.10.57 and on enemy Support line at O.32.a.37.13 to 38.10. Light Jun. 18 Rds cutting wire at O.32.a.20.15. Weather very cold. 1 Pec L.	

WAR DIARY
or
INTELLIGENCE SUMMARY.

(Erase heading not required.)

Army Form C. 2118.

Place	Date	Hour	Summary of Events and Information	Remarks and references to Appendices
BOIRY BECQUERELLE	28.	9.45	Shells found to be defective were returned to the dump for further examination. Short Mortar (mk I) fired 24 rds on selected targets in O.32.b. 6" fired 75 rounds on suspected T.M. positions at U.7.c.10.15. On Dugouts at O.32.c.50.40. and O.20.d.9.2 also on Trench Junction at O.26.b.55.45. From 10. am the Lst Battery of 34th D.A.H.A. came under the 34th D.T.M.O. command.	
	29.		Heavy Mortars fired 19 Rds obtaining good bursts on O.32.N.O.9. O.32.h.4.9. and O.2.1.4.3.9. 6" fired 40 Rds on CHERRY WOOD and Dugouts &c at O.25.e.5.2. Left Sector = fired 25 bds on HANDY TRENCH and Sunken Roads in vicinity. Weather very wet.	

WAR DIARY
or
INTELLIGENCE SUMMARY.
(Erase heading not required.)

Army Form C. 2118.

Place	Date	Hour	Summary of Events and Information	Remarks and references to Appendices
TARA BECOURELLE	30.	11am to 11.30am	1/6 Heavy Mortars fired 41 Rds on isolated targets on O.32.b.0.32.c. 2 inch fired 25 Rds badly damaging wire at O.32.a 10.45 " " 30 " " " " " and O.32.a " " 6 " " on trench J.O.26.a.30.35 & O.26.c.60.21 " " and 20 " " " U.2.a.25.15. Light mortar fired 41 rnds on FAY ALLEY and KENDY TRENCH and sunken road at U.8.a.6.7.	
	31.		Heavy Mortars fired 23 rds on O.26.d.1.0 and O.32.c.2.45 and O.33.a.65.00 2 inch fired 123 rnds on tang J.O.26.c.5 to O.32.a.39.0 and O.26.c.5.3 to T.K stump? causing considerable damage on support line 6.1.b.90.50 to O.1.b.80.60. and on Tm trench at O.32.c.4.7. Sunken road U.8 central to U.8.c.10.30 and on COPSE TRENCH.	
			The total number of rounds fired by 34th T.M. Coy during the past month = 2363. Rounds " T.M. E. 413 " T.M. F. 288 " T.M. K 236 " T.M. K	Capt & ?? 34 T.M.O.

Army Form C. 2118.

WAR DIARY
or
INTELLIGENCE SUMMARY.
(Erase heading not required.)

Army Form C. 2118.

D.T.M.O.
34 Divn Arty

Month of January 1918

Place	Date	Hour	Summary of Events and Information	Remarks and references to Appendices
BOITY / BECQUERELLE	1.	1 a.m.	In accordance with "Concentration Scheme" Heavy Mortars fired 32 rounds, 6 in fired 136 rounds, on selected targets in O.26.c. 9.d. O.32.c.	
		11.20 a.m.		
		2.40 p.m.		
		11.35 p.m.	Left Sector Hof Bn fired 83 rds 6" on U.1.b. and U.2.a. on S.O.S. lines for registration. on U.S.a. MATCH ALLEY. FAG ALLEY. & COPSE TR.	
	2.		Short (M.L) Mortars fired 14 rds on O.32.b. 10.45. 6 inch " 30 " " T.M. position at O.32.c. 45.65. on U.2.a. 80.10. and SENSEE TRENCH. 2 in L fired 30 rounds clearing old gaps in wire at O.32.a. 15.30. 40H Bn fired 70 rounds 6" on COPSE TR. SUNKEN RD in U.S. central. U.S.a.25.65. U.S.a. 40.65.	
	3.	2 a.m.	3/6 N.T.D. Mortars 13/160, packed to Y.34.K. Y.M.B.	
		1.0	Heavy Mortars fired 25 rds into CHERISY at O.32.b. 10.50 and O.32.d. 05.95 and on O.33.a.0.4.	
		3 pm	6 in fired 95 rds on selected targets in O.26.c. O.32.a. & c. U.1.b. & d. and U.2.a. (40H Bn) fired 91 rds 6 inch on Junction of FAG ALLEY & JUNKER RD. COPSE TR. & CEYLON TR.	

WAR DIARY or INTELLIGENCE SUMMARY

Army Form C. 2118.

5TMO
24 D

Place	Date	Hour	Summary of Events and Information	Remarks and references to Appendices
BOIRY BECQUERELLE	July 4	1.30	H. & L. 6. Own trenches on fire.	
		1.	Howr (9.45) fired 23 rds on O.32.b.58 and O.33.a.2.6.	
		2.30	in retaliation about 12. L.T.M.S.	
		2.pm	6 inch fired 8 rds: Enfilading "ROOF LANE" from O.32.c.75.45	
		3 pm	to O.32.c.5.9 and on Trench from O.32.a.55.42	
			2 inch fired 9 rds, obtaining good bursts & removing stakes	
			wire at O.32.a.1.4 and 30 rds on	
			SENSEE TRENCH U.2.a.9.1, U.1.b.95.90 and U.2.a.20.49.	
	5	11 pm	Z. Battery returned from 2nd Army School of Mortars	
			from a 6" T.M. Course	
			Heavy Mortars fired 30 rds, and 6" fired 35 rds on selected	
			targets in O.26.c.&d. O.32.a.b.&c. and U.1.b.&d.	
			In retaliation nil.	
			(No M. Bur) fired 140 rds 6" on selected targets as per programme	
	6		10 men attached to T.M's during the absence of L.10/41	
			were issued to H.Q. D.A.C.	

Army Form C. 2118.

WAR DIARY
or
INTELLIGENCE SUMMARY.
(Erase heading not required.)

5TMO
24 Bn

Place	Date	Hour	Summary of Events and Information	Remarks and references to Appendices
BOIRY BECQUERELLE	Jan 6	9.45 (Short)	Fired 18 rds North of CHERISY. O.26.c.70.05. Retaliation: heavy. 6" fired 131 rds. Enfilade on BLOCK LANE in O.32.a Were at O.32.a O.675 on rebels target in O.32.c. U.1.b. U.2.a. U.8.a. Lot and U.14.b. Defensive positions, cut wire, [called?] "BROWN LINE" — 6" Newton T.M. fired [?] more in dugout at O.31.c.2.9. Good progress being made	
		2.30 to 3 pm	9.45 (Short) fired 8 rds on O.32.b.1.1. Retaliation: a few 5.9 M — 6" mort. fired 110 rds on targets:- O.32.a.4.c. U.1.b. U.8.a. BLOCKLANE and C.T. Junction of SUNKEN ROAD and FAG ALLEY and KANDY TR 2" fired 10 Rds on wire at O.32.a.1.4.	

Army Form C. 2118.

WAR DIARY
or
INTELLIGENCE SUMMARY.

(Erase heading not required.)

BTMo
24 Div

Place	Date	Hour	Summary of Events and Information	Remarks and references to Appendices
BECQUEREL	July 8	2.15 to 3.15 pm	9.45" M.R.T. fired 10 Rds on Crow Rd in O.32 Central 6 inch " " 82 " Selected targets in O 32 c & d, U.1.b and U.2.a. 2" fired 5 rds on Went at O.32 a 15 45.	
		9.15 am to 10.30 am	9.45" M.R.T fired 15 rds on selected targets on enemy's 6" " 133 " newtons " with Bombardment Programme	
		10"	6 inch fired 158 rds on FAG ALLEY. SUNKEN RD. and COPSE TR on targets in U.1.6. U.2.a. O.26.c. & d. and O.32.c. Capt of Rams returned from leave.	
		11"	2 inch fired 10 Rds (Gr Shrale) O.T. at O.32 a 20.20. 6" " 114 " on M.G.s at O 32 a 9 7. Dugouts O 32 6.1.4. T.M. at O.26.d. 35.75. Trenches at O.26 c. O.40.15 to O.26.d. 35.90. and in O.26 d U.2.a. U.8.c and U.14.c.	

Army Form C. 2118.

WAR DIARY
or
INTELLIGENCE SUMMARY.
(Erase heading not required.)

BT Mo
24 Bn

Place	Date	Hour	Summary of Events and Information	Remarks and references to Appendices
BOIRY X BECQUERELLE	Jan 12	11.30 1 am 2.30 pm	9.45" (M.F.) Fire 15 rds on dugouts at O.32.b.5.8. O.32.b.15/15 and O.26.d.2.0 Retaliation :- 50 - 15 cm in our position at O.31.b.0.9. 6 cms fired 52 rnds on dugouts at O.32.b.70.45. T-S – O.32.c.32.60 to 32/62 and O.32.e.60.70 and on FAG ALLEY.	
	13	12.1 3.35 4 pm	2 mks fired 6rds damaging dump at O.26.a.85.20 9.45" (M.F. 1 & M.F. III) each fired 10 rnds on O.32 b.2.2. O.26.d.4.0. O.32.b.35.00. O.26.a.85.65. 6 cms fired 189 rounds on dugouts O.26.d.0.9. O.26.c.35.30. T.M. at O.26.d.35.15 and O.32.a.9.6 KANDY TRENCH, COPSE TR. and unlocated targets U.1.b. O.26.b.x.d. O.32.b.x.c. New sub led in/laid in M.F.III heavy hostile which was damaged by shell fire.	

Army Form C. 2118.

WAR DIARY
or
INTELLIGENCE SUMMARY.
(Erase heading not required.)

27th Siege Bn

Place	Date	Hour	Summary of Events and Information	Remarks and references to Appendices
BOIRY BECQUERELLE	J/14		Heavy 9.45" fired 22 rds on Cross Roads O.32 Central and O.26.d.75.70	
			6 inch fired 90 Rds on TANDY TK, CEYLON + OUNCE TKS. Dugouts and Trench O.26.c.50.15. O.32.b.45.05. SENSEE TK U.2.c.30.80 to 50.90 U.2.a.00.70 and O.32.d.00.90.	
			2 inch Trench Mortars fired and unreplyed Bt. H.Q T.M. O.26.d.35.15	
			2 inch Trench Grds on Trench O.26.a.8.2	
	15		Heavy 9.45" fired 20 Rds on O.26.d.40.00 + 70.65	
			6 inch " 15 " " O.26.d.2.0	
			2 " " 60 " " O.32.a.20.15 Sap + M.G	
	16		6 inch fired 10 Rds on dugouts O.32. e.50.55 to 50.90 U.2.d.50.00 to 95.20, U.2.a.20.80 to 30.95	
			2 inch fired 10 rds on U.2.a.	
	17		9.45" M.A fired 10Rds on O.32.b.40.00. + 40.10.	
			6 inch fired 15 Rds on SENSEE VALLEY U.2.a.50.00 to 9.0.15. very good shot.	
			2 " " 20 " " C.T. O.32.a.35.40	

WAR DIARY or INTELLIGENCE SUMMARY

Army Form C. 2118.

57 M.O.
24 Div

Place	Date	Hour	Summary of Events and Information	Remarks and references to Appendices
BOIRY BECQUERELLE	Jan 18		6 inch fired 5 rds on OUNCE TRENCH, this being the only T.M. activity to-day.	
	19		Heavy Mortars fired 2 rds on T.M. + selected targets in O.32.c. (The T.M. was silenced at O.32.6.20.20.) Cmdt fired 2 rds on OUNCE TRENCH 2" " 35 " damaging wire at O.26.a.8.2.	
	20		6 inch fired 4 rds on KANDY T.K. Lieut. T.E. Owen returned from leave. One 6" howitzer in BROWN line completed, and progress made with 3 more.	
	21		6 inch fired 10 Rds on KANDY T.K. The 2 inch Newton Guns were removed from the line. 4/Lt A.C. Angell from B/60 posted to Y.34th T.M.B. 4/Lt A. James " " B/60 " V. " H.T.M.B. Both were killed by an accident on Jan 24th

WAR DIARY or INTELLIGENCE SUMMARY

Army Form C. 2118.

BTMO 3d Div

Place	Date	Hour	Summary of Events and Information	Remarks and references to Appendices
BOIRY BECOURT/FLERS	22		Heavy Mortars fired 26 rds on O.32.b.40.00, O.32.b.50.15, and Rifle M.G. emplacement at O.32.b.30.45. (a light retaliation). 6 inch fired 60 rds on U.2.a. 40.60, 70.55. (a light retaliation) and on KANDY TRENCH. 2 inch fired 20 rds on U.1.b. 85.95.	a.71.91 a.85.10 and U.5.a
	23		6 inch fired 58 rds on suspected T.M. emplacement O.32.c.90.55. on O.32.c.50.30. KANDY TRENCH. and Junction of CEYLON TR: and VALLEY ROAD. 2 inch fired 40 rds on O.32.b.00.05 and U.2.a. 25.85. Orders were issued that 100 rounds of ammunition was to be kept in reserve at each trench position and 50 rds at each 9.45" position, in the event of there being a relief.	
	24		Heavy Mortars fired 13 rds on O.32.b.22.22. and O.26.d.8.7. 6 inch fired 70 rds on T.M. at O.32.c.50.55. KANDY TR and VALLEY ROAD. Junction of CEYLON TR and VALLEY ROAD. KANDY TR and TUNNEL at U.8.a. 20.60. 2 inch fired 26 rds on O.32.c.30.10. U.2.a.23.95 U.2.a. 0.8. and TRENCH at U.2.a.30.95.	

Army Form C. 2118.

WAR DIARY
or
INTELLIGENCE SUMMARY.

(Erase heading not required.)

5TMG
su Bn

Place	Date	Hour	Summary of Events and Information	Remarks and references to Appendices
BOIRY BECQUERELLE	Jan 25		Heavy mortar fired 10 rds on O.32.b.2.2. Good bursts and no retaliation. 6" fired 35 rds on junction of CEYLON TR and FONTAINE — BULLECOURT RD and on KANDY TR.	
	26.		Heavy Mortars fired 12 rds on O.32.b.2.2. O.32.b.30.45. In retaliation to hostile Minnie; good shooting obtained. 6 inch fired 1 rd for registration and UAP 21. [illegible]	
	27	9.45	"MK III fired 12 rds on O.32.c.9.8. 6" fired 70 rds on O.26.c.4.7. and 8.6. No retaliation also on U.1.b.70.75. 90.75 on O.32.c.15.25 and O.32.c.3.1. ½ Lt to Macduff proceeds on leave.	

Army Form C. 2118.

WAR DIARY
or
INTELLIGENCE SUMMARY.
(Erase heading not required.)

JTMo
2n Bn

Place	Date	Hour	Summary of Events and Information	Remarks and references to Appendices
BOIRY BECQUERELLE	Jan. 28		Heavy Long Mortar carried out a shoot with "aeroplane observation" on the hostile T.M. position at O26 c 78.78 — 22 rds were fired and result very satisfactory. 6 inch fired 90 Rds on hostile T.M. O26 b g3 65. U2a O.7. and selected targets in U.1.6. U2.a. and O32.a. T.M. was extended at O32.a. 30.06. 40 R.D. was fired 69 rds. 6 inch on UAP21. UAP4. Dugouts at U8.6.2.9} KANDY TR and function of OUNCE and COPSE TR (and at U.F.a.5 g3) 6" D. continued on leave.	
	29		Heavy Mortars fired 12 rds on O26 at 30.00. and 10. 70. 6 inch fired 122 rds on selected targets, and railway on action at U2 b-25.46.	
	30		6 inch fired 70 Rds on O26 d 35 70. UAP21. UAP4. on OUNCE and KANDY TR TRENCHES. Weather fine.	

Army Form C. 2118.

WAR DIARY
or
INTELLIGENCE SUMMARY.
(Erase heading not required.)

Instructions regarding War Diaries and Intelligence Summaries are contained in F.S. Regs., Part II. and the Staff Manual respectively. Title pages will be prepared in manuscript.

Place	Date	Hour	Summary of Events and Information	Remarks and references to Appendices
BY BECQUERELLE	Jan 31		6 inch fired 50 Rds on O.32.c.80.32. O.32.c.65.25. U.16.00.95. on hostile Machine Gun at U.16.95.95. and on U.2.a.05.70. T.M. ammunition expended during the last month — 2643. Rounds. T.M.G. 322. " T.M.B. 196. " T.M.F. 179. " T.M.K.	

J. Mains Capt,
D.T.M.O. 34th Div.

Army Form C. 2118.

WAR DIARY
or
INTELLIGENCE SUMMARY.
(Erase heading not required.)

VA 20
DTM 034 Duncan

Place	Date	Hour	Summary of Events and Information	Remarks and references to Appendices
BOIRY BECQUERELLE	February 1	11.30 to 11.45 am	6 inch Newton Mortars fired 9 rounds on O.26.c.7.1. O.26.d.6.0. O.32.c.15.65. M.G. 6.T.S. in O.32.c. T M Position O.32.c.55.70 and on Support Line V.2.a.20.80. Retaliation nil. Weather was fine but cold.	
	2		The Long Mark III fired 25 rds on ST MICHAEL'S STATUE, at O.27.c.30.95 and on O.26.d.95.65 and obtained good hits. 6 inch fired 153 rds on selected targets in O.26.d. O.27.c. O.32.c. U.2.a. U.8.d. U.8.a. OUNCE TR and FONTAINE — BULLECOURT ROAD on KANDY and CEYLON TRS.	
	3	1 pm	6 inch continued very active, firing 150 rds on the usual selected targets. Weather rough and cold.	
	4		Heavy Mortars fired 56 rounds on selected targets in O.32.b. 6 inch " 176 " " " as usual. Considerable movement of transport seen on PURY-HENDECOURT RD. Evidently always taking place. 6 inch mortars fired on parties and dispersed them.	

Army Form C. 2118.

WAR DIARY
or
INTELLIGENCE SUMMARY.
(Erase heading not required.)

Instructions regarding War Diaries and Intelligence Summaries are contained in F. S. Regs., Part II. and the Staff Manual respectively. Title pages will be prepared in manuscript.

Place	Date	Hour	Summary of Events and Information	Remarks and references to Appendices
BOIRY BECQUERELLE	Feb 5		The Long and Short Heavy Mortars carried out a successful shoot with aeroplane Observation - 25 rounds were fired on O.32.b.05.10. and O.32.b.55.90. 2 direct hits obtained. Enemy fired 10 rounds on the usual targets.	
	6		" 126 "	
	6		" 84 "	
			Heavy mortars fired 10 Rds on O.32.b.20.20. 3 Officers and 1 N.C.O. and 3 men for Battery of 3rd Div T.M.B came to learn the line and reconnoitre to in preparation of the forthcoming relief by the 3rd Div.	
		8.15 to 29.22	Capt Brown d.s.o. T.Y. Battery, proceeded to 2nd Army School of Mortars for duty, as an Assistant Instructor on prob taken.	
	7	11 am	42 N.C.O.s & men of the 3rd Div. arrived as to relieve the 5th K.T.M. in the line.	
			Enemy Mortars fired 67 Rounds, on O.26.c.7.3. and in reply to S.O.S. Many of the enemy observed at dressing station during the morning.	

Army Form C. 2118.

WAR DIARY
or
INTELLIGENCE SUMMARY.
(Erase heading not required.)

Place	Date Feby	Hour	Summary of Events and Information	Remarks and references to Appendices
BOIRY BECQUERELLE	9.	7-30 a.m	6 Officers and 80. O.R. left BOIRY BECQUERELLE by Lorries and proceeded to CANETTEMONT near FREVENT — the route taken was via ARRAS — AVESNES — le — COMPTE and ETREE WAMIN, arrived at destination by noon.	
		10.30 a.m	B.T.M.O. 3rd p.u. arrived with remainder of the personnel of 3rd T.M.B. and relief was completed by noon.	
	10	7.30 a.m	The D.T.M.O. and remainder of 34th T.M. Personnel, left BOIRY-BECQUERELLE, same route as above being taken — and arrived at destination by noon. (8 Lorries were allotted to T.M.s for the move).	
		9. a.m	Parade for all ranks who arrived on the 9th Orderly Officer Lieut. Weather, " Sergt. Sergt Gurvan.	
		9.15 to 12 noon	Box Respirator Inspection and drill and marching drill.	
		2-15 to 4 p.m.	Fatigues; cleaning billets and Improving the conditions of the Camp.	
			General remark: This to be continued daily. Weather was fine.	

Army Form C. 2118.

WAR DIARY
or
INTELLIGENCE SUMMARY.
(Erase heading not required.)

Instructions regarding War Diaries and Intelligence Summaries are contained in F. S. Regs., Part II. and the Staff Manual respectively. Title pages will be prepared in manuscript.

Place	Date	Hour	Summary of Events and Information	Remarks and references to Appendices
CANETTEMONT. (Sheet 51C).	11	9 am	Parade for Inspection. Orderly Officer, 2Lt. R. James. " Sergt. Cpl. Walton.	
		9.15 am to 4 pm	Box Respirator drill – Marching drill – & General fatigues, – as on previous day.	
	12	9 am to 4 pm	Parade, S.B.R. drill and fatigues – as above. Orderly Officer 2Lt Bly Thr " Sergeant Cpl. Barker.	
	13	9 am to 4 pm	Parades & as above. Orderly Officer; 2Lt K. J. Franklin, " Sergeant; Sgt Harrison 12 – 2 inch Medium Mortars were taken and handed over to D.A.D.O.S. at LA-CAUROY. 4 – 6 inch Newton Mortars arrived – Have being for instructional purposes. 10 N.C.Os and men of "V" Bty commenced a course under 2 Medium Bty N. C. O.S. 1 Tailor arrived from the D.A.C. for 10 days with T.M.2 and was placed at the disposal of "V" Bty for 10 days and 2 days to each Medium Battery, for repairs to	

WAR DIARY or INTELLIGENCE SUMMARY

Army Form C. 2118.

Place	Date	Hour	Summary of Events and Information	Remarks and references to Appendices
CAETTEMONT	Feby. 13		A "Daily Programme of Training" was commenced (one copy attached herewith). 20 Rifles were loaned to T.M. from the D.A.C. for drill & Instruction purposes.	
	14th	9 am 4 pm	Parade. Training commenced according to "programme" Orderly Officer Lt Lanham " Sergeant Sgt Greig One N.C.O. of the I.P. & O. were on coal Squad of "Physical Drill" & the I.P. & O. were on coal Squad for 3 days and each A Physical Instructor arrived for 3 days and each afternoon a class was held exclusively for N.C.O's with for drill and Lectures.	
		5-30 pm	Lieut Lanham proceeded on Leave Weather was very dull.	
	15	9 am	Parade and Training continued as per programme Orderly Officer 2/Lt Crookes. 3 Gunners from X.T.V each from X.T.V were posted to the D.A.C. There were being issued to T.M.S.	

Army Form C. 2118.

WAR DIARY
or
INTELLIGENCE SUMMARY.

(Erase heading not required.)

Instructions regarding War Diaries and Intelligence Summaries are contained in F.S. Regs., Part II. and the Staff Manual respectively. Title pages will be prepared in manuscript.

Place	Date	Hour	Summary of Events and Information	Remarks and references to Appendices
CANETTEMONT	July 16		Parades, and training continued, according to programme.	Orderly Officer. Lt E.D. Cox.
	17		do	2/Lt Macduff.
	18		do	Lieut Heather W.
	19		do	2/Lt Blythe W.L.
	20		do	2/Lt Franklin K.J.
	21		do	Lt Cox E.D.
	22		Capt P. Filkins proceeded on leave. Parades, Physical; Rifle; and marching drill and Telephony squad, continued.	2/Lt Macduff.
	23		do	Lt Heather W.
	24		do	2/Lt Blythe W.L.
			A Revised programme of training was commenced (see copy attached) and proceeded to the Third Army Mining school for a course on dug-out construction.	

1. 11. 60. and 3. Wt. W12839/M1293: 75,000. 1/17. D.D. & L., Ltd. Forms/C.2118/14. (A7092).

Training Programme – for week commencing
Saturday 24th Feby 1918.

DATE.	TIME.	
Feby 24th	9. am.	Inspection Parade.
	11. am.	Football Match.
" 25th	9. am.	Inspection Parade
	9.15 to 10.30 am.	Rifle Drill – Physical Drill. Telephony – Squad as usual. 6 inch Gun drill for "V" Battery
	10.45 to 12 noon	— do —
	2.15 pm	Football Match.
" 26th	Morning	same as on 25th
	2.15 pm.	Paper chase & Physical Drill.
" 27th	Morning	same as on 25th
	2.15 pm.	Football Match & Parade Inspection by G.O.C. Division.
" 28th	Morning	same as on 25th
	2.15 pm.	Jumping: Wrestling: Boxing.
March 1st	Morning	same as 25th Feby.
	2.15 pm	Football Match.
" 2nd	Morning	same as 25th Feby.
	2.15 pm	Football Match.

18.2.18.

Capt.
D.T.M.O. 34th Div.

Army Form C. 2118.

WAR DIARY
or
INTELLIGENCE SUMMARY.
(Erase heading not required.)

Place	Date	Hour	Summary of Events and Information	Remarks and references to Appendices
CANETTEMONT	Feby 25	9 am to 12 noon & 2 pm to 4 pm	Parade, Physical training, rifle drill, Gas drill, & marching drill } according to programme	Orderly Officers 2/Lt Franklin R.T. Lt E.D. Cox 2/Lt Macduff L Lt Heathcote W.
	26	do	do	
	27	do	do	
	28	do	do	
			Weather fine.	
			Ammunition expended from Feby 1 to 8th inclusive.	
			933 Rounds S.M.L.E	
			45 " L.M.E	
			71 " S.M.K	

H Vans Capt
A/OC 7/H Div

Army Form C. 2118.

WAR DIARY
or
INTELLIGENCE SUMMARY 34 D TM By

(Erase heading not required.)

Instructions regarding War Diaries and Intelligence Summaries are contained in F.S. Regs., Part II. and the Staff Manual respectively. Title Pages will be prepared in manuscript.

Place	Date	Hour	Summary of Events and Information	Remarks and references to Appendices
CANETTEMONT.	March 1st	9 am	Inspection Parade. Box Respirator drill, and Marching drill.	
	2nd	9.15 am to 12 noon	same as on 1st. Weather fair.	
	3rd	8.30 am	The 3 Medium Batteries personnel left Canettemont to take over on the line from the 40th Divisional T.M.B. & arrived about noon, at ST LEGER.	
	4th	8.30 am	"V" Battery proceeded to ST LEGER to take over from 40th H.T.M.B. Weather very dull.	
ST LEGER.	5th		The relief was completed by noon. 12 enemy Newton Trench Mortars were taken over in situ (Nine in the front line system, three in alternate positions) nine Rand M were taken over in Billets.	
	6th		Registration shoots were carried out on KANDY TRENCH and on various targets. 2 enemy Mortars were handed over to the 59th H. Div. (complete).	

2449 Wt. W14957/Mgo 750,000 1/16 J.B.C. & A. Forms/C.2118/12.

Army Form C. 2118.

WAR DIARY
or
INTELLIGENCE SUMMARY

(Erase heading not required.)

Instructions regarding War Diaries and Intelligence Summaries are contained in F.S. Regs., Part II. and the Staff Manual respectively. Title Pages will be prepared in manuscript.

Place	Date	Hour	Summary of Events and Information	Remarks and references to Appendices
ST LEGER	March 6th		The reorganization of 54th S.M. took place. Two Heavy Batteries (each with 6 guns) to remain with the Division. The R.G.A. personnel were transferred to the Heavy Battery taken over by the 16 Corps.	
	7th		Destructive shoots were carried out on KANDY & OUNCE Trenches, & two hostile T.M. positions. 2 6 inch Newton Mortars were handed over to the 40th Div. Weather was very fine.	
	8th	5.25	6 inch fired on TRIDENT ALLEY, and on T Junction in U.9.c. 15.25	
	9th		Fire was carried out on various points in COPSE TRENCH.	
	10th		6 inch fired on various targets in U.8.d. U.15.a. & U.15.c. slight retaliation. Weather fine.	

WAR DIARY or INTELLIGENCE SUMMARY

Army Form C. 2118.

Place	Date	Hour	Summary of Events and Information	Remarks and references to Appendices
ST LEGER	May 11th		6 and fired on Hostile T.M. positions on U.2.c. Weather fine.	
	12th		41 rounds were fired on hostile T.M. at U.8.a.3.4. and on V.d.d. 20.00.	
	13th	11 a.m. to 7.30 a.m.	The enemy was observed to be massing forces and an attack was considered imminent. Harassing fire was put down on enemy trenches & forced crossings. 458 rounds were fired during this period. The enemy did not attack.	
	14th	7.30 to 6 a.m.	87 rounds were fired on COPSE TR. and on enemy working parties in FONTAINE, and on enemy party reported to be digging trench between DOG LANE & BEEF ALLEY.	
	15th	7.35 to 6 a.m.	106 rounds harassing fire on COPSE - KANDY - and OUNCE TRENCHES, and TRIDENT ALLEY. Weather continued to be fine.	

Army Form C. 2118.

WAR DIARY
or
INTELLIGENCE SUMMARY

(Erase heading not required.)

Instructions regarding War Diaries and Intelligence Summaries are contained in F. S. Regs., Part II. and the Staff Manual respectively. Title Pages will be prepared in manuscript.

Place	Date	Hour	Summary of Events and Information	Remarks and references to Appendices
ST LEGER	16/1/17	3 am to 6 am	161 rounds were fired on COPSE TRENCH and trench junction on U.15.a. and U.2.c. Weather very fine.	
	17	3 am to 6 am	135 rounds fired on the above targets. 2/Lt N.R.D. Crosby proceeded on leave to England.	
	18		50 rounds were fired in conjunction with L/H Group of 4/5 on hostile T.M. emplacements on U.2.c.	
	19	10	92 rounds fired on various selected targets in U.8.6. & U.9.c.	
	20	10	112 rounds fired on suspected T.M. in FONTAINE, on wire at junction of FAG and COPSE TRENCH, and at U.15.a.05.95. Weather fair.	

2449 Wt. W14957/M90 750,000 1/16 J.B.C. & A. Forms/C.2118/12.

WAR DIARY
or
INTELLIGENCE SUMMARY

Army Form C. 2118.

Place	Date	Hour	Summary of Events and Information	Remarks and references to Appendices
ST LEGER	March 21	4~am	The enemy heavily bombarded the lines and back areas. Enemy Trench Mortars retaliated on hostile T.M positions, on (S.O.S.) and Trench junctions. About 1600 rounds were fired during the morning very good shooting observed. The enemy having driven in our line on the south attacked our forces on the flank, this necessitated a withdrawal. The casualties during this period were:- 1. O.R. killed of "Y" Battery. 3. O.R. Wounded (gas) "Y" 2. O.R. " - " - V/VIII T.M.B. All 3H.K. T.M. personnel left ST LEGER and proceeded to the R.A.C. (No 3 station) at HAMELIN COURT.	
	22.		The Bat/C removed from HAMELINCOURT and proceeded to HENDECOURT - LEZ - RANSART. All available T.M personnel assisted No 3 Section to deal with Ammunition.	

Army Form C. 2118.

WAR DIARY
or
INTELLIGENCE SUMMARY

(Erase heading not required.)

Place	Date	Hour	Summary of Events and Information	Remarks and references to Appendices
HENDECOURT L52	March 23rd		All personnel of X Battery proceeded to work the ammunition dump at BOIRY-ST-RICTRUDE.	
KANSART	24th		Y Battery personnel searched No's 1. and 2 sections in taking ammunition to the line. Weather fine.	
	25th		—do—	
	26th	7.10pm	The D.A.C. & T.M. personnel withdrew from HENDECOURT and proceeded to BELLACOURT.	
	27th		The T.M. personnel assisted the Column to deal with Ammunition.	
	28th			
	29th			

Place	Date	Hour	Summary of Events and Information	Remarks and references to Appendices
	March 30	11.30 am	Removed from BELLACOURT and proceeded to GAUDIEMPRE and arrived at 4 pm. Part of X Battery were killed in the village, remained still covering the B.A.C. to deal with ammunition.	
	31st		Weather turned very wet.	

J. Spiers Capt R.F.A.
D.T.N.O. 34th Div.

34th Divisional Artillery

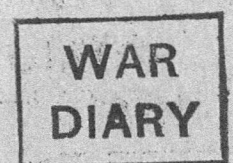

D. T. M. O.

34th DIVISION.

APRIL 1 9 1 8

WAR DIARY
or
INTELLIGENCE SUMMARY

(Erase heading not required.)

Instructions regarding War Diaries and Intelligence Summaries are contained in F.S. Regs., Part II. and the Staff Manual respectively. Title Pages will be prepared in manuscript.

Place	Date	Hour	Summary of Events and Information	Remarks and references to Appendices
GAUDIEMPRE	April 1	9 a.m.	Inspection parade. and "Box Respirator" drill.	
	2nd		do	
	3rd		All T.M. Personnel attached to the Sections, D.A.C. and 152nd & 160th F.A. Brigades, returned to their Batteries.	
		18.30 p.m.	Left GAUTEMPRE and proceeded to BAVINCOURT - arrived there at 4 p.m. (Weather very fine.) 6 Lorries were allotted to T.M. for the move.	
	4th	3 p.m. to 6 p.m.	Bath Parade for all N.C.O.s & men. Weather wet.	
	5th	9 a.m.	Left BAVINCOURT and proceeded by lorries to ST POL. (Route, via HERLIN-LE-SEC, near ST POL, via FREVENT - DOULLENS -). Arrived at destination at 1 p.m. Weather fair.	

INTELLIGENCE SUMMARY

(Erase heading not required.)

Place	Date	Hour	Summary of Events and Information	Remarks and references to Appendices
	April 6th	8.30 a.m.	Left MERLIN-LE-SEC & proceeded to ST. HILAIRE (nr ST VENANT) (Route taken — via ST POL – LILLERS) & arrived about 3pm. An advance party of 2 officers & 9 N.C.O.s proceeded to ST POL, to join party proceeding to ERQUINGHEM near ARMENTIERES, for making preparations for taken over from the 38th Div. I.M.B. Weather was fine.	
	7th	10.30 a.m	Move continued — the destination being HAVERSKERQUE. (for the day) arrived at 12 noon. Route — via LILLERS – ST VENANT. Weather very fine.	
	8th	10. a.m	Left HAVERSKERQUE, and completed the move, arriving at ERQUINGHEM at 4 pm. (Route — via NERVIL – ESTAIRES – STEENWERCK) Parties proceeded to the line, to take over from the 38th Div (S. Cecil Newton Mostock taken over in the line)	

INTELLIGENCE SUMMARY

or

(Erase heading not required.)

Instructions regarding War Diaries and Intelligence Summaries are contained in F.S. Regs., Part II. and the Staff Manual respectively. Title Pages will be prepared in manuscript.

Place	Date	Hour	Summary of Events and Information	Remarks and references to Appendices
ERQUINGHEM	April 9th	4 a.m.	The enemy heavily bombarded the town & the surrounding places, and later in the day succeeded in forcing back the PORTUGUESE who were holding the line to the right. This necessitated our own troops to withdraw. All the Newton Mortars were buried & the limbers recovered. There were no casualties to personnel. The T.M. personnel took up billets at STEENWERCK, with the 34th Div. H.Q. BLANC - MAISON near STEENWERCK. Weather very fine.	
	10th	10.30 p.m.	Left L-EPINETTE and proceeded to OUTERSTEENE.	
	11th	12 noon	Left OUTERSTEENE and marched to HAZEBROUCK. Arrived at 7 p.m., N.C.O.'s & men billeted in the schoolroom. Weather very fine.	
	12th		Remained at Hazebrouck.	

INTELLIGENCE SUMMARY

Place	Date April	Hour	Summary of Events and Information	Remarks and references to Appendices
	13	12.30 noon	Left HAZEBROUCK for MORBECQUE.	
MORBECQUE	14 to 20		All T.M. personnel took over at the Ammunition Dump.	
			— do —	
	21	2 p.m.	30. N.C.O.s + Men of X Battery, proceeded to 152 F.A. Bde. } for preparing 30. " " " Y " 160 " " } gun positions (in reserve). Remaining N.C.O.s + men still remained at the Ammun. Dump. Weather unsettled during this period.	
	22nd to 30		Working parties, assisted the F.A. Bdys, as stated above.	
	29		L.P. Banks (X Battery) returned from leave.	

Jas Perry Capt. R.F.A.
D.T.M.O. 34th Div.

WAR DIARY
or
INTELLIGENCE SUMMARY.
(Erase heading not required.)

Army Form C. 2118.

3rd Bn.t Trench Mortars

Vol 25

Place	Date	Hour	Summary of Events and Information	Remarks and references to Appendices
MORBECQUE	May 1st		60. N.C.O's and Men still arrived 152nd & 160th F.A. Bdes. preparing gun positions etc.	
	2nd		1. Gunner was slightly wounded by a (live) still falling the Ammunition Dump, in MORBECQUE. Weather very fine.	
	3rd		1. N.C.O & 6 men having completed their gun positions for the field Battery, carried the parts of the ammunition Dumps.	
	4th		Working parties - as above.	
	5th	am	20. N.C.O's & men from "X" Battery, & 10 from "Y" Battery proceeded to 160 FA.Bde. to prepare gun positions. (This party remaining with 160 Bde until the work is completed). Weather very wet.	

Army Form C. 2118.

WAR DIARY
or
INTELLIGENCE SUMMARY.
(Erase heading not required.)

Place	Date	Hour	Summary of Events and Information	Remarks and references to Appendices
MORBECQUE	May 6th	12.	O.i/c of 34th D.A.C. (temporarily attached to 30th D.A.C.) joined the party at the 2 Ammunition Dumps rented the 34th D.A.C. arrived in this area. Weather fair.	
	7.		Working parties as on the 4th inst.	
	8.	7.30 am	All available personnel proceeded to STEENBECQUE & erected Nissen Huts for 34th R.A. Hd Qrs.	
	9.		Completed erecting the above huts. Weather very warm.	
	10.	7.30 am	Left MORBECQUE and proceeded to STEENBECQUE. 3 Coilpls 2 Bders & 2 Guns were posted to D/160 F.A. Bde, & proceeded to the Wagon lines. Working parties remained with the Field Batteries.	

Army Form C. 2118.

WAR DIARY
or
INTELLIGENCE SUMMARY.
(Erase heading not required.)

Place	Date	Hour	Summary of Events and Information	Remarks and references to Appendices
STEENBECQUE	11.		The undermentioned personnel were posted to the Batteries as stated with effect from to-day.	
			"X" Battery. 7 Gunners to 152nd F.A.Bde.	
			1 Cpl 2 Gnrs A/160 "	
			1 n.c.o. & men B/160 "	
			5 " " D/160 "	
			Y Battery. 12 n.c.o. & men to 152nd	
			4 " " A/160 "	
			5 " " B/160 "	
			3 " " C/160 "	
			6 " " 1 min D/160 "	
			1 Sgt to 34th D.A.C.	
			The remaining personnel (7 Officers & 38 n.c.o. & Men remained at STEENBECQUE, Ammunition Dumps.	

Army Form C. 2118.

WAR DIARY
or
INTELLIGENCE SUMMARY.
(Erase heading not required.)

Place	Date	Hour	Summary of Events and Information	Remarks and references to Appendices
STEENBECQUE	May 12 to 18		1 Officer + 27 N.C.O.'s + Men received on the Ammunition Dump &c. Weather very warm during this period.	
	18.	8 pm	27 N.C.O.'s + Men from the Ammunition Dump were posted to 5th Div. T.M.B, and proceeded to 5th Div. Headquarters at THIENNES. Officers were posted away as under:—	

APPENDIX 1.   11th. May 1918.

(1)   Under instructions from 34th. Division the the 34th. T.M.B. parsonnel were drafted, as required, as reinforcements to other units of the 34th. Divisional Artillery, and to 5th. Divisional Artillery.

(2)   Captain J.A. Raine M.C., R.F.A., was posted to 13th. Corps H.Q.

(3)   Captain L.E. Lanham M.C., R.F.A., was posted to 3rd. Divisional Artillery.

for D.T.M.O.
34th. Division.

Army Form C. 2118.

WAR DIARY
or
INTELLIGENCE SUMMARY.

(Erase heading not required.)

Instructions regarding War Diaries and Intelligence Summaries are contained in F. S. Regs., Part II. and the Staff Manual respectively. Title pages will be prepared in manuscript.

Place	Date	Hour	Summary of Events and Information	Remarks and references to Appendices
	1918.			
STEENBECQUE. C.29.d.5.1.	June 26th		34th DIVISIONAL TRENCH MORTAR BATTERIES, re-formed with effect from 26th June 1918. (Authority: First Army, G.O.C.,R.A. No 100/172, dated 17/6/18.) Captain J.A. RAINE, (M.C.) R.F.A., appointed D.T.M.O., arrived at 34th Divnl Artillery Headquarters, from 13th Corps Hd.Qrs. to reconstitute "X" and "Y" Batteries. The undermentioned Officers were posted to Batteries as shown, with effect from 26th. Captain W. HEATHER. R.F.A. appointed O/C, "X" Battery, from 1st Army School of Mortars. Captain P. BANKS. -do- " "Y" " D/160th Bde. R.F.A. Lieut F.E.R. FRANKLYN. R.F.A., posted to X Battery from No 2 Section 34th Div.Amm.Col. 2/lieut W.L. BLYTHE. " " Y " " D/160th Bde. R.F.A. 2/Lieut R. JAMES. " " Y " " B/152nd Bde. " 2/Lieut S. ANGELL. " " X " " " " 2/Lieut N.R.D.Crookes. " " X " " No 1 Section 34th Div.Amm.Col. The Officers at the F.A. Brigades remained with their batteries until the 28th instant. 2/Lieut N.R.D. CROOKES. remained in charge of 34th AmmnReserve Park during the absence on leave of the senior Officer in charge.	

Army Form C. 2118.

WAR DIARY
or
INTELLIGENCE SUMMARY.
(Erase heading not required.)

Place	Date	Hour	Summary of Events and Information	Remarks and references to Appendices
STEENBECQUE. C.29.d.5.1.	1918. June. 26th.		Trained Trench Mortar Personnel were posted from Units as shewn. 19. N.C.O's and Men from 152nd Bde. R.F.A. 38. " " " " 160th " " 29. " " " " 34th D.A.C. 14. " " " " 5th Div. Trench Mortar Batteries. 1. " man " 1st Army School of Mortars. The above paraded at Headquarters, 34th Div.Ammn.Column., and billets were occupied at STEENBECQUE. (C.30.d.8.0.) sheet 36 A N.W. The Officers occupied billets in STEENBECQUE.	
	27th to 30th inclusive.)	9-.a.m. 9-30 a.m. to 12-30p.m. 2- p.m. to 4-30 p.m.	Inspection Parade. Box Respirator Drill. Physical Drill. and Marching Drill, carried out daily. In the anticipation of an early return to the line.	

[signature]
Captain, R.F.A.
D.T.M.O., 34th Division.

Army Form C. 2118.

WAR DIARY or INTELLIGENCE SUMMARY.

X and Y 34th Med. Trench Mortar Batteries.

(Erase heading not required.)

July 1918.

Place	Date 1918.	Hour	Summary of Events and Information	Remarks and references to Appendices
Steenbecque. C.30.d.8.0.	July 1st	9 a.m. to 12-30 p.m.	Physical training - Box Respirator drill. Marching drill.	
		2- p.m. to 4-30 p.m.	--do--	
	2nd		--do--	
	3rd		--do--	
	3th	6.p.m.	4 Lorries from Divisional Supply Column arrived at STEENBECQUE in readiness for the move on the 4th inst; to BELGIUM.	
	4th	9 a.m.	2 Lorries per battery conveying Personnel and Stores departed STEENBECQUE and proceeded to RUBROUCK, route via LYNDE - EBBLINGHEM - CASSELL - ARNEKE, and arrived at 1 p.m., and billetts were occupied for the night.	
	5th	9 a.m.	Departed RUBROUCK and proceeded to PERA CAMP in HAANDEKOT AREA - BELGIUM. (route via CASSELL - WINNEZEELE - WATOU,) arrived at 1 p.m.	
	6th		Box Respirator and Marching drill.	

Army Form C. 2118.

WAR DIARY
or
INTELLIGENCE SUMMARY.
(Erase heading not required.)

Instructions regarding War Diaries and Intelligence Summaries are contained in F. S. Regs., Part II. and the Staff Manual respectively. Title pages will be prepared in manuscript.

Place	Date	Hour	Summary of Events and Information	Remarks and references to Appendices
PERA CAMP (HAANDEKOT- Area.) Sh/27.	1918. July 6th.		The following 6inch Trench Mortar Positions were approved by IInd Corps R.A., and work on same commenced immediately. 2 positions at each location. viz: G.9.c.3.6. G.9.b.6.6. A.28.c.6.3. A.22.c.0.0. Platforms for the above were laid down in such a way so that the bed and gun can be mounted at very short notice, pointing in any direction. 2/Lieuts S. ANGELL X Battery) proceeded on 14 days leave to ENGLAND. 2/Lieut W.L. BLYTHE. Y Battery.)	
	7th 8th) to) 14th)		10. 6inch Newton Trench Mortars received from ORDNANCE. complete. Work on 6inch T.M. positions carried on daily., weather was fine during this period and good progress was made on these positions. 2. 6inch T.M.s complete received, to complete authorized Establishment.	
	15th		2/Lieut R. JAMES. Y Battery proceeded on leave to ENGLAND.	

Army Form C. 2118.

WAR DIARY
or
INTELLIGENCE SUMMARY.
(Erase heading not required.)

Instructions regarding War Diaries and Intelligence Summaries are contained in F.S. Regs., Part II. and the Staff Manual respectively. Title pages will be prepared in manuscript.

Place	Date	Hour	Summary of Events and Information	Remarks and references to Appendices
PERA CAMP. HAANDEKOT- AREA. BELGIUM. Sh/27.	1918. July 15.		Both Batteries made preparations for the forthcoming move to SOISSONS AREA.	
	16th		Lieut F.E.H. FRANKLYN and one N.C.O., proceeded by the First Train, leaving HEIDEBECK Station at 1.a.m. in advance of batteries to reconnoitre billets in new Area. "X" Battery left HEIDEBECK Station at 2.p.m. "Y" " " MAANBERG " 6.p.m. All guns were taken together with Stores, 4 G.S. Wagons were loaned for this purpose from 34th Divisional Ammn Column.	
	17th		Proceeded by rail via BERGUES- CALAIS - BOULOGNE - CRAIL. arrived and detrained at LOUVRES at 2.p.m. Batteries then marched to PLAILLY were billets were occupied for the night.	
	18th		Box Respirator Inspection and drill.	
	19th	6.a.m.	Departed from PLAILLY and marched to FRESNOY (Nr Crepy) (route via:- SENLIS and CREPY.)	
	20th		General fatigues.	
	21st	7.a.m.	Departed from FRESNOY and proceeded to VIVIERS via:- VILLERS-Cotterets and arrived at 11.a.m.	
		2.p.m.	All personnel from X Battery marched to take over Ammunition Dump on LONGPORT Road Y Battery proceeded to MORIENVAL to deal with Ammunition arriving at Railhead.	

Army Form C. 2118.

WAR DIARY
or
INTELLIGENCE SUMMARY.
(Erase heading not required.)

Instructions regarding War Diaries and Intelligence Summaries are contained in F. S. Regs., Part II. and the Staff Manual respectively. Title pages will be prepared in manuscript.

Place	Date	Hour	Summary of Events and Information	Remarks and references to Appendices
	1918. July 21st contd.		12. Trench Mortars with stores remained with transport at 34th Divnl Ammn Column.	
	22nd to 27th		Dealing with Ammunition on the respective dumps as stated.	
	28th		Left Ammunition dumps as stated above and proceeded to new dumps near BILLY - S/OURCQ. Ref. French Sheet OULCHY-LE-CHATEAU.(1/20,000) 79.62. and at VAUMOISE.	
	29th to 31st.		Dealing with ammunition as above.	

[signature]
Captain, R.F.A.
D.T.M.O., 34th Division.

Army Form C. 2118.

WAR DIARY
or
INTELLIGENCE SUMMARY

X and Y. 3rd Medium Trench Mortar Batteries R.F.A.

August 1918

Place	Date	Hour	Summary of Events and Information	Remarks and references to Appendices
OULCHY-LE-CHATEAU VI.I. Trench sheet 1/40,000.	August 1918 1st		Personnel of "X" Battery carried on dealing with ammunition Dump at 79.62.	JR 27
	2nd		" " "Y" " " " do " VAUMOISE.	
	3rd		— do —	
			Lieuts CROOKES and ANGELL, and 20 N.C.O.s & men proceeded by lorry to forward gun positions in VIERZY area to collect surplus ammunition left there by the field batteries, who had moved out to the rear, to move away from this front.	
	4th	9am	"X" Battery left dump near BILLY SOURCES and proceeded by Lorries to NANTEUIL-LE-HAUDOUIN (Ref. sheet BEAUVAIS 1/200,000) route via LONGPONT — VILLERS Cotterets — and VAUMOISE. arrived at destination by 4pm.	
	5th	10pm	Lieuts FRANKLYN and CROOKES, and 3 N.C.Os & men remained behind to clear up ammunition dumps. Personnel of "X" Battery proceeded to entraining station nr LE PLESSIS, for move to BELGIUM.	

Army Form C. 2118.

WAR DIARY
or
INTELLIGENCE SUMMARY.
(Erase heading not required.)

Instructions regarding War Diaries and Intelligence Summaries are contained in F. S. Regs., Part II. and the Staff Manual respectively. Title pages will be prepared in manuscript.

Place	Date	Hour	Summary of Events and Information	Remarks and references to Appendices
(but not) HAZEBROUCK J.A.	Aug 1918 5th		Remaining personnel of "Y" battery left VAUMOISE ammunition dump & proceeded to DAMMARTIN station to entrain.	
	6.		X. Battery arrived at BERGUES detraining station at 11 pm. and proceeded by motor lorry, (loaned by Divisional Supply Column) to "BORDEN CAMP" at K.3.d.8.5.	
	7.		Y. Battery arrived at REXPOEDE detraining station at 9 pm. & marched with No. 2 Section, 2 A.C. to camp.	
	7.		Y. Battery left K.2 Section D.16 & marched to billets at K.3.d.8.5.	
BORDEN CAMP. K.3.d.8.5.	8.	9 am.	Parade. Camp fatigues during remainder of the day.	
		6 pm.	R.E.O.'s men who remained behind at the Ammunition dumps returned to their respective batteries.	

Army Form C. 2118.

WAR DIARY
or
INTELLIGENCE SUMMARY.
(Erase heading not required.)

Place	Date	Hour	Summary of Events and Information	Remarks and references to Appendices
BORDEN CAMP N.3.d.E.5.g (Ref. Sheet 27) 1/40,000	August 1918 8	9 a.m. 9 " 9 " to 12.30 2 p.m. to 4.30 p.m.	Inspection parade. Marching drill. Physical drill. 1 Bn. Respirator drill & inspection. Orderly Officer 2/Lt W.G. Blythe	
	10		do	
		10 a.m.	2/Lieut L. Argyle & 2/Lt 60 N.C.O.s & men proceeded to ROUSBRUGGE — HARINGHE station to collect 12 Canl. Newton Trench Mortars & stores. 3 Motor Lorries loaned by the Divnl Supply Colmn conveyed these to Camp.	
	11	Church parade alone	Marching drill & Physical drill. Orderly Officer 2/Lt R. Innes	
	12	5 a.m. 8	1 N.C.O. & 4 men & 1 Battery proceeded to Trench Mortar School of Instructions for Light Trench Mortar Course. Marching & Physical drill as above. Orderly Officer 2/Lt E. MacDuff	

Army Form C. 2118.

WAR DIARY
or
INTELLIGENCE SUMMARY.
(Erase heading not required.)

Instructions regarding War Diaries and Intelligence Summaries are contained in F. S. Regs., Part II. and the Staff Manual respectively. Title pages will be prepared in manuscript.

Place	Date	Hour	Summary of Events and Information	Remarks and references to Appendices
E.10.a.5.h. (Ref. Sheet 27) (1/40,000)	1918 11th Aug 12th		10th Battalion moved away from "BORDEN CAMP" & proceeded to billets at E.10.a.5.h.	
			4 G.S. Wagons were drawn from the D.A.C. to carry pack stores &c.	
	13th	6 am	Reveille. Men from each battery attended a signalling course assembling at Division Hd. Qrs. at SOUTHOVE CHATEAU.	
		9.10 12.30 2 pm 5 pm	Marching drill - physical drill Lecture Officers Lt. Blythe W.C.	
	14th		do	
			Men were knocking about & somewhat "the hedge"	
	15th	9 am 12 noon	Morning drill - physical drill & L.B. in innumerable drill. Lecture officers 2/Lt. R. James.	

Army Form C. 2118.

WAR DIARY
or
INTELLIGENCE SUMMARY.
(Erase heading not required.)

Instructions regarding War Diaries and Intelligence Summaries are contained in F. S. Regs., Part II. and the Staff Manual respectively. Title pages will be prepared in manuscript.

Place	Date	Hour	Summary of Events and Information	Remarks and references to Appendices
E 10. or Bellevue (Sheet 27) (Ypres)		11.30am 12.30pm 2.30pm 10pm	Marching drill. Physical drill. Bayonet & musketry drill carried out daily.	
	19		Capt. M. HEATHER proceeded on 14 days' leave to England.	
	20	Funeral	Musketry drill & re-out lectures.	
	21	as above	" "	
	21	5 pm.	2 motor lorries loaned by the Divisional Supply Column conveyed "L" Battery ammunition to park near the line from Ypres to 40th (6 R) Division.	
	22	9 a.m.	The above lorries conveyed "L" Battery ammunition stores to new camp at Chateau (Sh.27.L.27.c.+.6.) and arrived at 10.30 a.m.	
			Relief of the 29th D.A.H.Q. as Frenel Mortar H.Q. was completed. No casualties	
			6" Trench Mortars were taken over	

Army Form C. 2118.

WAR DIARY
or
INTELLIGENCE SUMMARY.
(Erase heading not required.)

Place	Date	Hour	Summary of Events and Information	Remarks and references to Appendices
SH 28/. A.27.b. & T.9.b.	August 25th		Locations of 34th T.M.B. (Ref. Sht. 28)	
			T.M.O. A.27.c. 70.90.	
			H.Q. X/34 T.M.B. A.24.c. 70.90.	
			H.Q. Y 34 T.M.B. T.14.a. 70.60.	
			Enemy Newton Trench Mortars.	
			1. Position at T.14.a. 25.59. 1. Pozen. at T.9.c. 65.05	
			1. " " T.14.a. 58.50. 1. " " T.3.d. 35.40.	
			1. " " T.8.d. 05.49. 1. " " T.14.a. 40.30	
			1. " " T.8.d. 10.55. 2. Pozens. " H.H.b. 80.15.	
			1. " " T.9.c. 65.02. 2. " " H.11.b. 85.45	
			The above positions were found to be in very good order.	
	8 pm		1030 Rounds T.M.G. ammunition were taken over at these	
	8.5 pm		positions.	
	10.15 pm		Enemy shelled areas T.14.a. & T.13.b., with bursts of	
	10.20 pm		Shrapnels.	
	10.30			
	10.35 pm			

WAR DIARY or INTELLIGENCE SUMMARY

Army Form C. 2118.

Place	Date	Hour	Summary of Events and Information	Remarks and references to Appendices
Sh28/ A.27.a.2.6	1916 Aug 24th		6" Trench Mortars fired 17 rounds on the following targets:- CRUMP FARM. I.5.a.9.5. & checking Zero Fines	
		5pm to 7.30pm	a number of gas shells were fired by enemy on front line. RAMPARTS was shelled with 4.2"	
	25th	6.15 to 7pm	28 rounds 6" T.M. were fired on:- New Cotts I.5.a.3/1. CRUMP FARM. I.5.a.9.5. Trench road I.5.a.98.95. The STABLES I.5.b.3.5. (Something set alight at I.5.b.2.5.) Ground moist all day made observation difficult. Hostile Artillery shelled YPRES with about 50 rounds 5.9" during the day.	
	26th		6" T.M. fired 20 rounds on:- Enemy trench from I.5.b.0.5. to I.5.a.99.99.	
		10.15am to 1.45pm	A very consistent shooting obtained. Hostile artillery shelled YPRES & north of POTIJZE road around I.4.a.90.20. I.4.a.90.50. with 4.2" & 5.9"	5.9"

Army Form C. 2118.

WAR DIARY
or
INTELLIGENCE SUMMARY.
(Erase heading not required.)

Places	Date	Hour	Summary of Events and Information	Remarks and references to Appendices
A27.0.2.6 (R.8)	1918 Aug 26th	6"	T.M's did not fire owing to Infantry working parties being out. Hostile artillery paid the usual attention to YPRES during the night. (about 135 r.d. of 5.9").	
	28th	6"	T.M. did not fire owing to Infantry relief. X Battery relieved Y Battery personnel in the line.	
	29th	6" 10 pm	Heavy Trench Mortars fired 45 r.ds on — THE STABLES I.5.a.6.30.55, RUM FARM & ENTRY ROAD I.5.a.2. & direct hits were obtained on enginery & MARN.	
		11.15 pm	NEW COT 8, I.5.a. & direct hits on dugouts in I.5. a J.5.7.0. Guns fired on Hel O.P., Hostile Artillery shelled I.3 & I. Infantry positions & paid special attention was paid during night on I.13.c. & I.9. out Hostile harassing fire continued intermittently on TOTNES ROAD.	

WAR DIARY
or
INTELLIGENCE SUMMARY.

(Erase heading not required.)

Army Form C. 2118.

Place	Date	Hour	Summary of Events and Information	Remarks and references to Appendices
A.2.C.2.6 (S.W).	1918 Aug 30	6"	6" T.M's fired 30 rounds on TRENCH I.5.a.97.80. & I.5.b.12. Direct hits obtained & Stokes aerials & carriers thrown in the air.	
		8.30pm	Enemy paid the usual attention to YPRES. Approaches during night, but had been unusually quiet during day.	
		4 am	Army Fires went easy, 10 minute bursts of ad. & delibr on Ypres.	
	31	6.30 am	1 section each × 1st T.M.B personnel proceeded to 16 A.24 to relieve ×/34 T.M.B. (1st R. Bde T.M.B. relieving 34th T.M.B.) on the line as night 31/1st & 1/2nd Sept 1918. Relief was duly completed & all guns & stores handed over to 34th T.M.B. personnel proceeded from the line & arrived at Battery Horse lines (A.24 c 2.6) at 2.am.	

M. ..... Capt R.H.A.
O.C. 1st MD ....

Army Form C. 2118.

WAR DIARY
or
INTELLIGENCE SUMMARY.
(Erase heading not required.)

Op. August 1918. 34th Div. Trench Mortar Battery. R.F.A.

VOL 27

Instructions regarding War Diaries and Intelligence Summaries are contained in F. S. Regs., Part II. and the Staff Manual respectively. Title pages will be prepared in manuscript.

Place	Date	Hour	Summary of Events and Information	Remarks and references to Appendices
A.27.c.26. Sh28/1/10000.	1st	8 p.m.	X Battery were relieved in the line by the 114 & 115 T.M.B., all personnel arrived safely at Camp, & preparations made for move next day.	
	2nd	7 a.m.	Lorries loaned by D.I.C. made 3 journeys conveying both battery personnel & stores to new camp, to be taken over from 6/6 D.T.M.O. situated at 56/29. L. 2. d. 6. 6.	
	3rd		Relief of the 6th Div Trench Mortars completed by noon. All Aer. Photos & maps were duly handed over for their aid.	
	4th	7 a.m.	Lieut. H.E.H. Franklyn with 30. R.60. 4 min proceeded to Ammunition dump to clear up etc.	
		4 p.m.	returned to camp.	
	5th	7 a.m.	2nd Lt. L.G. Lythgoe proceeded with the above party to new Ammunition Dump situated at L.24.d.5.5 (SK28). This party removed there and rations taken up daily until work is completed or T.M's go into action. Weather for above period remained fair.	

Army Form C. 2118.

WAR DIARY
or
INTELLIGENCE SUMMARY.
(Erase heading not required.)

Instructions regarding War Diaries and Intelligence Summaries are contained in F.S. Regs., Part II. and the Staff Manual respectively. Title pages will be prepared in manuscript.

Place	Date	Hour	Summary of Events and Information	Remarks and references to Appendices
A24.c.2.6 1/40,000	Sept 6 to 7th		Party as stated on 5th remained at Ammunition Dump.	
	8th	7 am	Lorries loaded by Divisional Supply Column made 3 journeys & conveyed both Batteries to new billets situated at Sh.27-1/L.29.6.5. 2 in relief of the 112th Div T.M. Btys., & relief completed by noon. Weather very wet.	
	9th	9 am	Parade for inspection. Orderly Officer 2/Lt R. Jones	
		9.15 to 12.30pm	Cleaning billets &c.	
			10 men returned to Camp from party at Ammunition dump.	
	10th		3 Officers & 31 N.C.O's & men proceeded up the line to Wulverghem 6" T.M. positions These were situated as follows:-	

contd---

Army Form C. 2118.

WAR DIARY
or
INTELLIGENCE SUMMARY.
(Erase heading not required.)

Instructions regarding War Diaries and Intelligence Summaries are contained in F. S. Regs., Part II. and the Staff Manual respectively. Title pages will be prepared in manuscript.

Place	Date	Hour	Summary of Events and Information	Remarks and references to Appendices
L.29.6.5.2.	Sept 1918.	10a	1. 6" position at N.19.d.9.8.	
			1. " " N.29.a.27.40.	
			1. " " N.23.b.27.22.	
			1. " " N.23.b.21.35.	
			Weather turned very wet, but progress was made on these positions.	
	11th to 13th		Work carried on the above positions almost completed. Ammunition was taken up to guns firing next day.	
	14th 15th		6" Trench Mortars fired 60 Rounds on targets :— Hostile Trench Mortar at N.30.c.5.3. SPANBROEKMOLEN CRATER. WARSAW CRATER. Direct hits were obtained on front parapets of both the craters. Weather very unsettled.	

D. D. & L., London, E.C.
(A8004) Wt. W1771/M231 759,000 5/17 **Sch. 52** Forms/C2118/14

Army Form C. 2118.

WAR DIARY
or
INTELLIGENCE SUMMARY.
(Erase heading not required.)

Place	Date	Hour	Summary of Events and Information	Remarks and references to Appendices
L.29.d.9.2.	Sept 15	5 pm	All personnel, guns, stores etc, were withdrawn from the line to rear billets, in anticipation of a move from this sector.	
		12 noon	The 17. N.C.O.'s & men returned to billets from 31st A.R.P. Billets were watched at L.29.b.5.2. and new billets taken over at L.29.d.9.2.	
	16	9.a.m	Parade. General Camp fatigues during remainder of day.	
	17	9.a.m	Parade. All guns mounted & thoroughly cleaned. Weather fair.	
	18	9.a.m	Parade. Box Respirator drill & inspection.	

WAR DIARY
or
INTELLIGENCE SUMMARY.
(Erase heading not required.)

Place	Date	Hour	Summary of Events and Information	Remarks and references to Appendices
Refer map Sheet 27.	August 1918 19th	4 p.m.	Both batteries moved from billets at L.29, d.9.2., and occupied camp near 34th Divisional Reception Camp situated at L.34.a.6.8.,	
			6. G.S. Wagons loaned by 34th D.A.C., conveyed stores, guns, &c., to new camp.	
			4th L.G. LYTHGOE. 1/4th Cheshire Regt, proceeds on 14 days leave to England.	
	20th		Preparations for move to new sector. 34th French Mortar Batteries to go into action on the BELGIAN front forthwith.	
SK28/. E.1.a.4.4. BREWERY CAMP.		6 p.m.	4 G.S. Wagons loaned from 34th D.A.C., conveyed personnel, stores &c, to new Headquarters situated at BREWERY CAMP (B.1.a.4.4.) near WOESTEN.	
			The wagons to remain with T.M.B's during the stay in this sector for conveying ammunition to the line.	
		8 p.m.	6 Lorries conveyed personnel & guns, stores &c, required for the line to HAMMOND'S CORNER (WEILJE) & remained there for the night.	

Army Form C. 2118.

WAR DIARY
or
INTELLIGENCE SUMMARY.
(Erase heading not required.)

Instructions regarding War Diaries and Intelligence Summaries are contained in F. S. Regs., Part II. and the Staff Manual respectively. Title pages will be prepared in manuscript.

Place	Date	Hour	Summary of Events and Information	Remarks and references to Appendices
BREWERY CAMP. (B.1.a.4.4.) (26.28).	1916 Sept 21st		During the night, work was commenced in view of operations to take place on this front in the near future. 6 positions were selected as follows:— 3 Positions at C.23.a.9.1. ⎫ 3 — " — C.23.a.7.9. ⎬ "X" Battery 2 — " — C.23.a.7.9½. ⎭ 2 — " — C.11.a.0.3. ⎫ "Y" — " — 2 — " — C.10.6.9.3. ⎭	
	22nd		Work on the above positions carried on during night. 300 rounds T.M.G. taken up to positions, these were conveyed by copies to BOUNDARY ROAD, then taken forward by G.S. Wagons.	
	23rd		Work on positions continued. Weather was fair today during the last 3 days which enabled much progress to be made on positions.	

Army Form C. 2118.

WAR DIARY
or
INTELLIGENCE SUMMARY.
(Erase heading not required.)

Instructions regarding War Diaries and Intelligence Summaries are contained in F. S. Regs., Part II. and the Staff Manual respectively. Title pages will be prepared in manuscript.

Place	Date	Hour	Summary of Events and Information	Remarks and references to Appendices
BREWERY CAMP. (B.1.a.H.H.) (Sh.28)	Sept. 23. 1916	24 hrs	1. Cpl., 1 Bdr, & 5 Gunners were working on the 2 positions at C.11.a.0.3. The enemy put down a very heavy barrage in the neighbourhood and undoubtedly the men took shelter in a shell-hole nearby. The enemy raided this area and penetrated to the right rear of the fell-hole. 2 of the above men, not having returned by daylight 2 N.C.O's went out to search for them, but found no trace, & it is feared that the men were taken prisoners.	
	24.		Work on position continued. 9 new positions for these were commenced at C.10.d.5.6. The 2 guns from C.11.a.0.3. were removed during night. 600 rounds T.M.G. taken up to positions during night, making a total of 900 rounds this amount to be expended during the initial stage of the attack.	

WAR DIARY
or
INTELLIGENCE SUMMARY.
(Erase heading not required.)

Army Form C. 2118.

Place	Date	Hour	Summary of Events and Information	Remarks and references to Appendices
BREWERY CAMP (B₁ a H.15) (K.20)	1916 Sept 25		Good progress made on the 2 new positions.	
	26.		All positions completed, and ammunition in positions.	
	27.		The Order of Battle was as follows:—	
			Commanding Officer .... Capt J.E.Maine. M.C.- R.F.A.	
			P.T.M.O. 34th Div	
			Headquarters : Brewery Camp : WOESTEN.	
			Battle Headquarters. C.21.b.15.85. (H.2)	
			O/C. X. B⁴y. Capt W. HEATHER : 9/6. Y. B⁴y. Capt P. BANKS.	
			X. Battery. Y. Battery.	
			3. Guns. C.23.a.9.1. Commanded by 2 Guns. C.23.a.7.9. Commanded by	
			Lt L. Ruccorff. 2/Lt R James.	
			Pos. 1. Corpl D. Mason. 2 " C.10.b.9.3.–" Lt W.Blythe	
			Bdr H. Macey. 2 " C.10.d.5.6.–" Capt R Banks.	
			Bdr R. Bartam.	
			3. Guns. C.23.a.7.9. Commanded by Pos. 1. Corpl H. Scott.	
			Capt W. Heather. Bdr O. Kellon.	
			Pos. 1. Corpl J. Later. Cpl L. James.	
			Bdr D.K.Bunton. Sgt H. Pitone.	
			Gnr Crosfield. Bdr A. Fowlis.	
			Cpl J. Smith.	

WAR DIARY
or
INTELLIGENCE SUMMARY.

(Erase heading not required.)

Army Form C. 2118.

Place	Date 1918	Hour	Summary of Events and Information	Remarks and references to Appendices
BREWERY CAMP B.1.a.4.4. (28S).	Sept 28	5.am.	In support of the attack to take place; 6" French Mortars fired 855 rounds on enemy pill-boxes – M.G. emplacements & selected targets. Casualties: 2 1. Bdr. Wounded.	
	29.		All guns brought from positions to rear Hd Qrs, ready for move.	
	30		5 Lorries conveyed personnel & part of stores from BREWERY CAMP (B.1.a.4.4.) to KEMMEL. remainder of stores were brought on the 6 G.S. Wagon. Weather turned very wet.	

[signature] Capt R.H.A.
34th D.T.M.B.

WAR DIARY
or
INTELLIGENCE SUMMARY.

(Erase heading not required.)

Army Form C. 2118.

3rd Divisional Trench Mortar Battery R.F.A.

Vol 28

October 1918.

Place	Date	Hour	Summary of Events and Information	Remarks and references to Appendices
KEMMEL	1st Oct	2 p.m.	X & Y Batteries marched from KEMMEL by WHYCHAETE to HOUTHEM. Arrived at 4 p.m.	
	2nd		Enemy heavily shelled HOUTHEM on roads with H.E. & Shrapnel during day & night.	
	3rd		Both Batteries moved from HOUTHEM and marched to CAMP BELGE, via VOORMEZEELE.	
	4th		Commencing to-day, ammunition was rcd from gun positions and dumped to D.C.L.G. section lines Sly Lorry for transport to HOUTHEN DUMP. The following from 4th T.M.B's were detached for carting ammunition:— 2 Officers & 30 O.R. at the following locations:— N.3 to O.3 / N.14 a 2.4 / N.14.b.5.8. / N.14.b. / N.5.C. / N.15.c.2.4. to N.15.1.4.5. 1 Officer & 30 O.R. to DINITRI DUMP & HESSIAN M.3.C.1.7. to cart ammunition on lorry Haulbach Salient taken for W.M. Coy.	

Army Form C. 2118.

WAR DIARY
or
INTELLIGENCE SUMMARY.
(Erase heading not required.)

Instructions regarding War Diaries and Intelligence Summaries are contained in F. S. Regs., Part II. and the Staff Manual respectively. Title pages will be prepared in manuscript.

Place	Date	Hour	Summary of Events and Information	Remarks and references to Appendices
CAFE BELGE			Ruled were attached each for relieving ammunition on the 7th inst. In addition an officer and men looked amm. from gun positions to our billets. This was seen by fogs to near the action RHO for moving away.	
	8th		Capt. P. BANKS Y.3H T.N.B. proceeded on 14 days leave to England. Parties salved ammunition as zero above.	
	9th		" "	
	10th		" "	
N.3.a.2.1. 2/28.	10th	9.30	Moved from CAFE BELGE and proceeded to HALLEBAST CORNER at N.3.a.20.10.	
	11th		Parties salved ammunition as above.	

Army Form C. 2118.

WAR DIARY
or
INTELLIGENCE SUMMARY.
(Erase heading not required.)

Instructions regarding War Diaries and Intelligence Summaries are contained in F. S. Regs., Part II. and the Staff Manual respectively. Title pages will be prepared in manuscript.

Place	Date	Hour	Summary of Events and Information	Remarks and references to Appendices
HALLEBAST CORNER SK.28/N.3.a.2.1.	Oct 12		Details for ammunition loading, as follows:— Lieut James and 20 men with 6 lorries to clear CAFE BELGE.	
			" Angell and 10 men with 4 lorries to DIMITRI.	
			" Franklyn and 2 " with wagons to clear near BUTTERFLY FARM.	
			" Lythgoe and 10 " " to " Dranoutre.	
	13.		Working parties as detailed above.	
	14.		" " " "	
	15.		" " " "	
			Lieut Blythe with 1. N.C.O. and 17. men proceeded to ABEELE to collect remounts.	
	16.	9.a.m.	Batteries moved from HALLEBAST CORNER and proceeded to BASSEVILLE Cabaret. Route via VOORMEZEELE — SPOILBANK — VERBRANDMOLEN — HILL 60 — KLEIN ZILLEBEKE., and arrived at destination about 3 p.m. Weather was wet & dull.	

Army Form C. 2118.

WAR DIARY
or
INTELLIGENCE SUMMARY.
(Erase heading not required.)

Instructions regarding War Diaries and Intelligence Summaries are contained in F. S. Regs., Part II. and the Staff Manual respectively. Title pages will be prepared in manuscript.

Place	Date	Hour	Summary of Events and Information	Remarks and references to Appendices
BASSEVILLE Cabaret.	October 17		Lieut James and 4 men with 1 lorry salved ammunition in vicinity.	
	18.		Lieut Angell with 21. R.O.L. and men proceeded to 160 F.A. Bde for attachment to Batteries. Lieut James with 22. R.O.L. and men to 152 Bde for temporary attachment to Batteries.	
	19	9 a.m.	Lieut F.C.H. Franklyn & Battery proceeded on 14 days leave to England. Remaining personnel moved from BASSEVILLE Cabaret and proceeded to R.10.a.y.5. just East of MENIN. Arrived at destination about 10. a.m. Weather - very dull.	
	20		Billets employed 1 R.O.O. and 4 men returned from A.H.Q. (from attachment)	
	21		Batteries moved from R.10.a.y.5. and proceeded to R.14 area in (LAUWE). Route via pontoon bridge	

Army Form C. 2118.

WAR DIARY
or
INTELLIGENCE SUMMARY.
(Erase heading not required.)

Instructions regarding War Diaries and Intelligence Summaries are contained in F. S. Regs., Part II. and the Staff Manual respectively. Title pages will be prepared in manuscript.

Place	Date	Hour	Summary of Events and Information	Remarks and references to Appendices
M.9.c. 45.35. LAUWE (Sh 29.)	Oct 21		Crossing the LYS. now on M13. Arrived at 4 pm and billets occupied at M.9.c. 45.35. and M.14.a. 80.70. 2/Lt L.G. Lythgoe with 2 N.C.O.s and 9 men proceeded by Lorry from the Refilling point to ZYPTEENE to collect remounts for 34th Div. T.6.	
	22		Lieut W.L. BLYTHE, X. Battery, posted to D/160 Bde R.F.A. with effect from 21.10.18., and joined his new unit forthwith.	
	23	9 am	Horses cleaning etc. B.S.M. MacDuff S.10/1 regains from leave.	
	24	8.30 a.m.	Battery moved from LAUWE and proceeded to ROLLEGHEM. (Sh 29. N.25.d. 3.5.) route via AELBEKE. arrived about noon.	

Army Form C. 2118.

WAR DIARY
or
INTELLIGENCE SUMMARY.
(Erase heading not required.)

Place	Date	Hour	Summary of Events and Information	Remarks and references to Appendices
ROLLEGHEM. 25. N.25.a.3.5.	25		Lieut LYTHGOE with party return with remounts for 2nd R.A.C.	
	26		Capt P.BANKS. rejoined from Leave.	
	27		Lieut L.G. LYTHGOE and 11 men (3 from X Bty. 8 from Y Bty.) proceeded to 2nd Army School of Mortars for 6" T.M. Course, commencing 29th inst.	
	28		Battery moved from ROLLEGHEM with the 3rd K.D.A.C. and proceeded to BEVEREN, and occupied billets at C.25.d.95.80. Route:- WALLE - COURTRAI RLY. STN, look No 9. (H.27/a) STACEGHEM - HARLEBEKE. Arrived destination at 1 pm.	

Army Form C. 2118.

WAR DIARY
or
INTELLIGENCE SUMMARY.

(Erase heading not required.)

Place	Date	Hour	Summary of Events and Information	Remarks and references to Appendices
BEVEREN J.29 (C25 d.9580).3/5	October 29th	7am to 8am	1 hour rough earease each morning for all animals attached to T.M.B's. Parties of N.C.O's and men provided daily to 34th Ammunition Dump to assist in dealing with ammunition.	
		17.30	Guard from T.M.B's consisting of 1 N.C.O. & 3 men found daily for this dump.	

M. Mailler
Capt. R.F.A.
34th D.T.M.B.

Army Form C. 2118.

WAR DIARY
or
INTELLIGENCE SUMMARY.
(Erase heading not required.)

November 1918. 34th Trench Mortar Battery R.F.A.

Instructions regarding War Diaries and Intelligence Summaries are contained in F. S. Regs, Part II. and the Staff Manual respectively. Title pages will be prepared in manuscript.

Place	Date	Hour	Summary of Events and Information	Remarks and references to Appendices
BEVEREN Sh.29/ C.25.d.9586.	November 1st		2. N.C.O's & 10 men proceeded to ammunition dump at C.26.c. to assist in dealing with ammunition. Guard for this dump was found daily, at 17.30 hours consisting of 1.N.C.O. and 3 men.	
	2nd		Lieut MacDuff & Battery with 1.N.C.O & 3 men proceeded to new ammunition dump at I.19.c. near VICHTE.	
	3rd		Horse parties joined their Batteries. Both Batteries moved away and proceeded to KLOETHOEK near WEVELGHEM. Transport moved with the 34th D.A.C., Route via HARLEBEKE - COURTRAI - BISSEGHEM - WEVELGHEM, and then to billets situated in KLOEFHOEK at Sh.28/L.36.c.5.3. Weather very fair.	

WAR DIARY
or
INTELLIGENCE SUMMARY.

(Erase heading not required.)

Army Form C. 2118.

Place	Date	Hour	Summary of Events and Information	Remarks and references to Appendices
WEVELGHEM. SH.29.q.10. L.36.c.5.3. 6⁺⁰	Nov 7ᵗʰ		Parts of 20 K.O.D. Ymen awaited the D.A.C. to deal with ammunition.	
			Batteries to be reorganized on a mobile 2 gun establishment, to be maintained at a strength of 1 Captain, 2 Subalterns and 32 O.R. remaining personnel to be attached to D.A.C. to replace casualties.	
			S. Limber G.S. Wagons to be transferred by L.A.A. Section, 34th D.A.C. (4 to each Battery) On reorganization being completed, X Battery will be attached to 152. F.A. Bde, & Y. Bty to 160 F.A. Bde, for tactical purposes.	
	8ᵗʰ			
	&		All surplus stores and equipment were taken to the Divisional Stores in LAUWE, pending	
	9⁻		their withdrawal by Ordnance 34th Div.	

Army Form C. 2118.

WAR DIARY
or
INTELLIGENCE SUMMARY.
(Erase heading not required.)

Instructions regarding War Diaries and Intelligence Summaries are contained in F. S. Regs., Part II. and the Staff Manual respectively. Title pages will be prepared in manuscript.

Place	Date	Hour	Summary of Events and Information	Remarks and references to Appendices
	Nov 10th	10"	Batteries marched from WEVELGHEM with Hd Qrs 34th D.A.C., and proceeded to ESSCHER. Route via BISSEGHEM – COURTRAI – SWEVEGHEM – and thence to billets in ESSCHER.	
	11th		Guns & carriages, limbers &c thoroughly cleaned.	
	12th	12 noon	Batteries marched from ESSCHER and proceeded to HARDHOEK. Route via STEENBRUGGE – STACEGHEM – COURTRAI – WEVELGHEM, and thence to billets at J.K. 28. L. 28. a. 4. 2.	
	13th 14th		Billets improved & pony wagons, carriages &c cleaned	

WAR DIARY
or
INTELLIGENCE SUMMARY.

(Erase heading not required.)

Army Form C. 2118.

Place	Date	Hour	Summary of Events and Information	Remarks and references to Appendices
	Nov 15	9.am	Batteries marched from WEVELGHEM and proceeded to ST GENOIS, arrived there at 4pm. Route via LAUWE — AELBEKE — ROLLEGHEM — BELLEGHEM. Thence to Billets.	
	16	9.am	Left ST GENOIS and marched to ANVAING, route via HELCHIN — CELLES and CORDES.	
	17	"	Wagon & harness cleaning, & general fatigues.	
	18	10.30 am	Left ANVAING and proceeded to STOCQ. Route via ELLIGNIES — LEZ-FRASNES — CONTRE-PRÉ & LAHAMAIDE. Arrived destination at 3pm.	
	19	"	Wagon & harness cleaning, & general fatigues.	

WAR DIARY
or
INTELLIGENCE SUMMARY.

(Erase heading not required.)

Army Form C. 2118.

Place	Date	Hour	Summary of Events and Information	Remarks and references to Appendices
STOCQ.	Dec 20/17 to 30 inc.		The following programme was carried out daily (except Sunday) 7. am. Physical Exercise. 9.30 am Swedish Barracks. 11.30 Rifle drill or Route march. 2 pm football & games.	

W Healey Capt R.A
3rd A.S.M.C.

WAR DIARY
or
INTELLIGENCE SUMMARY.
(Erase heading not required.)

Army Form C. 2118.

34 DTM 8 / 9830

Place	Date	Hour	Summary of Events and Information	Remarks and references to Appendices
STOCQ	1st to 11th		Physical Exercise, Marching drill, Riding drill & Rifle practice. There were taken daily by the Orderly Officer.	
	12	9 am	Batteries moved from STOCQ to BOIS-DE-LESSINES, route taken was OSTICHES, WANNEBECQ, OPHIGNIES.	
	14	9 am	Continued the march, to West of NORRUES, en route via BOURGON-LILLY – arrived destination at 3 pm.	
	15		Remained at above Village.	
	16	9.30 am	March continued, destination for the day being HOUDENG-AIMERIES, route – via SOIGNIES, & ROEULX, arrived at destination about 3 pm.	

Army Form C. 2118.

WAR DIARY
or
INTELLIGENCE SUMMARY.
(Erase heading not required.)

Instructions regarding War Diaries and Intelligence Summaries are contained in F. S. Regs., Part II. and the Staff Manual respectively. Title pages will be prepared in manuscript.

Place	Date	Hour	Summary of Events and Information	Remarks and references to Appendices
	17th		The march continued to ROUX.	
			armentieres via LA LOUVIERE, CHAPELLE-LEZ-HERLAIMONT,	
			& COURCELLES.	
			arrived at 3 p.m.	
	18th		March continued to CHATELINEAU.	
		am	Route via LODELINSART and GILLY.	
			arrived at 2 p.m.	
	19th	9am	March continued to ST. GERARD.	
			Route taken via FOSSE. arrived at 2 pm	
	20/9		Remained at ST GERARD	
	21/9			
	22		Battn. moved from above place to FALISOLLE	
			via FOSSE. Billets occupied in FALISOLLE.	
			Weather very dull.	

Army Form C. 2118.

WAR DIARY
or
INTELLIGENCE SUMMARY.
(Erase heading not required.)

Place	Date	Hour	Summary of Events and Information	Remarks and references to Appendices
FATSOUL A.	Dec/17 22. 10.26.		In accordance with instructions received the following were despatched from 34th I.M.B.³ for Demobilisation to England.	
			DISPERSAL STATION. COALMINERS. PIVOTAL. LONG SERVICE. Officers O.R. Officers O.R. Officers O.R.	
			PURFLEET	
			OSWESTRY . . 1 . . .	
			RIPON . . 3 . . .	
			CHISELDON . . 5 . . 1	
			SHORNCLIFFE . . 15 . . .	
			TOTAL . . 24 . . 1	
			The above N.C.O.'s & men proceeded to Corps Concentration Camp at NEUILLY by Lorry, for despatch to England.	

Army Form C. 2118.

WAR DIARY
or
INTELLIGENCE SUMMARY.

(Erase heading not required.)

Instructions regarding War Diaries and Intelligence Summaries are contained in F.S. Regs., Part II. and the Staff Manual respectively. Title pages will be prepared in manuscript.

Place	Date	Hour	Summary of Events and Information	Remarks and references to Appendices
FALISOLLE (Ref sheet Namur 8)	23rd to 31.	9.00	Daily Inspection Parade. Remainder of day, on general fatigues.	
	29th		Captain W. HEATHER. R.F.A. D.T.M.O. appointed 34th R.A. Education Officer; I assumed duties forthwith, and joined R.A.H.Q. 34th Divⁿ at PROFONDEVILLE.	

W. Heather
Captⁿ R.F.A.
34th D.T.M.O.

X & Y. 34th Trench Mortar Batteries. R.F.A.

WAR DIARY
or
INTELLIGENCE SUMMARY

Army Form C. 2118.

JANUARY. 1919.

Place	Date	Hour	Summary of Events and Information	Remarks and references to Appendices
FALISOLLE	January 1st		Lieut L. MACDUFF, R.F.A., appointed Acting Captain while commanding X Battery — vice — A/Captain W. HEATHER appointed D.T.M.O, 34th Div. Both H/C above to date from 30/11/18.	
	5th		A/Captain P. BANKS, Y Battery, granted 14 days (special) leave to England.	
	10th		2/Lieut J. ANGELL, returned from leave.	
	11th		A/Capt L. MACDUFF, X By, proceeds to Base for Demobilization (Group 43 Student).	
			A/Capt A.S. YOUNGS. R.F.A. joins X/34th T.M.B. from H.R Army H.Q to take over command of X Bty from A/Capt L. MACDUFF.	
	13th		2/Lt O.T. proceed to join 113(A) F.A. Bde, for attachment as observer in view of the forthcoming move to Germany.	

34th Div. T.M. Bs. R.F.A.

Army Form C. 2118.

WAR DIARY
or
INTELLIGENCE SUMMARY.
(Erase heading not required.)

Place	Date	Hour	Summary of Events and Information	Remarks and references to Appendices
FALISOLLE	January 1919.			
	14		2/Lt S ANGELL, X Battery, proceeded to join H.Q. 34th D.A.C. on being appointed TOWN MAJOR of MORNIMONT. (occupied by H.Q. Nos 1 & 2 sections D.A.C.)	
	16		12 N.C.Os & men join the D.A.C. for attachment.	
	18		Capt W. HEATHER D.T.M.O. proceeds on 14 days leave to U.K.	
	27		Batteries move by train to Germany, and are stationed at Siegland	
	29		Batteries move by road to Zundorf	
	"		2/Lieut. S. Angell returns to unit.	

B Newey
Capt RFA

34th Div. T.M.Bs. R.F.A.

Army Form C. 2118.

WAR DIARY
or
INTELLIGENCE SUMMARY.
(Erase heading not required.)

Place	Date	Hour	Summary of Events and Information	Remarks and references to Appendices
FALISOLLE	January 1919. 23rd		The following personnel have been demobilized during the month :- 	

CATEGORY.	X. Battery		Y. Battery		REMARKS
	Officers	O.R.	Officers	O.R.	
COALMINERS.		3			
DEMOBILIZERS & PIVOTAL					
STUDENTS & TEACHERS.					Capt to MACDUFF
A.F.Z.56.					
GUARANTEE LETTER.					
Long Service.					
WATFORD DETAILS.					1
Over 41 years of age.					
TOTALS.	Off. 1	O.R. 4			

R. Stone (Major)

X & Y 34th French Mortar Batteries. R.F.A.

Army Form C. 2118.

WAR DIARY
or
INTELLIGENCE SUMMARY.
(Erase heading not required.)

February 1919.

Vol 32

Instructions regarding War Diaries and Intelligence Summaries are contained in F. S. Regs., Part II. and the Staff Manual respectively. Title pages will be prepared in manuscript.

Place	Date	Hour	Summary of Events and Information	Remarks and references to Appendices
Lindorf.	February 1919			
	1st		Lieut S. Angell joined No.1 Section 34th D.A.C. for attachment.	AA
	6th		Captain P. Banks struck off the strength of 34th T.M.B's, having been over 30 days on leave and not having returned; Authority No. A.Y.p. 840/156/14/P3 Capt. C. S. Youngs attached to 34th D.A.C. as Acting Adjutant. dated 24/1/19. 2 Other Ranks sent to 34th D.A.C. for attachment.	AA AA AA
	11th		Lieut R. James proceeded to United Kingdom for 14 days leave.	AA
	13th		Lieut J. E. A. Franklyn returned from Refresher course at Locomotive Works, St. Etienne, and is attached to 34th D.A.C.	AA
	14th		All remaining Other Ranks (11) attached to 34th D.A.C.	AA
	16th		4 Other Ranks despatched to Concentration Camp for demobilization.	AA
	22nd		3 Other Ranks despatched to Concentration Camp for demobilization.	AA
	28th		Lieut R. James returned from Leave to England	AA

March 1st 1919

B. Young Capt.
R.F.A.
for O.I.M.O. 34 Bn

X & Y Eastern Trench Mortar Batteries R.F.A. March 1919

Army Form C. 2118.

WAR DIARY
or
INTELLIGENCE SUMMARY.
(Erase heading not required.)

Vol 33

Place	Date	Hour	Summary of Events and Information	Remarks and references to Appendices
	March			
	17th		2/Lieut Angell S. Granted Leave to United Kingdom from 14/3/19 to 28/3/19	
			14 men returned from 113th Brigade R.F.A. and attached to Eastern D.A.C.	
	24th		4 men despatched to concentration camp for demobilization	

F. Mount Capt. R.F.A.
for Eastern E.T.M.B.

WAR DIARY of 2nd Eastern L.T.M.B.

Army Form C. 2118.

INTELLIGENCE SUMMARY. from 10.5.19 to 31.5.19.

(Erase heading not required.)

Place	Date	Hour	Summary of Events and Information	Remarks and references to Appendices
HENNEF	10/5/19		The 2nd Eastern L.T.M.B. formed to-day. Personnel drawn from 51st 52nd & 53rd Bns. Bedfordshire Regt. Present strength 3 officers and 31 O.R.s	
do	do		Capt. G.S. DEXTER. 51st Bedfords. Officer Commanding Battery.	
do	do		Lieut. L.G. BUTLER. M.C. -do- 2nd in Command	
do	do		2/Lt. C.C. FYSON. 52nd -do-	
HENNEF	12/5/19	10:00	Battery inspected by G.O.C. 2nd Eastern Inf. Brigade	
HENNEF	15/5/19		Battery moved to WEINGARTSGASSE.	
WEINGARTSGASSE	22/5/19		Lieut L. HUMPHREYS. M.C. taken on strength from 53rd Bedfords	
do	23/5/19	12:00hrs	Battery inspected by G.O.C. Eastern Division	

34TH DIVISION

34TH DIVL AMMN COLUMN
JAN 1916-DEC 1918

1919 JLY

34TH DIVISION

34th D.A.C.
Vol 1

Tan

Jan '16
Dec '16

CONFIDENTIAL.

WAR DIARY

OF

34th DIV. AM. COL.
R.F.A.

From Jany 11th 1916 to Jany 31st 1916

Army Form C. 2118.

WAR DIARY
of 34th D.A.C.
INTELLIGENCE SUMMARY.
(Erase heading not required.)

Instructions regarding War Diaries and Intelligence Summaries are contained in F. S. Regs., Part II. and the Staff Manual respectively. Title pages will be prepared in manuscript.

Place	Date	Hour	Summary of Events and Information	Remarks and references to Appendices
CODFORD	11/1/16	4am to 12.45pm	The Column entrained for SOUTHAMPTON, total strength according to bar Establishments Pt VII (dated August 1st 1915).	Train Table Appendix I.
SOUTHAMPTON	11/1/16	7.15pm	Left SOUTHAMPTON for HAVRE.	Q.M.G
HAVRE	12/1/16	12 noon	Disembarked. Accommodated in Halle 3 GARE MARITIME for the night	Q.M.G Q.M.G
HAVRE	13/1/16	11.30 am	Entrained at GARE DES MARCHANDISES	Q.M.G Q.M.G
ST. OMER.	14/1/16	2 am	Detrained, and marched to ARQUES.	
ARQUES.	14/1/16	3 pm	Billeted & bivouacked E. of Le PONT A'ARQUES.	Q.M.G A.D.S.S.
ARQUES	18/1/16	2.30 pm	Drew 704 rounds 4.5" Howitzer Amn. from ARQUES STA.	Q.M.G
ARQUES	22/1/16		Ordered to leave ARQUES at 7.30 am tomorrow to go to new billeting area in NEUF BERQUIN — ESTAIRES road.	
ARQUES	23/1/16	7.30 am	Column marched for NEUF BERQUIN via EBBLINGHEM, HAZEBROUCK (rear of Column clear at 11.30 am) LA MOTTE, VERTE RUE, LA COURONNE.	Q.M.G
		2.30 pm	Arrived at NEUF BERQUIN. Billeted between NEUF BERQUIN and ESTAIRES, on main road.	

Com'g 34 D.A.C.
17/2/16

CONFIDENTIAL

WAR DIARY
OF
34TH DIVL. AMMUNITION COLN
R.F.A.

FROM FEB. 1ST 1916, TO FEB. 29TH 1916.

Army Form C. 2118.

WAR DIARY
or
INTELLIGENCE SUMMARY.
(Erase heading not required.)

Instructions regarding War Diaries and Intelligence Summaries are contained in F.S. Regs., Part II. and the Staff Manual respectively. Title pages will be prepared in manuscript.

Place	Date	Hour	Summary of Events and Information	Remarks and references to Appendices
ESTAIRES	Feb 15th 1916 4th	9 am	In accordance with instructions from G.O.C. 34th Div. Art., the following detail was detached to join 47th D.A.C., for supply of amtn. to B/147th (How.) Bde. R.F.A., now attached to 47th Div Art:- 1 Sjt., 10 Dr., 3 Gnrs.; 1 Horse, 20 mules; 3 wagons complete; 17 rounds Amtn.	J.M.G.
	19th.	10.30 am	In accordance with orders by G.O.C.R.A. 34th Divn., HQ and No.1 Section marched to new billeting area via TROU BAYARD and LE PETIT MORTIER.	
	"	12 noon	Handed over to 23rd D.A.C. at ESTAIRES gun ammunition as follows:- 18 pdr Q.F. Shrapnel 6648 rounds; 4.5" Howitzer Lyddite 558 rounds.	J.M.G.
STEENWERCK	"	"	Took over from 23rd D.A.C. at A.27.d.5.5. (Sheet 36) following ammunition:- 18 pdr Q.F. Shrapnel 648, H.E. 576 rounds; 4.5" How. Shrapnel 112, Lyddite 298, Amatol 88 rounds.	
	"	2 pm	Ammunition supply begun, the Division having taken over a portion of the line of defence.	J.M.G.
	"	11 pm	Ammunition received from Bnl. Amtn. Sub-Park to complete No.1 Section to establishment.	
	20th.	12.15 pm	No 2 Section took over new billeting area, marching by the same route as HQ and No.1 Section.	J.M.G.
	"	2 pm	Ammunition received from Sub-Park to complete No 2 Section to establishment.	J.M.G.
	21st.	11.30 am	No 3 Section took over their new billeting area, marching by the same route as HQ and No.1 Section.	
	"	3 pm	Ammunition received from Sub-Park to complete No 3 Section to establishment.	
	"	"	Amtn. supply organized as follows:- AC/152nd Bde. R.F.A. to be supplied by No.1 Section; AC/160th Bde. R.F.A. by No 2 Section; AC/175th Bde. R.F.A. by No 3 Section ; AC/176th Bde. R.F.A. and Divl. Troops by Section on Duty.	J.M.G.

March 1st 1916

Chrisford Capt. R.F.A.
Cmm'g 34th D.A.C.

34. Dic A.e
vol 3

Army Form C. 2118.

WAR DIARY
or
INTELLIGENCE SUMMARY.
(Erase heading not required.)

Instructions regarding War Diaries and Intelligence Summaries are contained in F. S. Regs., Part II. and the Staff Manual respectively. Title pages will be prepared in manuscript.

Place	Date	Hour	Summary of Events and Information	Remarks and references to Appendices
STEENWERCK	MARCH 1916 18th	11 am	In accordance with instructions from G.O.C. 34th Div. A.T. HQ and No1 Section 34th Div. Amn Col. marched to new billets at A.17.d.2.5 vacated by the Divl. Cavalry. [Reference Map. Sheet 36]	John G

1 APR 1916

.... COL. R.F.A.
COMDG. 34th DIV. AMTN. COL.

2353 Wt. W3544/1454 700,000 5/15 D. D. & L. A.D.S.S. Forms/C 2118.

34th Divisional
Ammn. Column
Vol II

34 DAC
AC
vol 4

Confidential

War Diary

of

34th Divisional Ammunition Column

From April 1st 1916

To April 30th 1916

Army Form C. 2118.

WAR DIARY
or
INTELLIGENCE SUMMARY.
(Erase heading not required.)

Instructions regarding War Diaries and Intelligence Summaries are contained in F.S. Regs., Part II. and the Staff Manual respectively. Title pages will be prepared in manuscript.

Place	Date	Hour	Summary of Events and Information	Remarks and references to Appendices
STEENWERCK	APRIL 1916 10th	8 am	4 G.S. wagons loaded with 18 pdr. amm., with sufficient personnel including an officer of No. 1 Section, were sent to position of 152nd B.A.C., to supply amm. if necessary, between time of departure of 152nd B.A.C. + time of arrival of relieving Australian B.A.C. (6th)	J.M.G.
		9 am	A similar detachment of No. 3 Section reported by 175th B.A.C. to supply amm. until relieved by the 4th Australian B.A.C.	
		5 pm	Both detachments reported to HQ as having been relieved by the respective Australian B.A.C's	J.M.G.
LE PETIT MORTIER	12th	8 am	O.C. No. 2 Section undertook supply of amm. from time of departure of 160th B.A.C.	
"	"	11 a.m.	All amm. + Very Lights handed over to 2nd Australian D.A.C. and responsibility for supply of amm. was also handed over.	J.M.G.
STEENWERCK	13th	9 am	By order of G.O.C. 34th Div. Art. the 34th D.A.C. marched to the billets recently occupied by the 2nd Australian D.A.C. at MOULIN FONTAINE, C.21.a.0.5. (Sheet 36A), via LE VERRIER, VIEUX BERQUIN, LA MOTTE, PAPOTE, MORBECQUE & LA BELLE HOTESSE. The unit reached its new billeting area at 2.30 pm.	J.M.G.
MOULIN FONTAINE	14th	9 am	Took over from Rear Party 2nd Australian D.A.C. full complement of amm. less 3 boxes S.A. Pistol WEBLEY and 4 rounds 18 pdr. Shrapnel. Also 1,019,000 rounds S.A.A. for supplying to B.A.C's were taken over and a guard of 1 N.C.O. + 3 men left over it until it could be removed by motor lorry.	J.M.G.
MOULIN FONTAINE	15th	6.30 am	The 34th D.A.C. continued its march to the Second Army Training Area, via BLARINGHEM, RACQUINGHEM	

Army Form C. 2118.

WAR DIARY
or
INTELLIGENCE SUMMARY.
(Erase heading not required.)

Instructions regarding War Diaries and Intelligence Summaries are contained in F.S. Regs., Part II. and the Staff Manual respectively. Title pages will be prepared in manuscript.

Place	Date	Hour	Summary of Events and Information	Remarks and references to Appendices
	APRIL 1916			
	15th (continued)		HEURINGHEM, WIZERNES and LUMBRES, reaching its new billeting area SENINGHEM & COULOMBY at 5 p.m.	
COULOMBY	15th	3.30 p/m 6 p/m	HQ & No1 Section are billeted at SENINGHEM, Nos. 2 & 3 Sections at COULOMBY	
"	16th	6 am	S.A.A. for B.A.Cs dumped at No 2 Section billets.	Jn. g
SENINGHEM	17th	7 am	Manage from S.Q.R.A. authorises issue of S.A.A. to B.A.Cs of 152nd 160th & 175th Bdes, R.F.A.	Jn. g
SENINGHEM	"	6.30 am	Training Programme begun. 8 Spuds sent daily to 175th A/M/RFA under a Subaltern Officer, for Gun Drill	Jn. g
			15 N.C.Os & men (INCD. 3 hr men h/ section) proceeded to TILQUES for a course of instruction at the Divisional Trench Mortar School	Jn. g
"	22nd	11.15 am	1 Officer & 40 other ranks proceeded to AMIENS (entrained at ST OMER) for attachment to 13th. Division as a working party.	Jn. g

_____ COL. R.F.A.
COMDG. 34th DIV. AMN. COL.

Confidential

War Diary

of

34th Divl. Ammn. Col.

from May 1st. 1916   to May 31st 1916

WAR DIARY
or
INTELLIGENCE SUMMARY.
(Erase heading not required.)

Army Form C. 2118.

Instructions regarding War Diaries and Intelligence Summaries are contained in F. S. Regs., Part II. and the Staff Manual respectively. Title pages will be prepared in manuscript.

Place	Date	Hour	Summary of Events and Information	Remarks and references to Appendices
	May			
SÉNINGHEM	5th	6 pm	Capt. H HOLMES and 40 other ranks proceeded to Fourth Army Trench Mortary School for course of instruction in Heavy Trench Mortars.	yes
	6th	3 pm	Under orders from GOCRA the Column commenced its move to Fourth Army Area; entraining stations WIZERNES & AMIENS. X/34, Y/34, Z/34 TMBs attained for the move, unnoted; no loading parties; the first 2 at AMIENS, the last at WIZERNES. 5 trains utilised	yes
LONGEAU	7th	11 am	The Column commenced to detrain at LONGEAU, and to march to LA HOUSSOYE via AMIENS & QUERRIEU. T2 TMB were detached at LONGEAU.	yes
LAHOUSSOYE	8th	7.30 pm	The Column continued its move to new billeting area D.23.d (Ref Map ALBERT 1/40,000)	yes
BRESLE	9th		HQ established at h/s billet BRESLE	yes
BUIRE	10th	7 pm	A 1252 rounds AX 470 rounds handed over to 5th DAC under instructions from GOCRA	yes
"	11th	-	2 Officers & 66 other ranks detailed for Heavy Trench Mortar course 28 days and Battery ranks for Machine	yes
"	16th	11 am	DAC reorganized under GHQ Letter OB/20 585 dated April 20th 1916. 18th BAC to become "A" Echelon DAC, absorbing the Horse BAC. The MC about to bring of Ammunition & the "B" Echelon DAC	yes
"	18th	-	3 Officers, 66 other ranks detailed for Medium Trench Mortar course	yes
"	21st	-	52 other ranks supplied to Brigades as working parties for different purposes etc	yes

Army Form C. 2118.

WAR DIARY
or
INTELLIGENCE SUMMARY.
(Erase heading not required.)

Instructions regarding War Diaries and Intelligence
Summaries are contained in F. S. Regs., Part II.
and the Staff Manual respectively. Title pages
will be prepared in manuscript.

Place	Date	Hour	Summary of Events and Information	Remarks and references to Appendices
	MAY			
BUIRE	25th	9am	Details, surplus to settlement of Divisional Artillery proceeded by road to ABBEVILLE via RONDE, conducted by Capt BARKER, R.M. & S.Q.M. rank	
DERNANCOURT	27th	10.30am	H.Q. D.A.C. established at DERNANCOURT, with Nos 1 & 2 Sections "A" Echelon	
	19th	8pm	Conducting Party for details returned	

Culwper-Mayor
Comg 34th D.A.C.

34 A.3 A.Col
Vol 6
June

Confidential

War Diary

of

34th. Divisional Ammunition Column.

From June 1st 1916   To June 30th 1916

WAR DIARY
INTELLIGENCE SUMMARY

(Erase heading not required.)

Army Form C. 2118.

Instructions regarding War Diaries and Intelligence Summaries are contained in F. S. Regs., Part II. and the Staff Manual respectively. Title pages will be prepared in manuscript.

Reference Map ALBERT 1/40,000

Place	Date	Hour	Summary of Events and Information	Remarks and references to Appendices
DERNANCOURT	June 1st 1916	7-8am	DERNANCOURT shelled slightly	
		8am	2 Officers & 66 other ranks W/34 Trench Mortar Batty. attached this unit were sent to front line to help dig in telephone wires.	Jm.g
		-	Under orders from G.O.C. 34th Div.Art., the 34th D.A.C. began to dump ammunition at gun positions.	Jm.g
	2nd	-	Intermittent shelling of DERNANCOURT, especially near No.1 Section horse lines.	
	3rd	-	Negligible shell of DERNANCOURT shelled. No casualties in DAC.	
	7th	-	Dump at gun pits completed. Also 75 rounds per gun 18pdr & 40 rounds per gun 4.5" How= distributed to batteries. Under orders from G.O.C. R.A. this dump is to be increased to 1000 rounds per gun 18pdr, 500 rounds per gun 4.5" How=, 250 rounds per gun 18pdr & 4.5" How= to be maintained at D.A.C. as Bulk Dump. This is also the dump for 16 guns 18pdr & 4 guns 4.5" How= of the 19th Divn. attached to this unit for ammunition supply.	
	8th	3am	During shelling of DERNANCOURT by 15cm H.V. gun one man of No.2 Section wounded.	Jm.g
	10th	-	In accordance with instructions from G.O.C.R.A. positions were reconnoitred for A & B Echelons. 34th DAC suitable for occupation during an advance. Positions selected were (1) for "A" Echelon, near BELLE VUE Farm & on further advance, in BECOURT WOOD (2) for "B" Echelon near MOULIN VIVIER.	Jm.g

Army Form C. 2118.

WAR DIARY
or
INTELLIGENCE SUMMARY.
(Erase heading not required.)

Instructions regarding War Diaries and Intelligence Summaries are contained in F. S. Regs., Part II. and the Staff Manual respectively. Title pages will be prepared in manuscript.

Place	Date	Hour	Summary of Events and Information	Remarks and references to Appendices
DERNANCOURT	June 1916 13th	—	Instructions received from HdQrs. R.A. to draw 1250 rounds lachrymatory 4.5" How? shell & to report when available for issue.	J.W.G
"	14th	11 pm	Revised Summer Time adopted. 11 pm. becomes 12 midnight.	J.W.G
"	16th	—	Owing to shelling of horse lines in the vicinity of No 1 Section "A" Echelon, that section moved ½ mile further west, just outside DERNANCOURT.	J.W.G
"	18th	—	Between the hours of 11 pm 17th inst. & 3 am on 18th, the 18ème Régiment d'Artillerie arrived at DERNANCOURT. Camp was prepared for them by the 34th D.A.C. to whom they were attached for amm. supply. [See Appendix "D"]	J.W.G
"		7 pm	Gumps at gunpits, as laid down on 7th inst., completed. [See Appendix "C"]	
"	19th	—	Instructions received from G.O.R.A. that in the event of the ground west of DERNANCOURT & south of the railway being shelled, Nos 1 & 2 Sections were to be moved N. of the railway to E.19.e.	
"		9 pm	Material for preparation of French gunpits taken to their gunpositions by the 34th D.A.C. 4.3 G.S. wagons were employed in the work.	
"	21st	—	IIIrd Corps Observation Balloon at D.23 shelled by 15 cm H.V. gun. Shrapnel & splinters of shell fell freely in lines of Sections 3 & 4, a horse being struck in No 3 Sec. No other casualties reported.	J.W.G

Army Form C. 2118.

WAR DIARY
or
INTELLIGENCE SUMMARY
(Erase heading not required.)

Instructions regarding War Diaries and Intelligence Summaries are contained in F.S. Regs., Part II. and the Staff Manual respectively. Title pages will be prepared in manuscript.

Place	Date	Hour	Summary of Events and Information	Remarks and references to Appendices
	June 1916			
DERNANCOURT	21st	9/pm	6948 rounds 75 m/m gas shell taken to French gun positions.	J in g
"	22nd	11/pm	Advanced ammunition dump started in BECOURT WOOD, with 352 rounds 15/phr amn.	J in g
"	24th	—	During the night June 23rd-24th, 18/phr amn was taken to the dump in BECOURT WOOD. While this was carried out, 1 horse was killed by a rifle bullet. 30 steel helmets were issued for the use of the men thus proceeding to the forward area.	
"	26th	6/pm	Working parties which left this unit last month for digging gunpits returned, except 1 NCO & 9 men kept employed by the 7 Heavy Artillery Group. Several shells from the 15 cm H.V. gun, fell in & around DERNANCOURT, one within 100 yards of the D.A.C. ammunition dump.	J in g
"	30th	11/pm	Capt BARKER with party consisting of 1 Sgt 6 men & 6 mounted orderlies, assumed control of the BECOURT WOOD Dump now increased to 5000 rounds 18/phr & 500 rounds 4.5" How Amtn	J in g
NOTE ①			Greatest amount of ammunition handled in one day, 24 hours ending 12 noon 27th inst.	

	Shrapnel	H.E.	How Shrap	How HE	18 phr 2880	4.5" How rounds	S.A.A.
ⓐ English Receipts	685	4497	—	2240		3464	471,000
Issues	11156	—	540				
Totals	11841	4497	540	2240		6364	471,000
ⓑ French Receipts	—	4020	—	—			
Issues	—	4620	—	—			
Totals	10,737	2240	540				

Army Form C. 2118.

WAR DIARY
or
INTELLIGENCE SUMMARY
(Erase heading not required.)

Place	Date	Hour	Summary of Events and Information	Remarks and references to Appendices
NOTE	(2)		English ammn handled in last 6 days of month of June 1916	

	Short.	H.E	H.E	S.A.A.
Receipts	53606	17696	12240	640,000
Issues	44914	14782	10996	811,000
Total	98,520	32478	23,236	1,451,000

CASimpson Colonel RMO
Cmdg 34th DAC

34th D.A.C.
(Ammunition Supply June 1916)

APPENDIX "B"

Week ending June 1916	Receipts 18 pdr Shrapnel	Receipts 18 pdr H.E.	Receipts 4.5" How. Shrap.	Receipts 4.5" How. H.E.	Receipts S.A.A. .303	Receipts S.A.A. Pistol Webley	Issues 18 pdr Shrapnel	Issues 18 pdr H.E.	Issues 4.5" How. Shrap.	Issues 4.5" How. H.E.	Issues S.A.A. .303	Issues S.A.A. Pistol Webley
3rd	1,568	1,120	–	720	–	–	1,237	730	–	400	123,000	–
10th	15,792	7,196	120	3,840	990,000	–	18,008	8,132	–	3,607	182,000	552
17th	26,057	9,160	–	10,420	540,000	–	25,779	8,061	120	10,184	165,000	1,608
24th	24,604	7,932	–	5,646	700,000	5,520	11,734	4,859	–	2,638	1,489,000	1,800
30th	53,606	17,696	–	12,240	640,000	–	44,914	14,782	–	10,996	811,000	2,760
	121,627	43,104	120	32,866	2,870,000	5,520	101,672	36,564	120	27,825	2,750,000	6,720

1 JUL 1916

J. Mylam Gittins Lieut. R.F.A.
Adjutant 34th DIV. AM^{TN} COL.

APPENDIX C

(Rounds per gun held in Division 19/6/16)

	In Echelons	At gunpits	With DAC	Remarks
18 pdr.	176	1000	250	C/175 & C/176 had 200 rounds per gun advanced from DAC
4.5" How.	108	900	150	D/152 had 800 rounds per gun only

19 JUN 1916

J. Mylam Gittins Lieut. R.F.A.
Adjutant 34th DIV. AM^{TN} COL.

Appendix D
French 75mm. Amtn.

Receipts					Issues				
Date	No 5 Special	No 6 Special	H.E.	Shrap	Date	No 5 Special	No 6 Special	H.E.	Shrap
June 1916					June 1916				
19th	11043				20th	405			
21st			9936		21st	6948			
22nd	2160			2385	22nd			4632	
26th		7497			23rd			2304	765
					26th		3240	2240	540
					29th	2025		760	
	13,203	7497	9936	2385		9378	3240	9936	1305

J. Mylam Gittins
Lieut. R.F.A.
Adjutant 34th DIV. AMTN COL.

34th Div.
III.Corps.

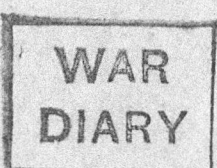

34th DIVISION AMMUNITION COLUMN.

JULY

1916

Attached:

Appendices "G" & "H".

Army Form C. 2118.

WAR DIARY
or
INTELLIGENCE SUMMARY

(Erase heading not required.)

Instructions regarding War Diaries and Intelligence Summaries are contained in F. S. Regs., Part II. and the Staff Manual respectively. Title pages will be prepared in manuscript.

34 D.A.C. Vol T

Place	Date	Hour	Summary of Events and Information	Remarks and references to Appendices
ALBERT area	July 1916 1st	7.30am	In conjunction with the VIII, X, XV and XIII Corps, the enemy's position was attacked.	
		8 am.	Four How Batteries of M.T. See attached to D/152nd Bde for ammunition supply in advance of BECOURT wood.	
			Orders were received for the Column to hold itself in readiness to move at the shortest notice.	
DERNANCOURT	"	2 pm	At the request of the O.C. 102nd Field Ambulance, the M.O./C. 34th D.A.C. assisted in tending the wounded at the Dressing Station. DERNANCOURT	
BECOURT WOOD	"		BECOURT WOOD came under shell & machine gun fire, and 4 men were wounded.	
DERNANCOURT	2nd		The Medical Officer continues to assist the 102nd Field Ambulance. Browns Houz & reactive Shell used to replace A.E P S A	
	3rd		Do.	
			30 rds: How Brown Shell with hard of 152" & 175" R A&RH Bde y	
"	6th		Orders were received that the arrangement in the BECOURT WOOD dump was to be removed explaining for the 34th Divn & the necessary instructions were issued to Capt. BARKER	
			6 Batteries of Medium Trench Mortars were attached to the Column for administrative purposes.	
BECOURT WOOD	10th		BECOURT WOOD was again shelled + 1 man of party in charge of the water dump there was wounded.	
DERNANCOURT			Notification received that "Shell Powder-Filled" will form part of C.Oks daily outfit of Horse amn.	
			500 rounds heavy Shell arrived from S.A.P.O.	
	17th		A party was detailed to clear the dugouts evacuated by C/175 Bde + to transfer the water to the dump in BECOURT WOOD. 250 rounds aerial (?) Shell were used to enrich D/152 and D/175.	

Army Form C. 2118.

WAR DIARY
or
INTELLIGENCE SUMMARY.

(Erase heading not required.)

Instructions regarding War Diaries and Intelligence Summaries are contained in F. S. Regs., Part II. and the Staff Manual respectively. Title pages will be prepared in manuscript.

Place	Date	Hour	Summary of Events and Information	Remarks and references to Appendices
BECOURT WOOD	July 1916 18th	8 am	At the request of the C.E. III Corps, 10 wagons were detailed to assist daily in making roads to new advanced artillery positions.	
BECOURT	19th		A party were detailed to collect amm. from the gun pits vacated by 15/17 6th Over 1900 rounds were collected & a balance left which cannot be dealt with until 21st inst	
	20th		Under orders from the C.R.A., the 34th D.A.C. moved to its new area at N19d - N20c. At the same time the Amm Refilling Point was transferred to W.27.b.11. Capt. FILLERY & 20 men were left in charge of EGGEHILL Amm Dump with orders to clear same as soon as possible. Full amm to be sent to new Refilling Point, and empty cartridge cases like types & put on trains for return to Base.	
ALBERT Area	21st		10 wagons detailed to clear cartn from ground gun pits occupied by batteries moving to forward positions. This is to be done daily until all pits are clean, amm. to be taken to Refilling Point.	
BECOURT	22nd		The transfer of amm. from EGGEHILL to new Refilling Point completed.	
ALBERT Area	23rd		The party clearing cartns to BECOURT WOOD Amm Dump came under shell fire & 1 man was slightly wounded.	
"	24th		A party of 1 Officer and 20 men was detailed to dismantle gun positions in AUTHUILLE WOOD vacated by C and D Batteries 175 H Bde at Q.4 sheet 57d. and to convey the material to BECOURT WOOD R.E. dump. The work was continued daily until completed.	

WAR DIARY
or
INTELLIGENCE SUMMARY
(Erase heading not required.)

Army Form C. 2118.

Place	Date	Hour	Summary of Events and Information	Remarks and references to Appendices
BERNANCOURT	July 4th		Trench carts transferred from EDGEHILL dump to Refilling Point by French Motor Lorries	App 3
			The EDGEHILL cart dump was thereal a Colonel Capt. FILERY & party opening the new V/34 Heavy Trench Mortar Batty attached to the DAC for administrative purposes	
ALBERT Area	27th	2pm	The 170 steel helmets required to complete the allotment of 200 to the DAC issued by Ordnance	App 3
		3pm	The party at work in AUTHUILLE WOOD were subject to heavy shell fire & were compelled to deepen from cover. 1 Mule was wounded by shrapnel	App 3
"	28th	2pm	Two Brigadiers were sent to 18th Regt d'Artillerie to remove ammn from their original gun positions to their new ones in advance.	App 3
"	29th	10am	300 rounds Exclamatory Shell received from Park Park 18th Regt d'Artillerie returned all surplus ammn to Refilling Point of this unit. 300 rounds Exclamatory Shell issued to 35th DAC	App 3
	30		Under instructions from GOC RA, 1 Officer & 10 men were detailed from each section to proceed to three affiliated French five batteries in Gunnery.	App 3
	31st		Six balloons Medium Trench Mortar Batteries attached to this unit for administrative purposes	App 3

[Offences & Ammunition Act
H Congratulatory message (A)]

C. H. Sunderland Colonel R.F.A.
Comg 34 DAC

APPENDICES "G" & "H".

Appendix G

34th D.A.C. Amm. Acct.
July 1916.

Week Ending	Receipts						Issues					
	18 Pdr		4.5" Howr		SAA .303		18 Pdr		4.5" Howr		SAA .303
	Shrapnel	H.E.	H.E.	Thermit		Shrapnel	H.E.	H.E.	Thermit	
Select Onward	24059	19451	5769	124	1934000	54117	9090	17421	720	2000,000
8th	39206	11409	13471	—	1909000	30151	6789	8212	—	158,040
15th	25744	9090	8374	664	336000	18421	2470	3618	064	173,040
22nd	11619	7222	3900	200	590000	4722	5772	734	—	158,040
29th	5793	1691	1852	—	591000			2047	—	
31st	3697	742	985	—	—					
Total	116912	40907	33383	988	5359,000	114423	38,730	32022	620	2,799,000

* Includes 18 Pdr Shrapnel 84,53 rounds } collected from
  " H.E. 2,161 " } original gun
  4.5" Howr H.E. 720 " } positions
  Incendiary (Thermit) 164

Jhingiam bttein G.R.F.A.
Adjt 34th D.A.C.

Appendix H Page 1

Special Order of the Day
by
Major General E. C. Ingouville Williams, C.B. D.S.O.
Commanding 34th. Divn.

The following telegrams have been received and despatched respectively, in connection with recent operations:-

To:- 34th Division.

"General Rawlinson wires as follows:- Please convey to the 34th. Division my hearty congratulations on their successes. Whilst regretting their heavy casualties I desire to express my gratitude for and admiration of the determination and gallantry with which they carried out their difficult task."

From 3rd Corps.

To:- 3rd Corps

"The 34th. Division very much appreciate the good opinion the Army Commander has formed of them as expressed in his telegram to you."

From 34th Division.

(sd) O.R. Chance Lt Col.
A.A.+Q.M.G. 34th Division

Appendix H Page 2

G.O.C
  34th. Division.

   Would you please convey to Brigadier General Kirby and the Officers under his command my appreciation of and hearty thanks for the extremely efficient and prompt support which he afforded to the 19th. Division during the time the 34th. Divisional Artillery was covering its front.

                              (sgd) H. Bridges
H.Q 19th. Division   Major General
11th July, 1916   Commanding 19th Division

C.R.A,
   34th Division   34th. Division. No 6502.

   Forwarded. It is a matter of great satisfaction to the G.O.C. Division to have received this letter.

                              (sgd) H.R. Blore. Major
11-7-1916   G.S. 34th Division

   Forwarded for information

                              (sgd) a main
                                 Major
                              Brigade Major R.A
12-7-1916   34th Division

Appendix H Page 3
Headquarters, R.A.
IIIrd. Corps.

    The Commander-in-Chief visited Corps Headquarters this evening and when leaving directed me to convey not only his own warm personal thanks, but that of the whole Army to all ranks of the Royal Artillery of the Corps that have taken part in the battle now in progress for the gallantry, skill, devotion and endurance with which they have carried out their duties in every particular.

    He stated that he had issued an Order of the Day to the Army at large in which the services of the Royal Artillery in general had been specially mentioned but wished his appreciation and thanks to be conveyed more specifically to all ranks of the R.A. III Corps of which every individual officer, N.C.O and many, had worthily upheld the great traditions of the Royal Regiment of Artillery, beyond which no higher praise can be given

(sd) H. Uniacke
Brig. General
Commanding Royal Artillery
III Corps.

9 July 1916

Appendix H Page 4

The Divisional Commander wishes me to express to the Divisional Artillery his satisfaction with their work during the recent fighting. He realises how long and arduous the work has been and considers they have done splendidly.

I can thoroughly endorse the Divisional Commander's words and take this opportunity to thank every Officer, Non commissioned Officer, and man for their excellent work.

I am proud to command such Artillery.

(sd) A.J. Kirby
Brigadier General
Commanding Royal Artillery
34th Division

11-7-16

34th Divisional Artillery.

34th DIVISIONAL AMMUNITION COLUMN

AUGUST 1 9 1 6 :::

34/

34 DAC. Vol 8

<u>Secret</u>

<u>War Diary Volume 8</u>

of

<u>34th. Divisional Ammunition Column</u>

<u>From August 1st- 1916</u>   <u>To. August 31st 1916</u>

Army Form C. 2118.

WAR DIARY
or
INTELLIGENCE SUMMARY.
(Erase heading not required.)

Instructions regarding War Diaries and Intelligence Summaries are contained in F. S. Regs., Part II. and the Staff Manual respectively. Title pages will be prepared in manuscript.

Place	Date 1916 August	Hour	Summary of Events and Information	Remarks and references to Appendices
ALBERT			REFERENCE MAPS ALBERT 1:10 19/8/16 AMIENS 17 1:50 21/8/16 SHEET 36 1:10 31/8/16 cloudy continues	
ALBERT	1st.		The R.E. road fatigue of 10 wagons (G.S.) New area for D.A.C. reconnoitred.	Jm 9
"	2nd		The Column moved to its new bivouac at W27, adjacent to the ALBERT-BOUZINCOURT Road	Jm 9
"	3rd		S.A.A. taken to lonely Copse stump, R.27. d.3.1.	Jm 9
		11pm	V/34 Heavy Trench Mortar Battery joined the Medium T.M.Bs in their camp at W.19. central.	Jm 9
"	4th.		Partial stampede of mules caused by hostile shelling Establishment of "A" Echelon D.A.C's. increased by 15 Gunrs., 5 per Section.	Jm 9
			Amn. reduced to A mid. AX 117 rounds BX 376 rounds at 12 midnight	Jm 9
"	5th	4pm	A 2700 rounds received from XV Corps as an emergency supply.	Jm 9
"	6th	7:30pm	ALBERT & neighbourhood shelled. One shell fell within a few yards of Nos. 2 & 3 Sections lines. Second batch of 4 Officers & 40 men attached for duty to RFA Brigades.	Jm 9
			Dismantling of gun pits in AUTHUILLE WOOD completed, the material having been all conveyed to the RE Dump BECOURT WOOD	
"	12th	2am	Splinter from shell fell in No.3 Section lines. No casualties.	Jm 9
"	13th		Third batch of 4 Officers & 40 men attached for duty to R.F.A. Brigades.	Jm 9
"	15th	11pm	Neighbourhood of DAC camp shelled.	Jm 9

Army Form C. 2118.

WAR DIARY
or
INTELLIGENCE SUMMARY.
(Erase heading not required.)

Instructions regarding War Diaries and Intelligence Summaries are contained in F. S. Regs., Part II. and the Staff Manual respectively. Title pages will be prepared in manuscript.

Place	Date 1916	Hour	Summary of Events and Information	Remarks and references to Appendices
ALBERT	August 16th	7am	One man wounded by shrapnel from A.A. gun whilst shelling hostile aeroplanes passing our horse lines	J. in g.
"	17th		V/34 (Heavy) T.M.B. and M/34, O/34, P/34 (Medium) T.M.B's disbanded. Personnel transferred to D.A.C. after X/34 & Y/34 & Z/34 (Medium) T.M.B's were completed to establishment plus 5 men per battery reserve.	J. in g.
"	18th	7pm	Neighbourhood of Camp shelled, a direct hit being made on an auto wagon belonging to another unit 20 yards SW. of No 4 Section lines.	J. in g.
"	19th		Half-Section 50th D.A.C. marched in to relieve 34th D.A.C. By order of the G.O.C. R.A. the 34th D.A.C. moved by Sections to its new area at FREHENCOURT, commencing at 6am, at 1 hour's interval. Responsibility for amtn. supply handed over to O.O. 50th D.A.C. at 12 noon.	J. in g.
FREHENCOURT	21st		By order of G.O.C. R.A. began to move to new area in accordance with "Q"/34's train programme.	J. in g.
STEENWERCK	22nd		The Column completed its move, assembling in the STEENWERCK Area.	J. in g.
"	23rd		A draft of 59 O.R. Ranks reposted from the Base, were taken on the strength of this unit.	J. in g.
"	24th	11am	Responsibility for amtn. supply taken over from 18th D.A.C., the supply being carried out from the Refilling Point used by that unit. By order of the G.O.C. R.A. 34th Divn, there was handed over to the 18th D.A.C. A 2997 BX 868 rounds.	J. in g.
"	25th		X/34 & Z/34 (Medium) T.M.B's moved up to Trenches.	J. in g.

Army Form C. 2118.

WAR DIARY
or
INTELLIGENCE SUMMARY.
(Erase heading not required.)

Instructions regarding War Diaries and Intelligence Summaries are contained in F. S. Regs., Part II. and the Staff Manual respectively. Title pages will be prepared in manuscript.

Place	Date 1916 August	Hour	Summary of Events and Information	Remarks and references to Appendices
STEENWERCK	26th		V/34 (Heavy) T.M.B. re-formed by order of G.O.C. R.A., and made up to full establishment.	In g.
	27th		Y/34 (Med.) T.M.B. marched to forward area.	In g.
	28th		V/34 (Heavy) T.M.B. moved to new billeting area, ERQUINGHEM. The 34th 2nd Artillery (4/4) were re-organised into 6-gun batteries. The surplus officers are attached to the D.A.C. pending news of further orders as to their disposal.	In g.
	29th		Surplus vehicles taken over from Artillery Bdes pending orders as to their evacuation.	On g. In g.
	30th		The 34th D.A.C. took over the billets vacated by the 18th D.A.C. Five ammunition officers posted to the 18th 2nd Artillery.	
	31st		60 men of the column attached to the D.T.M.C. for digging emplacements. 60 men also sent to Arty. Bdes for building O.P's, both parties being detached from the column. 100 men to go to fort 34th Div. Signals officer daily until further notice (commencing today) for the purpose of digging in telephone wires.	In g.

Wilson Colonel, R.F.A.
Commanding 34th Div. Am. Col.

Vol 9

<u>Secret</u>

<u>War   Diary (Volume 9)</u>

of

<u>34th. Divisional Ammunition Column</u>

<u>From Sept 1st-1916</u>   <u>To Sept-30th-1916</u>

Army Form C. 2118.

WAR DIARY
34th D.A.C.
INTELLIGENCE SUMMARY.
(Erase heading not required.)

Page 1

Instructions regarding War Diaries and Intelligence Summaries are contained in F. S. Regs., Part II. and the Staff Manual respectively. Title pages will be prepared in manuscript.

Place	Date 1916	Hour	Summary of Events and Information	Remarks and references to Appendices
STEENWERK	Sept 2nd		2760 grenades delivered to Light Brigade Bomb Store	J.L.g
"	4th		Arrangement on the re-organization of the Divisional Artillery. L.D. horses were received from Artillery Brigades.	J.L.g
"	6th		26 L.D. horses from Brigades sent to Mobile Veterinary Section for despatch to Base on 7th inst. 1 G.S. wagon lent to each Battery R.F.A. — Men all — for work on O.P.s etc.	J.L.g
"	9th		3 Officers transferred to 7th Divisional Artillery, 9 & 4 Officers transferred to 14th Divl. Artillery	J.L.g
"	11th		The C.O., M.O. and 1 Officer & 2 N.C.O.s per Section attended 34th Divl. Gas School for instruction in use of new Small Box Respirator.	J.L.g
"			The men attached to T.M. Batteries 30/8/16 rejoined their Sections	J.L.g
"	13th		1 Officer attached to R.H.A. 2nd Cavalry Division. Surplus vehicles evacuated, 4 Cooks Carts	J.L.g
"	14th		Following surplus vehicles evacuated. 1 Telephone wagon, 1 Maltese Cart, 1 Flat Cart. 1 extra G.S. wagon lent to each Battery R.F.A. for use in building wagon lines — making 22 wagons in all on loan.	
"			34.R.A. Signalling Class commenced, 15 O.R. D.A.C. attending.	
"			1 Officer attached to Caestre, STRAZEELE, for 5 day Ordnance Course of Instruction	J.L.g

Army Form C. 2118.

WAR DIARY
INTELLIGENCE SUMMARY.
(Erase heading not required.)

Page 2

Instructions regarding War Diaries and Intelligence Summaries are contained in F. S. Regs., Part II. and the Staff Manual respectively. Title pages will be prepared in manuscript.

Place	Date 1916	Hour	Summary of Events and Information	Remarks and references to Appendices
	SEPT		Reference maps Sheets 36 + 28	
STEENWERCK	16th		1 Officer + 12 O.R. attached to Second Army Trench Mortar School, BERTHEN, for a 10 days and 14 days course of instruction.	Jn g
"	20th		1 Officer attached to Reilhed, STRAZEELE, for 5 days Ordnance Course of Instruction	Jn g
"	22nd		The 100 men employed digging in Telephone wires return to duty on completion of the work	Jn g
"	"		No 3 Sec. 34th D.A.C. and Y/34 T.M.B. transferred to "FRANKS" Force.	Jn g
"	23rd		Instruction given to 1 Officer + 50 O.R. by R.E. in Straw hat making for men's helts.	Jn g
"	"		Ammunition in possession of No 3 Section + handed over to FRANKS Force at 12 noon :— A 145 AX 644 BPF 20 BX 240 SAK(4×)B 35,600 Pkt Webby 828 rounds.	Jn g
"	26th		5 guns 15 pdr. B.L.C. drawn from B.13.a.6.1. (Sheet 36)	Jn g
"	27th		10 "P.B." Men attached to No 1/Sec. for instruction in packing empty cartridge cases.	Jn g
"	"		2 wagons 15 pdr. drawn from S.22.a.1.2. (Sheet 26).	Jn g
"	"		12 men to be sent daily to assist R.E.s in construction of new Refilling Point at H.11.c.6.8.(Sheet 35)	Jn g
"	30th		173 rounds 15 pdr. Shrapnel drawn from 19th D.A.C. amm for 5 gun team was antillant	Jn g

Vol 10

SECRET

War Diary (Volume 10)

of

34th Divisional Ammunition Column

From Oct 1st 1916   To Oct 31st 1916

Army Form C. 2118.

WAR DIARY
34TH of D.A.C.
INTELLIGENCE SUMMARY.

Volume 10.

Page 1

(Erase heading not required.)

Instructions regarding War Diaries and Intelligence Summaries are contained in F. S. Regs., Part II. and the Staff Manual respectively. Title pages will be prepared in manuscript.

Place	Date	Hour	Summary of Events and Information	Remarks and references to Appendices
STEENWERCK	1916 Oct 5		Reference Map Sheet 36.	
	5th		One 15 pdr. gun with full detachment proceeded to front line under Lieut. APPLEBEE, and was attached to "C" Batty, 152nd A/B.	
	7th		Corpl D. Sargeant, No 1 Sec. "A" Echelon, D.A.C., in charge of DAC party working on O.P. of C/152 was killed by shell fire.	Jm g
	8th		6 R and 11 LD Remounts received. Daily working parties of 1 N.C.O. & 9 men detailed for work on gun emplacements of D/175 & A/116 respectively. Echelon consisting of 1 N.C.O. & 23 men, 24 horses & 24 mules, 4 horsed wagons & 4 G.S. wagons arrived from 516th (T.) Ammt Batty. & were taken on the strength of this unit.	Jm g Jm g
	11th		Daily road fatigue of 5 wagons detailed for carting stone for Corps Roads.	Jm g
	12th		Whilst Medium T.M Bntn was being moved forward by this unit, one mule was killed by M.G. fire.	Jm g
	14th		All Guns & S.A. Amtn transferred to new Amtn Refilling Point at H.1.0.6.8. T.M. Amtn remain at A.27.d. 5.0. & Grenades with Sectns.	Jm g
	17th		By order of C.R.A. the horses & mules of new echelon returned to C/175 to be kept in working isolation on account of ringworm.	Jm g
	18th		A second 15 pdr. gun taken up to front line & attached to C/160. Detachment formed from originals detachment sent up on 5th inst.	Jm g

Army Form C. 2118.

WAR DIARY
34TH D.A.C.
INTELLIGENCE SUMMARY.

(Erase heading not required.)

Page 2   Volume 10

Place	Date	Hour	Summary of Events and Information	Remarks and references to Appendices
STEENWERCK	1916 OCT. 21st		61 G.S. Wagon Loads of Amm. drawn from Advanced Railhead.	In. 9
"	24th		L.D. 11 Remounts received.	In. 9
"	25th		Reinforcements, 1 Fr: Staff Sergt. & 27 Telephonists arrived from R.A. & R.F.A. Base Depot, HAVRE	In. 9
"	26th		The G.O.C. R.A. 34th Divn. selected 16 "other Ranks" for Medium Trench Mortar Course at 2nd Army School, BERTHEN, commencing Nov 1st	
"	27th		Reinforcements received 25th inst. posted to Brigades. Six "other Ranks" sent to Z/34 T.M. Batty. for attachment for 14 days.	In. 9
"	31st		Extra daily fatigue of 2 G.S. wagons detailed for R.E. work. The 15pdr gun attached C/152 withdrawn from action. Lieut APPLEBEE and first detachment returned to D.A.C.	
			81 G.S. Wagon Loads of Amm. drawn from Advanced Railhead.	In. 9

A. Simpson Colonel R.H.A.
Cmdg. 34th D.A.C.

Secret.

War Diary (Volume XI)

of

34th Divisional Ammunition Column

From Nov- 1st 1916   To Nov 30th 1916

Volume 11

Army Form C. 2118.

WAR DIARY
34TH D.A.C.
INTELLIGENCE SUMMARY.

(Erase heading not required.)

Page 1 Volume XI

Place	Date 1916 Nov	Hour	Summary of Events and Information	Remarks and references to Appendices
STEENWERCK	1st.		16 Other Ranks "proceeded to BERTHEN for Trench Mortar Course of Instruction	Jn. 9
"	4th		The 34th Divl. Arty Signalling Class terminated	Jn. 9
"	5th		1 N.C.O. & 9 men were attached to A/160 for accommodation etc whilst working on B/175 gun position	Jn. 9
"			1 N.C.O. & 9 men were similarly attached to C/152 whilst working on D/175 gun position.	
"	9th		Six signallers (from the last course were attached to the Right & Left groups to control O.P. Exchanges (Telephone)	Jn. 9
"	10th		60 G.S. wagon Loads of Amtn. were drawn from the advanced Amtn. Railhead.	Jn. 9
"	15th		2 N.C.O. & 14 men returned from T.M. course commenced on 1st inst	Jn. 9
"	16th		9 men were attached to X/34 T.M. Battery, 6 men to Z/34 T.M. Batty	
"	19th		1 Officer & 17 "O.R." proceeded on Trench Mortar Course to Second Army T.M. Sch. C, BERTHEN	Jn. 9
"			2. Lieut. P. Banks who entered Base Hospl. HAVRE on 11/9/16, rejoined the D.A.C. from Hospital for duty	Jn. 9
"			23 Other Ranks reported from the Base in reinforcements	Jn. 9
"	20th		8 men from each Bde. attached to undergo course of "Signalling", 8 men of DAC. also joining the class.	
"			12 efficient drivers were exchanged with 12 drivers from C/175 for the purpose of instructing drivers belonging to that Batty.	Jn. 9

Army Form C. 2118.

WAR DIARY
34TH ~~or D.A.C.~~
INTELLIGENCE SUMMARY
(Erase heading not required.)

Page 2   Volume XI

Instructions regarding War Diaries and Intelligence Summaries are contained in F. S. Regs., Part II. and the Staff Manual respectively. Title pages will be prepared in manuscript.

Place	Date 1916	Hour	Summary of Events and Information	Remarks and references to Appendices
	NOVEM			
STEENWERCK	21st		1 Gunner reported from the Base as reinforcement	gmg
"	25th		26 Remounts (Mules) received	gmg
"	29th		3 N.C.O. & 25 men proceeded to Arien Railhead at STRAZEELE for fatigue duty until 13th prox.	gmg
"	30th		Capt H.F. BARKER attached A/175.	gmg

Wilkinson Colonel V.C.

Army Form C. 2118.

WAR DIARY
34TH of D.A.C.
INTELLIGENCE SUMMARY.

(Erase heading not required.)

Page 1   Volume 12

Place	Date 1916	Hour	Summary of Events and Information	Remarks and references to Appendices
	Dec.			
STEENWERCK	2nd		10,000 Rounds drawn from R.E. yd and taken forward for construction of O.P's	Jhg
"	5th		18 "Other Ranks" reported from the Base as Reinforcements.	
			Capt. T.C. KEWLEY, R.F.A.(T), 62nd D.A.C. attached to the unit for a course of instruction.	Jhg
"	11th		28 Wagon loads (G.S.) of Amtn. drawn from Advanced Amtn. Railhead.	
			1 N.C.O. + 11 men were attached to Right Group for work on gun Positions.	Jhg
"	12th		Capt. KEWLEY returned to England, and unem tle attached.	
			2nd Lieut H.E. PITT, R.F.A. was attached to this unit for duty.	
			One Gunner sent to Second Army School of Signalling at ZUYTPEENE for a course of instruction in visual signalling.	Jhg
"	13th		1200 bricks taken forward for construction of an O.P. This is also done daily until 10,000 bricks have been taken up.	Jhg
"	15th		40 G.S. Wagon loads of Amtn. drawn from Advanced Railhead	Jhg
"	19th		2 Officers proceeded to ST OMER to attend a practical Veterinary Demonstration at No. 23 Veterinary Hospital	Jhg
"	20th		16 "Other Ranks" posted to Left Brigade	Jhg
"	21st		19 "Other Ranks" reported from the Base as Reinforcements	Jhg
			The working party of 28 men rejoined the unit from Railhead, STRAZEELE.	

Army Form C. 2118.

WAR DIARY
34TH D.A.C.
INTELLIGENCE SUMMARY.
(Erase heading not required.)

Page 2 VOLUME 12

Place	Date 1916	Hour	Summary of Events and Information	Remarks and references to Appendices
ERQUINGHEM	DEC. 22nd		The 34th Division was inspected by the Commander-in-Chief on the ERQUINGHEM—BAC ST. MAUR Road. The D.A.C. was represented by the C.O., the Adjt., 1 Capt., 2 Subalterns & 80 "Other Ranks"	
	25th		16 Other Ranks were attached to the Light Group for work on Gun Emplacements.	Gn.5
	26th		2nd Lieut. R. Cooper, admitted Hospital.	Gn.5
			119 G.S. Wagon Ranks of Ammn. drawn from Adv. Railhead	Gn.5
	27th		117 " " " " " "	Gn.5
	28th		115 " " " " " "	Gn.5
	29th		Lt. Col. J.O. STITT, R.F.A.(T.), commanding 57th (W.L.) D.A.C. attached to this unit for instruction	Gn.5
	30th		2nd Lieut. T.S. CARROLL, attached to 175th Bde. R.F.A. for duty	Gn.5

Bally Maj. R.F.A.
Comdg. 34th Div. Am. Col.

D.A.C.

Army Form C. 2118.

WAR DIARY
34th or DAC.
INTELLIGENCE SUMMARY.

(Erase heading not required.)

Volume 13

Instructions regarding War Diaries and Intelligence Summaries are contained in F. S. Regs., Part II. and the Staff Manual respectively. Title pages will be prepared in manuscript.

Place	Date 1917	Hour	Summary of Events and Information	Remarks and references to Appendices
STEENWERCK	JANY 3rd		Two 15pdr guns limbers & 1 15pdr austn. wagon handed over to RTD Base St MAUR for transmission to Ordnance Officer.	JM g
"	4th		Three " " " " " two " " " " "	JM g
"	12th		The limbers of Nos. 4, 2 & 1 Sections DAC were inspected by the Second Army Commander.	JM g
"	13th		48 horses, harness etc. handed over to end of D/152 & 3/140 from No 3 Sec DAC	JM g
"	14th		The following horses were taken over from 0/175 :- 47 by 1 Sec. which remained at 0/175	
"			wagon lines, and 46 by No 2 Sec.	JM g
"	15th		Reorganization of DAC completed. No 3 Sec became 175th Brigade Austn Column. No 1 Sec "B"Echelon became No 3 Sec. "B" Echelon	
"	16th		1 Officer & 12 other Ranks proceeded in Trench Mortar Course to Second Army School (BERTHEN)	JM g
"	20th		The D.A.C. received orders to hold itself in readiness to move to METEREN – 28 shot	
"	27th		Instructions received that the Column would not leave its present billets until further orders	
"			Responsibility for Austn. Supply passed to 3rd Australian DAC. & from 12 noon	
"			Austn. in respect of Echelon Establishment handed over to 3rd Austln. DAC.	JM g

CHSaunders Colonel RHA
Comdg 34th DAC

2353 Wt. W2544/1454 700,000 5/15 D. D. & L. A.D.S.S. Forms/C. 2118.

Army Form C. 2118.

WAR DIARY
34TH D.A.C.
INTELLIGENCE SUMMARY.
(Erase heading not required.)

VOLUME 14

Instructions regarding War Diaries and Intelligence Summaries are contained in F.S. Regs. Part II. and the Staff Manual respectively. Title pages will be prepared in manuscript.

Reference Map:— HAZEBROUCK Sheet 5A, 1/100,000
LENS Sheet 11, 1/100,000

Place	Date 1917 Feby	Hour	Summary of Events and Information	Remarks and references to Appendices
STEENWERCK	1st		2nd Lieut NICHOLS and 8 "Other Ranks" proceeded on course to Second Army Trench Mortar School, BERTHEN.	Initials
	10th		Two Officers and 25 "O.R." proceeded to Third Army T.M. School, LIGNY ST FLOCHEL for course of instruction	Initials
	13th		By order of G.O.C. R.A. 34th Divn. "B" Echelon D.A.C. (with V/34 Heavy T.M. Battery & part of R.A. 111 R~s~ attached) marched to HAZEBROUCK via LE VERRIER, VIEUX BERQUIN, and LA MOTTE	Initials
HAZEBROUCK	14th		The above party continued to march to FONTES.	Initials
FONTES	15th		March continued to LA THIEULOYE	Initials
FRÉVIN CAPELLE	16th		"B" Echelon & attached further arrived in new area at FRÉVIN CAPELLE	Initials
STEENWERCK	19th		In accordance with orders received from G.O.C. 34th Divn, R.A. Group 34th Divn. (Col. Simpson R.F.A. Commander) marched to STEENBECQUE area — March Programme attached [Appendix 1]	Initials
STEENBECQUE	20th		R.A. Group continued its march to Third Army area according to attached Programme [Appendix 2]. D.A.C. billeted at FONTES	Initials
FONTES	21st		Column continued its march [See Appendix 3]. H.Q. D.A.C. at ANTIGNEUL CHATEAU. No 1 Section at GRICOURT, No 2 Section at MAREST	Initials
ANTIGNEUL CHATEAU	22nd		HQrs DAC and Sections remain in their billets occupied yesterday; awaiting further instructions. 1 Officer & 25 "O.R." proceeded to LIGNY ST FLOCHEL on Trench Mortar Course at Third Army School.	Initials

Signature

Army Form C. 2118.

'34 D Ass Col

Sgt /5

WAR DIARY
34TH OR D.A.C.
INTELLIGENCE SUMMARY.
(Erase heading not required.)

Instructions regarding War Diaries and Intelligence Summaries are contained in F. S. Regs., Part II and the Staff Manual respectively. Title pages will be prepared in manuscript.

Page 1.   VOLUME 15

Place	Date 1917	Hour	Summary of Events and Information	Remarks and references to Appendices
	MARCH		Reference Maps: Lens Sheet 11. 1/100,000 Sheet 51C. 1/40,000	
ANTIGNEUL CHN	2nd.		By order of the G.O.C.R.A. the column resumed its march as follows:- Hd Qrs & No 1 Sec to BETHONSART,	Jn. 6.
BETHONSART	4th		No. 2 Sec. to HERLIN-LE-VERT.	Jn. 6.
FREVIN CAPELLE	8th		Hd.Qrs. moved to VILLERS BRULIN	Jn. 6.
"	9th		Amtn. Supply resumed by "B" Echelon.	Jn. 6.
"	10th		6 G.S Wagons (complete turnouts) from "A" Echelon attached to "B" Echelon to assist in Amtn Supply.	Jn. 6.
			An additional 12 G.S Wagons of "A" Echelon with teams & personnel, attached to "B" Echelon.	Jn. 6.
E17 central	11th		Six 18pdr or 4.5in Hows Amtn Wagons per Battery sent from "A" Echelon for attachment to Brigades with full complement of N.C.O.'s, officers etc. to assist in supply of Amtn to "Z" Divl. Arty.	Jn. 6.
HERLIN LE VERT	12th		No 2 Sec. marched from HERLIN-LE-VERT to VILLERS BRULIN.	Jn. 6.
FREVIN CAPEUS	13th		35 "Other Ranks" attached Trench Mortar Batteries	
	16th		No 23112 Driver T. Taylor, No 3 Sec. wounded, whilst carrying forward material for Trench Mortar emplacement	Jn. 9.
	17th		"B" Echelon moved from FREVIN CAPELLE to "B" Camp E.16.b.8.1.	Jn. 9.
	18th		No 49927 Gnr Wood & No 4377 Gnr Wakefield of No 5 Sec. ("B" Echelon) wounded whilst transporting RE material	Jn. 9.
VILLERS BRULIN	19th		Remainder of Column moved to "B" Camp	
	20th		Whilst amtn. for "Z" Arty. was being taken to dumps, No 152381 Driver Jones, D wounded by hostile splinters	Jn. 9.
E.16.b.8.1.	23rd		Two officers attached, one from 311th Army F.A Bde & one from 84th Army F.A Bde.	Jn. 9.
	24th		Two more officers attached, commanding above two Army F.A. Bdes.	Jn. 8.

2353 Wt. W2544/1454 700,000 5/15 D.D.& L. A.D.S.S. Forms/C. 2118.

Army Form C. 2118.

WAR DIARY
34TH D.A.C.
INTELLIGENCE SUMMARY.
(Erase heading not required.)

Page 2   VOLUME 15

Place	Date 1917	Hour	Summary of Events and Information	Remarks and references to Appendices
E.16.b.	MARCH 26th		During transport of T.M. Amn. near St Nicholas, 4 "Other Ranks" were wounded, and 6 mules killed + 2 wounded by shell-fire :- No 25325 Dvr Mawbridge, 231382 Dvr Marson, 231332 Dvr Parkin, 146645 Dvr Reith, all of "B" Echelon.	Jan. 9
	27th		Drivers Mawbridge & Parkin, wounded yesterday, died of wounds.	Jan. 9
	28th		Amn. Supply for "Z" Division served.	Jan. 9
	29th		12 Howitzer Wagons detailed to assist daily in supply of water to 17th Divl Arty + D/56 + D/311 Batteries.	Jan. 9

AChumperformed RA,
Comdg 34 Div D.A.C.

Army Form C. 2118.

34 D A C

WAR DIARY
34TH D.A.C.
INTELLIGENCE SUMMARY.
(Erase heading not required.)

VOLUME 16

Instructions regarding War Diaries and Intelligence Summaries are contained in F.S. Regs., Part II. and the Staff Manual respectively. Title pages will be prepared in manuscript.

PAGE 1

Place	Date 1917	Hour	Summary of Events and Information	Remarks and references to Appendices
	APRIL		Reference Map :- { Sheet 51B 1/40,000 } { Sheet 51B }	
E.16.b (51c)	1st		2nd Lieut H. WILSON-JONES wounded whilst in charge of party digging emplacements, was evacuated to England 30/3/17 in heavy Trench Mortar	J.W.G.
			2nd Lt. J. WILLIAMSON (T.) proceeded to Third Army Trench Mortar School at LIGNY ST FLOCHEL for a course of instruction	J.W.G.
	2nd		1 N.C.O. & 11 men reinforcements from Base arrived & were posted to 152nd Bde. R.F.A. forthwith	J.W.G.
"	5th		Lieut. H.P. APPLEBEE, R.E.A. of this unit appointed Town Mayor of "B" (Camp) (E.16.b)	J.W.G.
"	9th		10 men joined from Reinforcement Depot & were posted to 152nd Bde R.F.A.	J.W.G.
"			"Z" Bay. By order of G.O.C. 34 Divn, 216 Mules with 108 drivers and 6 NCO's & 3 Shoeing Smiths, were attached to Infantry Transport of the Divn. to assist in supply of S.A.A. & bombs to the trenches	J.W.G.
"	10th		Two Amm. Wagon Sub Batterys (40 in all) were attached to 152nd & 160th Bdes R.F.A. to assist in Amn. Supply.	
			The D.A.C. received orders to move to new Wagon Lines N.E. of ANZIN Church (G.2.a.3.6. Sheet 51 B).	
			16 Remount Mules were received, reducing light draught animals deficient to 191. 115 N.C.O.'s & men joined from Reinforcement Depot.	
G.2.a.3.6. (51B)	11th		Move of D.A.C. to new area completed. 41 N.C.O.'s & men posted to 152nd Bde R.F.A., 57 to 160th Bde.	J.W.G.
—	12th		2nd Lt. C.O. LEMON. RFA joined from the Base.	J.W.G.
—	14th		8 men joined from Base Reinforcement Depot. The work of clearing gun positions vacated by 9" How: Bty. & 3/6th, 3/1st, 7/6th & 7/7th Bdes R.F.A. was begun. The	J.W.G.

Army Form C. 2118.

WAR DIARY
36th or DAC
INTELLIGENCE SUMMARY

(Erase heading not required.)

PAGE 2   VOLUME 16

Place	Date 1917	Hour	Summary of Events and Information	Remarks and references to Appendices
G.2.a (51b)	APRIL 15th (cont.)		Personnel of 4 French Motor Batteries (X/36, X/34, Y/34 & Z/36) were attached to the DAC to assist with road.	Ap.8
			11 prs of mules with drivers were attached to the Div. Infantry Transport	
"	16th		The above 11 prs of mules returned from the Infantry	
			2nd Lieut. C.O. Lemon posted to 160th Bde. R.F.A. 8 men were posted to 152nd Bde. R.F.A.	Ap.9
"	17th		By order of G.O.C. R.A. 36th Divn. an advanced Ammn. Dump was established at H.S.c.3.2 (½ mile St Laurent - Gavrelle Road). At least 10,800 rounds A+A.X. + 3600 rounds B.X. to be taken up before noon on 19th inst.	Ap.9
			2nd Lt. J. Williamson attached in charge of this dump	
H.S.c (61b)	18th		Gunner V. Ash (110196) wounded whilst unloading Ammn. at the advanced Dump.	Ap.8
"	19th		By 4 a.m. the following Ammn. had been taken up to advanced Dump (in much larger quantity than ordered)	
			By congested traffic routes between St Catherine & St Laurent :- A.7120, A.X.6260, B.X.3936.	
			36th Divn. Arty. came under orders of C.R.A. 4th Divn.	
			Following 3 subaltern officers joined from the base :- 2nd Lt. A. London, 2nd Lt. W.E. Blythe, 2nd Lt. K.J. Franklin	Ap.9
G.2.a (51b)	20th		C.R.A. 9th Divn. assumed control of 36th Divl. Arty.	
"	21st		7 men joined from Base Reinforcement Depôt	
"	22nd		All available amm. from DAC. was sent to advanced Dump. Whilst unloading there, DAC. parties sustained the following casualties :- Drivers Hamilton J., Staple W.G., Johnson T.R. wounded, and Drivers Busby & Crawley wounded	

Army Form C. 2118.

WAR DIARY
34th D.A.C.
INTELLIGENCE SUMMARY.
(Erase heading not required.)

PAGE 3   VOLUME 16

Instructions regarding War Diaries and Intelligence Summaries are contained in F.S. Regs., Part II. and the Staff Manual respectively. Title pages will be prepared in manuscript.

Place	Date 1917 APRIL	Hour	Summary of Events and Information	Remarks and references to Appendices
G.2.3.6.(S.16)	23rd		(remaining at duty). Animals killed, 9; wounded 10 (2 slightly). Deficiencies in animal strength now stand at Rdg 3 L.D. 227	
	24th	2 a.m.	2nd Lt A. LONDON posted to 152nd Bde R.F.A. Remounts received, 12 mules. 1 Officer & 10 "Other Ranks" forwarded to H15b to assist at Corps Ammn. Dump at present being formed. Notification received from 31st Divn. that Maj. J. DALBY who proceeded on leave on March 23rd. had been examined by a Medical Board, & should be struck off the strength of this unit.	Ap g
	26th		Remounts received Rdg 2, L.D. horses 3D. Mules 7.	Ap g
	27th	11 a.m.	Gnnr J Jones (71541) wounded by A.A. fire directed against enemy aeroplane which fired Observation Balloon close to DAC Camp.	Ap g
			By order of G.O.C. 31st Divn., the S.A.A. Echelons of the D.A.C. were attached to 102nd Infy. Bde. Transport at St NICHOLAS Gnnr Lynch, attached 160th Bde. W. Bgde. wounded.	Ap g
	30th	7 pm	The S.A.A. Echelons returned to the D.A.C. By order of C.R.A. 31st Divn. the 3 1/4th D.A.C. reports on Fly animals to 50th A.R.P.A.	Ap g

Deficiencies in Animal Strength:-

	Rdg.	Light Draught
April 1st	2	113
" 18	2	166
" 13th	2	191
" 20th	4	210
" 22nd	3	227
" 30th	1	159

C. H. Simpson, Major R.F.A.
Comg 34th D.A.C.

WAR DIARY
34th D.A.C.
INTELLIGENCE SUMMARY

Volume 17

Reference Map:- 51 B (1/40,000)

Place	Date 1917 MAY	Hour	Summary of Events and Information	Remarks and references to Appendices
In the Field G.2.a.3.6	3rd.		Owing to about 70 horses of B/160 being killed by shell-fire about 4 a.m., 12 teams with drivers, under 2nd Lt. HART, RFA(T), were temporarily attached to that Battery.	App. 1
"	5th.		20 Horses & 7 Mules (Remounts) were transferred to 160th Bde R.F.A.	App. 2
"	6th.		Received 100 horses from Remount Depot & issued 40 to 152nd Bde. & 60 to 160th Bde RFA	App. 3
"	7th.		Drew 85 mules (Remounts) from AUBIGNY	App. 3
"	8th.		Issued 40 mules to 152nd Bde. & 45 to 160th Bde. R.F.A.	
"	10th.		The party attached to 160th Bde on 5th inst rejoined. 2nd Lt. H.T. BIRD posted from 152nd Bde R.F.A. to D.A.C. 2nd Lt. Young, HIND, NELSON, ANDERSON, BANKS, OWEN H.E., already detached were posted to their respective units.	App. 4 App. 5
"	11th.		Control of 34th Divn. Arty. assumed by C.R.A. 17th Divn. 2nd Lt. MENZIES, attached 160th Bde., evacuated wounded.	App. 6
"	13th.		1 N.C.O. & 58 men arrived from Reinforcement Depot	App. 7
"	14th.		108 horses hundred of Ammunition supplied to Brigades. 1 N.C.O. & 18 men posted to 152nd Bde., & 26 men to 160th Bde., 2nd Lt. WILCOCK posted to 152nd Bde R.F.A.	App. 6
"	17th.		2nd Lt. Angell & 2nd Lt. Williamson posted to 152nd Bde. R.F.A.	App. 6 App. 6

Army Form C. 2118.

WAR DIARY
34th ∞ D.A.C.
INTELLIGENCE SUMMARY.

(Erase heading not required.)

Page 2 Volume 17

Instructions regarding War Diaries and Intelligence Summaries are contained in F.S. Regs., Part II. and the Staff Manual respectively. Title pages will be prepared in manuscript.

Place	Date 1917 MAY	Hour	Summary of Events and Information	Remarks and references to Appendices
G.2.a.3.6.			Reference Map:- 51 B (1/40,000)	
	19th		2nd Lt. HARKNETT rejoined from 152nd Bde R.F.A.	Ap. g
	22nd		46 Drivers & Gunners arrived from Reinforcement Depot	Ap. g
	23rd		23 Drivers & Gunners posted to 152nd Bde & 23 to 160th Bde, R.F.A.	Ap. g
			2nd Lt. H. JONES, reported, reported his arrival from the Base	Ap. g
	24th		2nd Lt. HARKNETT & BLYTHE attached 152nd Bde.	Ap. g
	26th		A party of 1 Officer & 50 Drivers proceeded to ABBEVILLE by train from AUBIGNY to draw 100 Remounts for 160th Bde	Ap. g
			Major E. C. Fleming struck off strength with effect from 21/5/17 on posting to D/311 A.F.A. Brigade.	E.G.W.
	27th		1 N.C.O & 21 men arrived from Reinforcement Depot	E.G.W.
	30th		1 N.C.O + 12 men arrived from Reinforcement Depot	E.G.W.
	31st		Drew 50 mules (remounts) from Aubigny	E.G.W.

C.W.Sunderland Rsk
Com'g 34th D.A.C.

Army Form C. 2118.

34 D Am Col
Volume 18
951/18

WAR DIARY
34TH ≠ D.A.C.
INTELLIGENCE SUMMARY.
(Erase heading not required.)

Instructions regarding War Diaries and Intelligence Summaries are contained in F.S. Regs., Part II. and the Staff Manual respectively. Title pages will be prepared in manuscript.

Page 1

Place	Date 1917	Hour	Summary of Events and Information	Remarks and references to Appendices
	JUNE		Reference Map: Sheet 51 B 1/40,000	
In the Field (G.2.a.3.6)	1st		2nd Lieut H.T. BIRD appointed O/C 34th Divl. S.A.A. Sump.	
			Control of 34th Div. A.Ty. resumed by C.R.A. 34th Divn.	Jm g
"	2nd		2nd Lieuts. R. VICKERS & E.B. LEMON reported their arrival from the Base	
			1 N.C.O. & 8 Gunners were posted to 152nd Bde R.F.A. and 9 Gunners & Drivers to the 160th Bde R.F.A.	
			1 N.C.O. & 14 Guns. & Drs. posted to the 34th T.M.B's	Jm g
"	3rd		2nd Lieut R. VICKERS posted to 152nd Bde. R.F.A. & 2nd Lieut E.B. LEMON to 160th Bde. R.F.A.	
			In accordance with instructions received from G.O.C.R.A. 34th Divn., 800 Phosphorus grenades & 3000 Smoke Candles were drawn from XVII Corps Amn. Park & a series of experiments carried out to ascertain the best method of forming a smoke screen in front of guns placed in advanced positions & concealing them & possible from aerial observation	Jm g
"	4th		Col. C.N. Sampson, Comdg., awarded the D.S.O. (London Gazette dated June 3rd 1917)	Jm g
"	5th		9 Pdrs., 9 13 gns. & Drs. arrived from Reinforcement Base Depot.	
			Received 9 Mules (Remounts) from 34th Divl. Train	Jm g
"	6th		8 Pdrs. & 1 Gnr. posted to 152nd Bde R.F.A., 5 gnrs posted to 160th Bde R.F.A.	Jm g
"			Capt. J.E. HUTCHINSON, A.V.C. reported from 14th Divn. for attachment to this unit	Jm g
	7th		Lieuts W. HOLDEN & P.W. STEWART reported their arrival from the Base	Jm g

WAR DIARY
34th D.A.C.
INTELLIGENCE SUMMARY

Army Form C. 2118.

PAGE 2   VOLUME 18

Place	Date 1917	Hour	Summary of Events and Information	Remarks and references to Appendices
In the Field (G.2.a.3.6)	JUNE 7th		4 G.S. wagons detailed as transport for 184th Tunnelling Coy. to be sent daily for alternate weeks commencing today.	J.M.G.
"	8th		A demonstration of the methods of forming a smoke screen for guns was carried out before the G.O.C. Division & the G.O.C. Divl. Artillery.	J.M.G.
"	9th		Signalling class commenced in 34th D.A.C. to bring number of signallers up to establishment.	J.M.G.
"	14th		R.A. Signalling Class commenced. 8 N.C.O.s & men per Brigade attached to this unit for the duration of the course. The D.A.C. Class was merged into the R.A. Class. 2nd Lieuts P.C. BELL & E.L. WILLIAMS and 12 N.C.O.s arrived as reinforcements from the Base.	J.M.G.
"	15th		Inspection of D.A.C. lines by G.O.C. R.A. 34th Divn.	J.M.G.
"	16th		2nd Lieuts A.W.L. BLYTHE & P.C. BELL posted to 152nd Bde., 2nd Lieuts K.J. FRANKLIN & E.L. WILLIAMS to 160th Bde., 2nd Lieut W. HOLDEN to Trench Mortar Batteries. 11 N.C.O.s posted to 152nd & 160th Bdes. R.F.A.	J.M.G.
"	19th		71 Remounts (51 horses & 20 mules) drawn from the Base.	J.M.G.
"	20th		Inspection of D.A.C. lines by G.O.C. Divn. Whilst a party of No.3 Section were taking rations to Trench Mortar positions, 1 mule was killed & 3 wounded by shell fire.	J.M.G.
"	22nd		C.R.A. 17th Divn. assumed control of the 34th Divl. Artillery. Capt. CRYSTALL, R.E., O/C R.A. Signals, attached to D.A.C. in connection with R.A. Signalling Class.	J.M.G.

Army Form C. 2118.

WAR DIARY
34th "D" D.A.C.
INTELLIGENCE SUMMARY.

(Erase heading not required).

PAGE 3   VOLUME 18

Place	Date 1917	Hour	Summary of Events and Information	Remarks and references to Appendices
In the Field (G.2.a.3.6.)	JUNE 24th		2 N.C.O.'s & 6 men posted to 152nd & 160th Bdes. R.F.A.	J.M.G.
"	29th		Echelons re-filled with ammunition in view of forthcoming move. 43 N.R. 18 pr. ammn reported from Pag	J.M.G.
"	30th		Defective Ammn. A66, AX74, BX4 rounds returned to XVIII Corps Salvage Dump MAROEUIL. A7, AX51. Handed over to 17th DAC following surplus ammunition; grenades & fuzes:- A7, AX51. ASmoke 113, BX17 rounds. S.A.A. 451 Boxes. Smoke Candles 1971. Phosphorus Grenades 571. Fuzes. "No.101" 217. "No.101E" 200. "No.106" 540. Under instructions from Corps R.A. the following BX without charges was returned to ANZAC DAC Dump:- 1066 rounds.	J.M.G.

C.H. Anderson Lieut RFA
Cmdg 34th D.A.C.

Army Form C. 2118.

WAR DIARY
34TH D.A.C.
INTELLIGENCE SUMMARY.

Volume 19

Page 1

Instructions regarding War Diaries and Intelligence Summaries are contained in F.S. Regs. Part II. and the Staff Manual respectively. Title pages will be prepared in manuscript.

Reference Maps:- { LENS, Sheet 11 } 1/100,000
{ AMIENS, "17" }
Sheet 62 c 1/40,000.

Place	Date 1917 July	Hour	Summary of Events and Information	Remarks and references to Appendices
FREVIN CAPELLE	1st		In accordance with 34th Division Orders, the 34th D.A.C. vacated its lines N.E. of ANZIN & marched to FREVIN CAPELLE where it took over the lines previously occupied by the 51st. D.A.C.	J.M.G.
"	3rd		11 Gunners reported their arrival from the Base as reinforcements.	J.M.G.
"	4th	12noon	The D.A.C. continued its march to new area via HAUTE AVESNES, WARLUS, BERNEVILLE & SIMENCOURT, halting for the night at MONCHIET.	J.M.G.
MONCHIET	5th	12noon	March resumed to COURCELLES-LE-COMTE area, via BEAUMETZ-LES-LOGES, RANSART, ADINFER, AYETTE, COURCELLES & GOMIECOURT, encamping for the night on the ground recently vacated by the 58th D.A.C.	J.M.G.
In the field	6th	11am	March to PERONNE resumed, via BEHAGNIES & BAPAUME, along the main ARRAS – PERONNE Road	J.M.G.
PERONNE	9th	11pm	The 34th D.A.C. marched to its new position in the line at the RAPERIE, Q13.d.88. (Sheet 62c)	J.M.G.
HANCOURT	10th	10am	Refilling Point & Ammunition dumps taken over from 59th D.A.C.	J.M.G.
Q.13.d.88.	12th		121 Remount Horses (Rdg. 21 & L.D.100) arrived from ABBEVILLE, by road.	J.M.G.
"	13th		Remounts, Rdg 18 & L.D. 4 handed over to 160th Bde. R.F.A. The balance, Rdg 3 & LD 96 were taken on the D.A.C. strength.	J.M.G.
"	16th		Capt. J.M. CURRIE, R.F.A.(T) reported his arrival from the Base & was attached to this unit.	J.M.G.
"	19th		31 Mules (L.D.) received as remounts.	J.M.G.
"	20th		Capt. CURRIE attached to 152nd Bde. R.F.A.	J.M.G.

Army Form C. 2118.

WAR DIARY
or
INTELLIGENCE SUMMARY.
(Erase heading not required.)

Page 2 . . . . Volume 19

Place	Date	Hour	Summary of Events and Information	Remarks and references to Appendices
Q.13.d.8.8.	21st		Reference Map: Sheet 62a 1/40,000	
			2 N.C.O's & 112 Gunners attached to 152nd Bde R.F.A. & a similar number to 156th Bde R.F.A. for instruction in gunnery, & an equal number attached to D.A.C. from Brigades for duty, etc.	J McG
"	25th		24 Gun'rs "Bers". reported from the Base as reinforcements	J McG
			Shoemakers' Shop for the whole of the 31st Divl Artillery opened under D.A.C. control. Establishment 1 N.C.O. 9	J McG
K.35.B.9.4.	26th		10 men. D.A.C. Tailors' Shop opened at the same time	J McG
Q.13.d.8.8.	30th		Work begun on new Amm. Refilling Point. MONTIGNY	J McG
			2nd Lt G. H. REID, R.F.A. reported for duty with D.A.C. on first commission (permanent), from 125th B.A.C.	J McG
"	31st		Strength of D.A.C :— Officers 21, Other Ranks 679; Riding Horses 77, L.D. Horses 307, L.D. Mules 496.	J McG

W Sunderson Colonel R.F.A.

Army Form C. 2118.

WAR DIARY
34TH D.A.C.
~~INTELLIGENCE~~ **SUMMARY.**
(Erase heading not required.)

Volume 20

Instructions regarding War Diaries and Intelligence Summaries are contained in F. S. Regs., Part II. and the Staff Manual respectively. Title pages will be prepared in manuscript.

Place	Date 1917	Hour	Summary of Events and Information	Remarks and references to Appendices
Q.13.d.8.8.	August 5th		Reference Map:- Sheet 62c. 1/40,000 4 N.C.O's & 36 drivers reported their arrival from the Base as reinforcements.	gm.g
"	7th		4 N.C.O's & 22 men posted to 160th Bde. R.F.A., 6 men to the 152nd Bde R.F.A. & 4 to the 34th T.M.Bo	gm.g
"	13th		The recently constructed Amn. Refilling Point at MONTIGNY was opened for receipts & issues. 15 men proceeded to the Third Army Trench Mortar School at LIGNY ST. FLOCHEL for a course of instruction in Heavy Trench Mortars.	gm.g
"	15th		24 additional wagons detailed for C.R.E. fatigues, bringing total up to 34 G.S. wagons daily. Mileage return for preceding 6 days, excluding 18pdr & 4.5" How. Amn. wagons :- 1880 miles loaded 2570 empty. Total 4450 miles.	gm.g
"	20th		8 x 500 rounds taken to D/152 gun positions, making 1500 rounds during past 3 nights. 180,000 rounds S.A.A. delivered to 101st M.G. Coy's positions.	gm.g
"	21st		150 canvas water buckets handed in to D.A.D.O.S. for use by infantry for carrying bombs in forthcoming operations. Re-organization of the 34th D.A.C. into 2 Sections similar to B.A.C's and 1 S.A.A. Section effected as from 12 noon. New establishment :- Officers 15, Other Ranks 605, Amn. Wagons 48, G.S. Wagons 52, Limbered G.S. Wagons 15, Water Carts 3, Maltese Cart 1, Riding Horses 73, Light Draught 664. 540,000 rounds S.A.A. delivered at 101st & 102nd M.G. Coys positions in readiness for forthcoming operations.	
"	22nd		2000 rounds 13pdr. Shrapnel delivered at gun positions of U Batty R.H.A., to assist in establishing the necessary dump for wire-cutting operations etc.	gm.g

Army Form C. 2118.

WAR DIARY
34TH or D.A.C.
INTELLIGENCE SUMMARY.

(Erase heading not required.)

Instructions regarding War Diaries and Intelligence Summaries are contained in F. S. Regs., Part II. and the Staff Manual respectively. Title pages will be prepared in manuscript.

Page 2   Volume 20

Place	Date 1917	Hour	Summary of Events and Information	Remarks and references to Appendices
Q.13.d.8.8	August 24th		Reference Map:- Shutluze 1/40,000	
			4 N.C.O.'s and 17 men posted to 160th Bde. R.F.A., 1 N.C.O. + 4 men to 152nd Bde. R.F.A., 1 S/S to II Corps R.A. 250,000 rounds S.A.A. delivered at Rvl. Bomb Store as Divisional reserve for operations of 26th inst. Mileage return for preceeding week, excluding ambn. wagons:- loaded 2180 miles, empty 2610 miles. Total 4790 miles.	J.M.g
"	25th		10 men proceeded to Third Army Trench Mortar School for instruction in T.M.s	J.M.g
"	28th		1 N.C.O. & 5 men posted to V/34 Heavy T.M. Battery. Surplus transport (18 G.S. waggons + 1 Maltese Cart) with 2 N.C.O.'s, 37 Drivers, 32 Horses & 8 mules were evacuated by road to Advanced H.T. Depôt, ABBEVILLE. During the 11 days ending 12 noon today, the following ambn.(A) have been handled by the D.A.C., in addition to smaller quantities of T.M. ambn. & of smoke & chemical shell	

(A)

	18 pdr		4.5in How.		13 pdr		Small Arms Ambn.
	Shrapnel	High Explosive	High Explosive	Shrapnel	High Explosive	Shrapnel	
Receipts	26,526	19,652	15,626	8,112	NIL	1,550,000 rounds
Issues	31,862	23,888	17,757	7,458	3,418	1,646,000 rounds
Totals	58,388	43,540	33,383	15,570	3,418	3,196,000 rounds
Receipts	6,000	NIL	2,000	NIL	NIL	500,000 rounds
Issues	7,368	4,220	2,366	644	NIL	476,000 rounds
Totals	11,368	4,220	4,366	644	NIL	976,000 rounds

(B) shows the greatest amount of ambn. handled in one day during the preceding period (24 hour ending noon 27th inst.)   J.M.g

Army Form C. 2118.

WAR DIARY
34TH or DAC
INTELLIGENCE SUMMARY.
(Erase heading not required.)

Page 3   Volume 2D

Place	Date 1917 August	Hour	Summary of Events and Information	Remarks and references to Appendices
Q.15.d.68.	31st		Reference Map:- Sheet 62c 1/40,000. Ammn for "A" Batty, R.H.A was conveyed by DECAUVILLE special train from MONTIGNY FARM to Railhead at Q.30.a.5.5., inaugurating this system of supply for all Artillery tasks in the neighbourhood of CAULAINCOURT. 2nd Lieut. E.B. LAWSON, R.F.A reported his arrival from the Base.	App 8

C.H.Simpson? Col RHA.
Comm 34th DAC

Army Form C. 2118.

WAR DIARY
34th D.A.C.
~~INTELLIGENCE SUMMARY~~
(Erase heading not required.)

Volume 21

Place	Date 1917	Hour	Summary of Events and Information	Remarks and references to Appendices
	Sept.		Reference Map:- Sheet 62c 1/40,000	
Q.19.d.9.6.	1st.		2nd. Lt. E.B. LAWSON, posted to 152nd Bde. R.F.A. and 2nd Lt. S. HARKNETT to 160th Bde. R.F.A.	J.M.G.
K.35.b.8.2.	4th.		Construction of extension of Ammunition Refilling Point at MONTIGNY was commenced.	J.M.G.
Q.19.d.9.6.	"		The N.C.O. & Gunners at Brigades for training in Gunnery rejoined, and men from Brigades with D.A.C. were sent back to their units.	J.M.G.
	6th.		174,000 rounds S.A.A. delivered to 102nd Infantry Brigade forward Dumps.	J.M.G.
	7th.		240,000 rounds S.A.A. delivered to M.G. positions & 72,000 to forward Dumps.	J.M.G.
K.35.b.9.2.	10th.		Owing to enemy counter-attack in afternoon & consequent heavy gunfire, all Ammunition Wagons & G.S. Wagons of the D.A.C. were utilised for supplying amn. to gun positions. The following amn. was received & issued after 7/km	
			A AX BX N NX S.A.A.	
			Receipts: 4000 1000 1000 — — rounds.	
			Issues: 3856 2900 1592 348 348 80,000 rounds.	
			Totals: 7856 3900 2592 348 348 80,000 rounds.	
			100,000 rounds S.A.A. delivered to M.G. by motors	J.M.G.
	11th.			J.M.G.
Q.19.d.9.6.	13th.		A party of 10 Gunners & Drivers proceeded to Third Army School of Mortars for course of instruction in Heavy & Medium Trench Mortars.	
			2nd Lt. R. COOPER attached to 160th Bde. R.E.A. for instruction in Gunnery (2nd Lt. LAWSON in exchange)	
	14th.		2nd Lt. C.G. WOODWARD attached to 152nd Bde. R.F.A. for same purpose (2nd Lt. HARKNETT in exchange)	
	16th.		2nd Lt. A.E. OWEN posted to 160th Bde. R.F.A. vice 2nd Lt W.H. CLARK posted to D.A.C.	
			8 men attached to T.M. Battevies as a working party.	J.M.G.

Army Form C. 2118.

WAR DIARY
34th D.A.C.
INTELLIGENCE SUMMARY.

(Erase heading not required.)

Page 2   Volume 21

Instructions regarding War Diaries and Intelligence Summaries are contained in F. S. Regs., Part II. and the Staff Manual respectively. Title pages will be prepared in manuscript.

Place	Date	Hour	Summary of Events and Information	Remarks and references to Appendices
Q.19.d.9.6.	1917 SEPT. 20th		Reference Map:- Sheet 62c 1/40,000 All 4.5in. How? Amtn. baskets exchanged for wooden steel ended trays.	Ph.G
	21st		6 G.S. wagons collected empties from D/152 gun positions. 2nd Lt. F.G. LEAMAN, R.F.A. reported his arrival from the 35th Div. Artillery.	Ph.G
	22nd		240 tents (C.S.L.) drawn from Ordnance Officer, Corps Troops, QUINCONCE & erected on Camp site at PERONNE, DOINGT & COURCELLES, ready for march-in of the 24th Div. Artillery	Ph.G
	23rd		12 G.S. wagons required nightly for conveying 60-cm. Tramway lines.	Ph.G
	27th		31 mules transferred to 152nd & 160th Bdes. R.F.A.	Ph.G
	28th		24 G.S. wagons detailed for daily work on roads. 2nd Lts. WOODWARD & COOPER rejoined the D.A.C. & 2nd Lts. HARTNETT & LAWSON returned to Bangalla. 6 men proceeded to Third Army School of Mortars for course of instruction in the Medium T.M.	Ph.G
	29th	12 noon	The 34th D.A.C., under orders of G.O.C. 34th Divn., handed over Camp at VRAIGNES, Amtn. Refilling Point at MONTIGNY and responsibility for Amtn. Supply to 24th D.A.C., and marched to its new camping ground N.E. of COURCELLES (J32 a & b)	Ph.G

CHSimpson Colonel R.F.A.
Comg 34th D.A.C.

Army Form C. 2118.

WAR DIARY
or
INTELLIGENCE SUMMARY.

(Erase heading not required.)

34. D.A.C.

Vol XXII

Place	Date	Hour	Summary of Events and Information	Remarks and references to Appendices
COURCELLES	Oct 1/17	10.30am	Signalling class assembled at D.A.C. H.Q.	G.S.1
"	2		training. Overhaul of Equipt & stores.	
"	3			
"	4			
"	5			
"	6			
"	7			
PERONNE	8th		D.A.C. entrained at PERONNE for YPRES Area and detrained on the 9th at PESELHOEK and marched to canvas grounds just south of CROMBEKE. One man of no 3 Section injured during the entraining.	G.S.1
	9th			
CROMBEKE	10	8.30am	Improving accommodation for personnel + animals – weather very wet during the period.	G.S.1
	11			
	12			

Army Form C. 2118.

WAR DIARY
or
INTELLIGENCE SUMMARY.
(Erase heading not required.)

Instructions regarding War Diaries and Intelligence Summaries are contained in F. S. Regs., Part II. and the Staff Manual respectively. Title pages will be prepared in manuscript.

Place	Date	Hour	Summary of Events and Information	Remarks and references to Appendices
CROMBEKE	Dec 1917 13	9 am	The Bn. marched to forward area (section of 70.E. SE.E.F.M. B.11.a) and B.D. sheet 28.1.40,000 - to this site had occupied for the night before by D 12" Hy of 245 Siege Batty, no preparation made to entertain enemy	
BOESINGHE	14	6 am	Preparation made in the entity of mounts to beltone infantry by pack animals. Camp bombed at 7 pm. no casual too - One H.A. observation balloon brought down in flames near camp by enemy aircraft.	
"	15	8 am	Commenced mountain supply with pack animals - Camp bombed at 7.10 pm. 1 Officer (CAPTN. J.M. GITTINS. Key) and 1 O.R. and 14 mules wounded. 1 G.S. wagon, officer's mess kit, and 2 tents damaged by fragments of bomb.	
"	16	6 am	Lt. finch returns pease of the deceased O'Bemet to mortuary quarter of mounts to by army. CAPTN. J.M. GITTINS. evacuates to Base. Camp shelled throughout the day.	
"	17	9 am	LIEUT. W. HOLDEN took over the duties of Hy Adjutant vice CAPTN. J.M. GITTINS. wounded.	
"	18	5.30 am	Camp shelled from 5-30 am. to 6-30 am. One dug out eleven men keeping one man who was dug out and found to be uninjured. Orders received to maintain 1800 yds per 18 Hr. battery & 750 rds per 6"Hn Gallery. Employed successfully maintains day & night.	

WAR DIARY
or
INTELLIGENCE SUMMARY.
(Erase heading not required.)

Army Form C. 2118.

Instructions regarding War Diaries and Intelligence Summaries are contained in F.S. Regs., Part II. and the Staff Manual respectively. Title pages will be prepared in manuscript.

Place	Date	Hour	Summary of Events and Information	Remarks and references to Appendices
BOESINGHE	Oct 1917 19th day		Special efforts to maintain supply of Ammn. to guns – No 2 team Lewes (casual) and 6 mule teams. Camp shelled heavily the day – no casualties from shell fire.	1. O.R.O.
"	20th		Great difficulty in getting Ammn. to guns due to heavy rain & derelict waggons etc. Roads to positions shelled day & night. 1.O.R. to 3 horses killed and 3 O.R. wounded.	1. O.R.O.
"	21st	5.30 am	Camp bombed at 5.30 am. Several dropped around men billets. No casualties – Camp invaded, shelled & bombed at 8-15 pm Ammn supply maintained throughout the day & night under great difficulties. 1.O.R. killed & 7 O.R. wounded during journey to battery positions – 2 mules missing & 7 injured on the line of shell fire – 2 O.R. wounded due to gas & evacuated to hear Repts of dischargers conducted of O.R.C. men in forward areas under heavy shell fire	U.A.
"	22nd day		Ammn supply carried on under great difficulties – killed 1 & 2 O.R. wounded in the line – 5 mules & 1 horse missing on forward area – Great increase of sick due to the trying conditions and completed rest and the 18th Divn. Ammn. Column taking our shells by enemy howitzer shells – 2 of which burst in the Camp. N.C.O & men of Ammn. took over duties of dumpr – further efforts were made & contact of O.R.C. dragoons on the line under heavy shell fire	1. O.R.O. U.A.

Army Form C. 2118.

WAR DIARY
or
INTELLIGENCE SUMMARY.
(Erase heading not required.)

Instructions regarding War Diaries and Intelligence Summaries are contained in F. S. Regs., Part II. and the Staff Manual respectively. Title pages will be prepared in manuscript.

Place	Date	Hour	Summary of Events and Information	Remarks and references to Appendices
BOESINGHE	Oct 1917 23	6am	Day fine – 81 men report sick. Permitr supply maintained. Reliefs of working parties and of men when in the line –	W
"	24	9am	Number of sick men increased to 100 – 8 mules and horses on the line – Permitr supply to Btters & Infantry continued – weather showery	
"	25	6am	Weather fine. Hand supply continued under difficulties – Camp left bombed at 1-10 hrs, one dugout blown in – no casualties –	
"	26	6am	Weather very wet. Column marches to rest area. Camp at WOESTON by road moving to new area at 12 noon. Tps over billets t standings from 29th Div.	H2dWA 1/40000
WOESTON	27	7am	Engineers continued work on standings for horses. 2 horses of No. 1 Sectn drowned in swamp. Salvage of derelict B. Sectn commenced under Reid CLARK. 7 G.S. and 1 G.S. arrived. Permitr supply continued.	Sht 28 1/40000
"	28	8am	Salvage party trying in 3 G.S. wagons making a total of 10 wagons. 8 Reinforcements from Base 12 from no 4 Camp CRAMBREKE and 11 from no 2 Camp arrived in the evening – Permitr supply continued – under very trying conditions – Pageant Camp + Aerodrome bombed during the evening	W

(A7099) Wt. W2859/M293. 750,000. 1/17. D. D. & L., Ltd. Forms/C.2118/14.

WAR DIARY or INTELLIGENCE SUMMARY

Army Form C. 2118.

Place	Date	Hour	Summary of Events and Information	Remarks and references to Appendices
WOESTEN	Feb/1917			
	29th	6am	Weather fine — Reinforcements to Bde: 1 to 136, 152 Bde 444 to 160 Bde — Enemy duffleg continues very quiet during the night. Camp bombed from 8.30 pm till 2.30 am — no casualties —	S.A.
-//-	30	5.30 am	Column Sump exploded(?) as BOESINGHE — LIEUT 9.40 MAS in charge with 19 reinforcements from SMS — 2 OR wounded. 47 hours shelled by sheet fire. 101 men reported sick — 66 had to be evacuated daily. Weather rives and stormy all day —	S.A.
-//-	31st		Weather foul — Bomb droppers enemy camp between 3 am + 4 am — no casualties — Camp shelled from 10 pm till 1 am — shelling of French continues but without casualty owing to humid of ash — What equal (to the Prussel; Prince of Km egs I Krumpses) causing the 5/1/2. The O.S.B. was in former array from 13th to 31st was as follows 8:— Killed = 3 O.R. — Died of wounds = 2 O.R. Wounded 1 Offcr. (CAPT. V.H. GITTINS RGN) + 14 O.R. Evacuated sick = 50 O.R. Died but not evacuated daily around 60 from 23rd Animals evacd by sheet fire + evacuated through various etc = 86 fat pigs, 5 13 to 31st of Transport — 105 Prayon +2 70 Purdon has to be abandoned on him in derelict condition — 10 G.S.P. + 2 limbers of R.S Purdon eventually salved —	S.A.

Army Form C. 2118.

WAR DIARY
or
INTELLIGENCE SUMMARY.
(Erase heading not required.)

Instructions regarding War Diaries and Intelligence Summaries are contained in F.S. Regs., Part II. and the Staff Manual respectively. Title pages will be prepared in manuscript.

Place	Date	Hour	Summary of Events and Information	Remarks and references to Appendices
WOESTEN	Oct 1917		Total Ammunition supplies to Arty & Infantry for period 13th to 31st as follows:-	
	31st			
				18/pr	High Explosive	4·5 How.	S.A. Amm.	
			Receipts	45,181	28,820	19,241	754,000	
			Issues					EA
			Total 93,242. All the ammunition sent to Guns & Infantry was supplied by Pack animals. —	

Lt.Col. Commdnt R.H.A.
Comdg 34th Bde.

WAR DIARY
or
INTELLIGENCE SUMMARY

Army Form C. 2118.

34 D Am Col

Place	Date	Hour	Summary of Events and Information	Remarks and references to Appendices
WOESTON	Nov 1917 1st	6am	Bombs burst early morning – no casualties – one man no.3 section wounded in the line – orders to maintain ammunition to 1000 Rds – weather fine but dull – ordered to be in readiness for move –	WA
"	2nd	9am	Day dull. Preparations for move to new area. Advance party of 242 A.Y.I. Bde (no 2 Secn) in the line – two animals killed at horse lines by Headquarters British time howitzer – no 2 horse lines & wagon lines over to 242 A.Y.I. Bde. No. 3 Secn drew teams to 345 A.Y.I. Bde. No.1 Secn camp known & tents returned to the Comsdt	
"	3rd	9am	A.C. marched to CROMBEKE via WOESTON ROAD arriving by at 1.30 p.m. weather fine –	WA
CROMBEKE	4th	9am	Inspection by Colonel Conrey & G.O.C. Preparations for march to new area.	WA

Army Form C. 2118.

WAR DIARY
or
INTELLIGENCE SUMMARY.
(Erase heading not required.)

Instructions regarding War Diaries and Intelligence Summaries are contained in F. S. Regs., Part II. and the Staff Manual respectively. Title pages will be prepared in manuscript.

Place	Date	Hour	Summary of Events and Information	Remarks and references to Appendices
CROMBEKE	5th Nov 1917	7 am	Commenced march to 3rd Army Area. Leaving CROMBEKE in following order. H.Q. from 7 am - No 2 Coy 7.30 am - No 3 Coy at 12 noon - No 4 Coy ECKE via POPERINGHE - ABEELE - Billets were alloted in STEENVORDE Area - the whole arriving in Billets at 5 pm. weather fine & dry.	W.D.
STEENVORDE	6th "	1.30 pm	Continues march from STEENVORDE to CALONNE sur LYS - Start 1.30 pm VIA CASTRE - STRAZELLE and MERVILLE - Column marching through arriving at 6 pm - Brownout billeted at farms - thrown in fields - weather fine -	W.D.
CALONNE	7th "	9.30 am	Marches from CALONNE sur LYS via CHOCQUES - ROBECQ to LABEUVRIERE arriving 12.30 pm - Billets occupied in huts & farms except No 2 Coy for who no accomodation secured. Regimented into huts for however & weather stormy & very wet.	W.D.
LABEUVRIERE	8th "	9.30 am	Continues march to BETHONSART arriving 2.30 pm - To 3 Coys occupied huts at CHOCOURT - Country very hilly round HOUDIN - roads very good - weather fine all day.	W.D.
BETHONSART	9th "	9.30 am	Concludes march to 3rd Army Area - VIA SAVY - ST. POL - ARRAS Road ARRAS - AVETTE - Road to BOIRY ST RIOTOUDE arriving at 4.30 pm weather stormy - roads good -	W.D.

WAR DIARY
or
INTELLIGENCE SUMMARY.

Army Form C. 2118.

Places	Date	Hour	Summary of Events and Information	Remarks and references to Appendices
BOIRY ST RICTRUDE	Nov 1917 10	9 am	Trench mortar Battery Mules (4 horses) to take over forward area. Batch's from 51st Divn Trench Mortars - T.M.B. wagons went to Capt W.J. with teams & personnel attached to T.M.B. for transport on forward area - Instructions received to take over camp from 62nd Divng D.H.C. on 11th near FICHEUX. S.7.C. (Sheet 51 B.S.W.)	
"—	11	12 noon	Marched to new Area camp - Took over camp & huts etc from 62nd Divn Divn Column - Accommodation for Officers - two nissen huts owned by detachment of T.O.C. huts to H.S. Qrs - Lieut. G. Lomas 150.R. took over Remtd at MERCATEL M.23.d.4.8. (Sheet 51.B.) man continue supply of Remts to Batterys from 12 noon. Camp visits by T.O.C. Divion - Weather cold.	
"—	12		Camp inspected by T.O.C. R.A. who gave authority for much work to be made for accommodation of officers. Arrangements to improve camp, accommodation for personnel & standing for animals. Weather fine & warm	

WAR DIARY
or
INTELLIGENCE SUMMARY.
(Erase heading not required.)

Army Form C. 2118.

Place	Date	Hour	Summary of Events and Information	Remarks and references to Appendices
BOIS Y of RIETRUDE	Jan 1917 13th	7 am	Work on roads, front and support trenches commenced – 16 F.S. engaged to AYETTE for stone metalled – Refilling scheme commenced. Egres. reinforcements received from Base – 2 NCOs & 17 OR to 160 Batt. 1 man posted to No. 13. Weather fine & warm. 2 minor trench recesses.	
"	14th	9 am	Continued work on camp. Reveries Eschelons arriving – 30 000 RB of St Andrew's drawn from Corps Dump & issued to 107 Inf y Bde. Weather fine – Capt McLINDNIA lecture at II Corps school.	62
"	15th	9 am	Work on camp continued – 8 hrs manual – 1 Sd engrs leave to brea Camp for farm work – 10 men from 77 & 192 R to take work on water front. For leave between R.E, I.S. & 62 " D.A.C. – 4 new hopters to camp. Weather fine & dry	62
"	16th	9 am	Re inforcements drafts to 152 F/160 S Bair. CAPT FILLER & 1 HOLDEN lecture at II Corps school 2. Improving camp generally & refitting eschelons.	62

Army Form C. 2118.

WAR DIARY
or
INTELLIGENCE SUMMARY.
(Erase heading not required.)

Place	Date	Hour	Summary of Events and Information	Remarks and references to Appendices
BOIS DE RIETRUDE	Sept 16th 1917	7 am	Road & water point construction – improving Brook Camp. Generally – 20 to the section for Infantry – 20 to R.E. for section for Pioneers. Lt Col from Canada Glass C.N. SIMPSON D.S.O. Revd R CROSER left for leave to ENGLAND. Weather fine & dry.	
"	17	9 am	Enhancements & youth on Camp. Antibouling at Welgeh & stores – 20 to S.S. waggons for Engineers fatigue – 6 S.S. waggons to draw brick. Bridges for 160 Bat. J. B. Reserve to R.M.O. for issue at Billets. Church parade under Capt YOUNG. Divisional Football in the afternoon no 2 beat no 1. 60 Section. Weather fine but cool. Major MOLLINDIN I.A. assumes command of O.C. Cork M 2nd WAR leave for leave to ENGLAND. weather fine.	
"	19	9 am	Voluntary inspection by AD.V.S. – took on water front they around Camp continuing – personnel on the afternoon – weather fine.	
"	20	9 am	work on Camp – Harness inspection – Horses Kingt Homley drawn from C.A.P. by no 3 section – other section freed. Hop Dr sent to S.J. M.O. to accompt sent transported to Jerusalem –	

WAR DIARY
or
INTELLIGENCE SUMMARY.

Army Form C. 2118.

(Erase heading not required.)

Places	Date	Hour	Summary of Events and Information	Remarks and references to Appendices
BOIS ST RICTRUDE	March 1917 21	9 am	Additional accommodation erected for personnel – Inspection of Clothing, kits etc. – Fatigue as fol. D.O.S. weather wet	WH
"	22	9 am	Wet & rough – Eoft or and around Camp generally – Football – Column v. 160 Bde vs Field team fur the tournament	WH
"	23	9 am	Party sent to collect 122 Remounts from BOISLEUX 46–14 ONT Animals picked 60 to No 2, 62 to No 3 Bty – 300 000 Rds S.A.A to Bomb store – 1 G.S. 2 Bodied R.E. drawn by 50 3 4	
	2 pm	to Cookelers. 1,000,000 Rds of S.A.A. more drawn to fire scheme – weather very rough & rain –	
"	24	9 am	10 Officers 146 reinforcements joined from Base – Improvements in Camp.	WH
	10 am	8 Reinforcements from Base –	
	2 pm	Football v. N.E. 152 Bde –	
"	25	9 am	Quarter & General work in Camp – Lieut CLARKE leave to ENGLAND – 10 G.S.Y. 10 R.S. Wagons for Engineer work – footballs in the afternoon – weather rough & showery	WH

Army Form C. 2118.

WAR DIARY
or
INTELLIGENCE SUMMARY.
(Erase heading not required.)

Instructions regarding War Diaries and Intelligence Summaries are contained in F. S. Regs., Part II. and the Staff Manual respectively. Title pages will be prepared in manuscript.

Place	Date	Hour	Summary of Events and Information	Remarks and references to Appendices
BOIRY ST GERTRUDE	Nov 1917 26	9am 6pm	Weather fair & wet. 20 to 1 reinforcements from base. Lt GRANT 1st/4th Leics 2 NCOs and 6 ORs sent to Base on P.B. - 6 Reinforcements to medical duty sent to Camp & 1st group Instructors of 15th Bn - weight in camp & 1st group Instructors of 11 NCOs men having been passed Swift military medal to Private congratulations of Corps Comm XIX Corps S.O.C. 32. Copy in C.O.C.M.	Copy of recom S.O.C. 32 Copy in "Weather"
" "	27	8.30am 9pm	Improvements in camp - Drainage Roads etc - 15/16 reinforcements from Base - Weather fine & dry. Footrace for Cup Tournament.	
" "	28	7am	Training - Fatigues - Improvement in Camp etc - Inspection by G.O.C. 9th who expressed his great pleasure with the general condition of the B.A.C. -	
" "	29	9am	Training & general improvement in Camp. Teams to head-works - weather fair & dry. Visit of Corps representative to view force dispositions.	

XIX Corps R.A. No. A.2569.
34th Div. Arty. Nos. H.A. 24, 25, 27 & 28.

C.R.A.
34th Divn.

The Corps Commander has pleasure in notifying the award of the MILITARY MEDAL to the undermentioned N.C.O's and Men.

Please convey the Corps Commander's congratulations to the recipients, adding the congratulations of G.O.C.R.A.

29118	Sgt.	W.H. Shaw	No 3 S.A.A. Sect. 34th DAC
10752	Dvr.	C. Heath	..
23666	"	J. Powers	..
11368	Sgt.	R. Dawson	No 1 Sect. 34th D.A.C.
11294	A/Bdr.	C. Sewendon	..
4283	"	H. Love	..
111777	Dvr.	G. Bradley	..
51113	Sgt.	A. Barnes	No 2
79670	S/S	J. Clarke	..
11472	Dvr.	R. Johnson	..
7758	Sadlr.	J.W. Gillico	..

(sd) W.J. Beddows, Capt. R.A.
Staff Captain R.A. XIX Corps

23.11.17.

-----2-----

Officer Commanding,
34th D.A.C.

Forwarded. Please add the congratulations of the C.R.A. to those of the Corps Commander and G.O.C.R.A.

(sd) A. Beal Capt.
Staff Capt.
34th Divl. Arty.

26.11.17.

True Copy

W. Holden
Capt. & Adj.
4.12.17

WAR DIARY
or
INTELLIGENCE SUMMARY.

(Erase heading not required.)

Army Form C. 2118.

Place	Date	Hour	Summary of Events and Information	Remarks and references to Appendices
BOIRY ST RICTRUDE	Nov 1917 30		Brigade notifies improvements in Camp. Footballs in the attainment — funds received from 1st to 3rd Battalions 3192 Ado of A & H X — Rum supply from 11th M Mckellar Camp. Capt. Comdg 34th by December	G.I.

WAR DIARY or INTELLIGENCE SUMMARY.

Army Form C. 2118.

(Erase heading not required.)

34 DAC

Place	Date	Hour	Summary of Events and Information	Remarks and references to Appendices
BOIRY ST. RICTRUDE	Dec 1917 1st	6.30 am	Road construction and general improvement of camp for personnel and animals. 4 S.A. wagons to 160 Bde. the Commandants fatigues and mules for permanent work. Weather fine & dry.	W.J.
"	2nd	9am	B.d. Major SMITH posted to the D.H.Q. from 9th Divl Amm Colmn. to replace R.S.M. HOLMES ordered to proceed to base as W.O. Batty Q. M. Sergeant – 1 O.R. wounded in forward area & (little) attached to 16 R.H.Q. 160 Bde R.F.A.	W.J.
"	3rd	9am	Reinforcements of 3 Sergeants & 2 Corporals received from base and joints to 152 & 160 Bdes. respectively. 7 S.A. wagons W.t. with Teams and Personnel attached to issued with Batteries.	W.J.
"	4th/5			W.J.
"	5th	9am 5 S.A. wagons to 160 Bde and issued teams & personnel for fatigues in forward area – mules to Horse Council for issue as transport.		W.J.
"	6th/7			W.J.

WAR DIARY
or
INTELLIGENCE SUMMARY.
(Erase heading not required.)

Army Form C. 2118.

Place	Date	Hour	Summary of Events and Information	Remarks and references to Appendices
BOIRY ST. RICTRUDE	Dec 8th 1917	2 pm	20 G.S. wagons and Officer to Engineers for work in forward area	WD
"	9th			WD
"	10th	8 am	2 Lieut REID sent to forward area to salve derelict transport - 20 G.S. wagons to DURHAM lines for transport work.	
"	10th	2 pm	4 G.S. Wagons and 12 men to forward area to collect parts etc. of derelict transport.	
"	12th	6.30 am	2nd Lieuts REID and CLARKE and 12 men attached to 152 & 160 WCs Coys respectively for taking empty wagons and GERMAN transport. - O.A.C inspected by Sub Commander Major General E.L. NICHOLSON. C.M.G.	
"	13th	9 am	R.S.M. HOLMES proceeds to base on a Beng P.M. Sergeant-list Aeroplane bombs dropped around camp at 6.30 pm - no casualties -	WD
"	14th	6.30 am	Area commdt. fatigues and mules and men for farming purposes	WD

Army Form C. 2118.

WAR DIARY
or
INTELLIGENCE SUMMARY.
(Erase heading not required.)

Instructions regarding War Diaries and Intelligence Summaries are contained in F. S. Regs., Part II. and the Staff Manual respectively. Title pages will be prepared in manuscript.

Place	Date	Hour	Summary of Events and Information	Remarks and references to Appendices
BORY ST. RICTRUDE	Sept 1917 15th			103
	16th			
"	17th	9am	R.S.M. SMITH proceeded to 91st Bde. R.F.A.	
"	18th	"	CAPT. A.W. MOLLINDINIA proceeds on leave to ENGLAND.	104
"	19th	9am	12 G.S. wagons to Div. A.G.R.D. for fatigues	105
			COLONEL C.N. SIMPSON, D.S.O. returned from leave to ENGLAND, and resumed command of the Column.	
"	20th	5.30	29 Remount Mules collected from BAPAUME and posted to the Column —	109
"	21st			104
"	22nd		3 Mules killed and 9 wounded by shell fire whilst on detachment with trench mortar batteries in forward area.	109

Army Form C. 2118.

WAR DIARY
or
INTELLIGENCE SUMMARY.
(Erase heading not required.)

Instructions regarding War Diaries and Intelligence Summaries are contained in F. S. Regs., Part II. and the Staff Manual respectively. Title pages will be prepared in manuscript.

Place	Date	Hour	Summary of Events and Information	Remarks and references to Appendices
BOIRY ST RICTRUDE	Dec 23rd 1917	6.30 am	25 G.S. wagons with teams held in readiness for work with Div S.H.Q.R.E. on new positions being carried.	WD
"	24th	—		WD
"	25th	9 am	8 G.S. wagons to Ordnance to replace lorries.	WD
"	26th	9 am	8 G.S. wagons to Ordnance 8 G.S. wagons to Bas and 5 to the H.Q. Q. do replace lorries.	WD
"	27th	—		WD
"	28th	—		WD
"	29th	—		WD
"	30th	—		WD
"	31st	—	A continuous frost for the last half of the month varying from 4° to 10° by day and from 10° to 25° by night interfered considerably with the out door work of the Column – feltering rugs and conditions to make the animals to be adequately exercised.	WD

A.W. Humphrey
Lieut Col
Com'g 34th D.A.C.

Army Form C. 2118.

WAR DIARY
or
INTELLIGENCE SUMMARY.
(Erase heading not required.)

34º D.T.C.

Place	Date	Hour	Summary of Events and Information	Remarks and references to Appendices
BOIRY ST. RICTRUDE	Jan'y 1st 1917	10ᵃ	Inspection of Sanitary and arrangements generally of detached transport with General mortars - weather fine - hard frost -	W.A.
"	2nd			W.A.
"	3rd			
"	4th		Recruits work owing to condition of roads	
"	"		CAPT. G.H. McEWEN marched and L/LIEUT. R. COOPER named of the military cross in New Years Honours Gazette.	
"	"		LIEUT. C.G. WOODWARD 2/LIEUT. W.H. CLARK 3 Sergeants and 4 others attached to Indian Cavalry Depot at ROUEN for instruction with horses.	
"	5th		One re-inforcement from base and posted direct to 152ⁿᵈ Coy M.H. 6 O.Rˢ attached to 152ⁿᵈ Bde ammn Colⁿ —	
"	6th		Three re-inforcements reported arrival from base –	W.A.
"	7th		Party of 10 O.Rˢ under LIEUT. HART proceed to BAPAUME to collect 12 L.G. horses and 8 mules by M.A.C. Weather mild - thawing earlier in the day - frost in the evening -	W.A.
"	8th		Heavy snow fall	W.A.

Army Form C. 2113.

WAR DIARY
or
INTELLIGENCE SUMMARY.
(Erase heading not required.)

34ᵈ D.A.C.

Place	Date	Hour	Summary of Events and Information	Remarks and references to Appendices
BOIRY ST. RICTRUDE	Jany 1918 9th	—	Visit of R.A. band under LIEUT. STRETTON - snowing hard and blowing a gale -	
"	10th	—	LIEUT. F. CANTY reported sick and several men have and attaching to No.2 Station -	
"	11th	9am	R.A. Band left for 4th Corps - snowing & thaw. Thaw precautions orders to be taken from midnight 11/12 -	WH
"	12th	—	8 G.S. Wagons to Ordnance to exchange wheels - 7 G.S. wagons to several motor Batteries vicinity -	WH
"	13th	—	5 G.S. wagons to Ordnance to replace ones owing to thaw precautions -	WH
"	14th	—	LIEUT F. CANTY and 30 O.R's attached to 152 Bde, 30 O.R's to 160 Bde, for ensuing reserve positions - 5 G.S. wagons to Ordnance to replace lorries -	WH
"	15th	—	8 G.S. wagons to D.A.D.O.S. for rations stores - 2 G.S. wagons to 160 Bde carrying stores to forward area	WH

Army Form C. 2118.

WAR DIARY
or
INTELLIGENCE SUMMARY.
(Erase heading not required.)

34 D A E

Instructions regarding War Diaries and Intelligence Summaries are contained in F. S. Regs., Part II. and the Staff Manual respectively. Title pages will be prepared in manuscript.

Place	Date	Hour	Summary of Events and Information	Remarks and references to Appendices
BOIRY ST. RICTRUDE	Jan'y 1918 16.		9 re-inforcements refugees arrived from base – 25 S.L wagons to 160 Bde. for next reinforcement area – 4 S.L wagons to D.A.D.S. for railhead next in place of lorries –	W.T.
"	17.		3 S.L wagons to Ordnance – 3 S.L wagons to 26 I.R.H.R. Bde. W.T. to collect and return forms &c to 34 I.R.R.D. – S.L to take over camp of 26 S.L & I.R. Bde. on their departure from area –	W.T.
"	18.		10 S.L wagons to D.A.D.O.S. – 2 S.L wagons to Area Comdts. Q.M. for tram-work – 20 re-inforcements refugees to 152 Bde. and 160 Bde.	W.T.
"	19.		31 re-inforcements arrived from base – 15 S.L wagons to rail-train – 2 S.L wagons to 160 Bde. 2 S.L wagons to Area Comdts. 4 S.L wagons to Ordnance –	W.T.
"	20.		15 S.L wagons to rail-train – 1 S.L wagon to 160 Bde. for work in forward area – 30 re-inforcements refugees to 152 Bde. and 160 Bde. – 4 S.L wagons to D.A.D.O.S – 1 S.L wagon to Area Comdt. for tram work –	W.T.

(A7092). Wt. W24591/M1293. 75,000. 4/17. D.D. & L., Ltd. Forms/C.2118/14.

WAR DIARY or INTELLIGENCE SUMMARY.

Army Form C. 2118.

34 STE

Place	Date	Hour	Summary of Events and Information	Remarks and references to Appendices
BOIS ST RICTRUDE	Jan 13 1918 21		15 S.A.A. wagons to Brit. sexn - 8 S.A.A. wagons to A.S.C. to S.A.A. dump railhead -	
"	22nd		5 S.A.A. wagons to MERCATEL for moving 2 A.T. mms for Infantry /H.Q. to forward area -	
"	23rd		2/Lieut. H.H. GRELLIER and 28 R.E. reinforcements reported on arrival at form base -	
"	24th		Capt. G.W. BAXTER, Lieut. J.B. BARTY, 2/Lieut. O. TURTON 4 O.R. reinforcements reported upon arrival from base -	
"	25th		Capt. G.W. BAXTER and 2/Lieut. H.H. GRELLIER posted to 152 Bty. Lieut. J.B. BARTY posted to 160 Bty. 2/Lieut. O. TURTON posted to 104 Cavalry Coy. Bn. 2 S.A. wagons to 104 M.G. Coy. - 2 S.A. wagons to 103 & M.G. Coy - 10 S.A. wagons to 105 Infty. Bn. to new area - 26 reinforcements to 152 & 160 Btys.	
"	26th		8 S.A.A. wagons to 130 & 146 R.F.A. to draw new ammn. 10 S.A. wagons to 1912 Infty. Bde. to move into new area.	

Army Form C. 2118.

WAR DIARY
or
INTELLIGENCE SUMMARY.

(Erase heading not required.)

34th S.A.C.

Instructions regarding War Diaries and Intelligence Summaries are contained in F. S. Regs., Part II. and the Staff Manual respectively. Title pages will be prepared in manuscript.

Place	Date	Hour	Summary of Events and Information	Remarks and references to Appendices
ROULEY St GERTRUDE	27 Jan/18		8 E.S. wagons to BONELLE to draw new huts. 16 E.S. wagons to 103 G. Supply Bde — 2 E.S. wagons to 104 G.S. Park Coy — 2 G.S. wagons to 102 S. Park Coy — no movements to new areas — 4 reinforcements to 15 m.t. horster. Escort to BOULOGNE to conduct Gunner ROSENTHAL an absentee belonging to RA. Huts No. 2 erected. Lieut C.A. WOODWARD proceeds on detachment to Camp Woodward on completion of Gunner of motors. Reliefs from ROUEN on completion of course of instruction.	W.H.
"	28th		14 E.S. wagons to 103rd Inf. Bde — 2 E.S. wagons to 203rd E.S Bde 2 E.S. wagons to 208th Coy Bde. — 26 G.S. wagons to 209 E.S. Coy no movements to new areas — 32 reinforcements posted from Base. Area round Camp bombed from 9.30 to 12 mn — no casualties —	W.H.
"	29th		Escort report arrival with E ROSENTHAL from BOULOGNE — 10 E.S. wagons to Asst Employment Coy — 10 E.S. wagons to 2nd HS G — 5 G.S. wagons to R.A. HS G — 1 G.S. wagon to bn m.t. very dead. No move units to new areas — 2 E.S. wagons to Asst Command for own work — 2 R.E. men attached for briefing in own work. No. 15. 1st expected 5 native personnel — R.S.M. E. CANTS reverts to 15th Bde R.H.A. Boer inmates of own m.t. branded under direction of G. Coster before march —	W.H.

(Ayop). Wt. W1859/M1293. 75,000. 1/17. D.D. & L., Ltd. Forms/C21834

Army Form C. 2118.

WAR DIARY
or
INTELLIGENCE SUMMARY.

(Erase heading not required.)

3rd DTC

Instructions regarding War Diaries and Intelligence Summaries are contained in F. S. Regs., Part II. and the Staff Manual respectively. Title pages will be prepared in manuscript.

Place	Date	Hour	Summary of Events and Information	Remarks and references to Appendices
BOURY ST RICTRUDE	January 30 1918		2 G.S. Wagons to 2nd Bns - Area Cmdt's fatigue and 5 miles for farm work -	
"	31st		4 Corporals and 6 Bombers posted to H.Q from 26 I.B.D. all under instruction from 6th Corps - 20 in for courses posted to 152 & 160 Bdes.	

M Simpson Capt
Cmm 3rd DTC

(A7092). Wt. W12859/M1293. 750,000. 1/17. D. D. & L., Ltd. Forms/C2118/14.

WAR DIARY
or
INTELLIGENCE SUMMARY

Army Form C. 2118.

34 D.A.C. Vol 26

Place	Date	Hour	Summary of Events and Information	Remarks and references to Appendices
BOIRY ST. RICTRUDE	February 1918 1st		Party of 1 Offr & 119 men from 152 + 160 Brigades under Lieut Laman proceed to ABBEVILLE to collect 68 remounts returns to camp. Lieut Colonel E.W. Spalding C.M.G. reported unwell. Boarding Board Camp from 10 p.m to 12 p.m.	6.B.O
" "	2nd		Instructions received to move to new area.	Aop
" "	3rd		Turnover of 18 pdr. + 4.5 Hows. ammunition — commencing with No 1 Section. G.S. wagon cont. to forward area to move mud.	Aop
" "	4th		Turnover of 18 pdr + 4.5 Hows ammunition of No. 2 Section. Wagons cont. to plot canal to meet Canal Coys. for animals. Nissen huts. Labour Coys. pickthanan. R.E. men finishing. Staff Captain R.A. + Lieut Cooper visited new area to allot huts etc. 35 R. Major Gent. to forward area to move mud. Lt. Col. E.W. Spalding proceed to VI Corps to inspect calibration range near ACHIET LE PETIT.	B.J.A
" "	5th		Instructions received to move to new area. Lieut Lorman & 2/Lieut _____ proceed 68 remounts (42 horses 26 mules) from Abbeville	A/A

Lieut Wt. W14390/M1393. 750,000. 1/17. D.D. & L., Ltd. Forms/C.2118/14. (A7092)

Army Form C. 2118.

WAR DIARY
or
INTELLIGENCE SUMMARY.
(Erase heading not required.)

Instructions regarding War Diaries and Intelligence Summaries are contained in F. S. Regs., Part II. and the Staff Manual respectively. Title pages will be prepared in manuscript.

Place	Date	Hour	Summary of Events and Information	Remarks and references to Appendices
BOIRY ST. RIOTRUDE	February 1918 6th	—	Preparations to move on 7th. G.S. wagon on scale to 152 & 160. & G.S. wagon each. 3 wagon complete with divisional animals to each battery. Jackson complete to R.A.H.Q. & Pioneer G.S. wagon complete to D.T.M.O. Distribution of ruminants by Staff Captain & Brigade S.A.C. as follows: Bde 14 L.D. 160 Bde 18 L.D. 15" Rifles D.A.C. 21 L.D.	B.G.m.
	7th	—	Camp handed over to area Commandant FICHEUX & Lieut. Jones. A guard of 1 Sgt & 6 men remained in charge of the following ammunition for landing over to 59th B.A.C. 756 Rds 18 Pdr., 792 Rds + 5 How: 984,000 Rds S.A.A. Column marched to SOUASTRE via ADINFER. MONCHY-AU-BOIS. BIENVILLERS arriving in billets at 1-40 p.m. G.O. CRA inspected the L.A.C. en-route & expressed his entire approval on its turnout.	
SOUASTRE	8th	—	Column marched from SOUASTRE to ETREE-WAMIN via COURTURELLE, SUS-ST-LEGER + BEAUDRICOURT arriving in billets at 2 p.m. Weather very inclement with much rain & snow. 2 Lieut. W.A. Henry reported arrived from France.	B.G.m.

Army Form C. 2118.

WAR DIARY
or
INTELLIGENCE SUMMARY.
(Erase heading not required.)

Instructions regarding War Diaries and Intelligence Summaries are contained in F. S. Regs., Part II. and the Staff Manual respectively. Title pages will be prepared in manuscript.

Place	Date	Hour	Summary of Events and Information	Remarks and references to Appendices
ETREE-WAMIN	February 1918 9	—	Settling in billets - completion of horse lines & huts.	EPG
~	10		Lieut Loman to Handicount. Lieut Loamor proceed to PARA Sch Sanitary course.	EPG
~	11		6 G.S. Wagons to T.M. In store etc. 10 G.S. Wagons to PREVENT to dig work emplacements. Training commences. Received from exploration to A.C & D. Batteries 152nd Brigade, to instruction on Gun Drill.	EPG
~	12		12 G.S. Wagons & 10 L.R. Wagons to CROUCHES to collect 18 Pdr + 5.5 How + SAA Ammunition taken over from 59th DAC Conference at R.A HQ Gr 6 Division. Lieut D.A Henry posted to 160 Brigade RFA. Draft of 9 Gunners posted from Base after having been temporarily attached to 152nd Bde in the mean time. Weather fine, but very dull.	EPG
~	13		Transport Lt T.M's Horatio Quin attached to D.A.D.R. 9 H G.S. wagons to CROUCHES to complete collection of Ammunition taken over from 59th DAC. 30 Reinforcement reported arrived from Base.	EPG

(A7908) Wt. W30/M1293. 750,000. 1/17. D. D. & L., Ltd. Forms/C.2118A.

Army Form C. 2118.

WAR DIARY
or
INTELLIGENCE SUMMARY.

(Erase heading not required.)

Instructions regarding War Diaries and Intelligence Summaries are contained in F. S. Regs., Part II. and the Staff Manual respectively. Title pages will be prepared in manuscript.

Place	Date	Hour	Summary of Events and Information	Remarks and references to Appendices
ETREE-WAMIN	February 1918			
	13th		9 Gunners received on 12th inst posted to 160 Bty.	8910
	14th		All Arabs in ETREE-WAMIN recommended by Lieut Cooper James & report in-inspected to R.A.H.Q.	8910
	15th		6 Gunners posted from T.M. Bde to B.A.C.	830
	16th		Sergt Cooper 1st Cork Farm attached R.A.C as instructor in Lewis Gun Drill. Sergt Fuller 10th Royal Dublin Fusiliers attached R.A.C. as Physical Training instructor for 3 days	8910
	17th		8 Reinforcement posted to 152nd Bty 4/3 to 160 2nd Bayols	8910
	20th		2 Lieut Greenwood & Lieut Mitchell Lewis Gun Officers Lewis Gun reported arrived from Base	8910
	21st		2 Lieut Greenwood Lewis Gun Officer posted to 152nd Btn. Lieut Gun Lieut Mitchell posted to 160th Bty with effect from 20-2-18. 6 Pl Credite Patrick R.H. No 2. Section 3rd D.A.C posted to 276 2nd Brigade A.F.A.	8910
			(Cuthbg Erly) 3rd Col Mur R.A 904 dated 20-2-18	

Army Form C. 2118.

WAR DIARY
or
INTELLIGENCE SUMMARY.
(Erase heading not required.)

Place	Date	Hour	Summary of Events and Information	Remarks and references to Appendices
ETREE-WAMIN	February 1918			
	24th		Lieut Lomas & 96 Other Ranks arrived from France & Joined the ABBEVILLE to form the 1st Bn 6th Central	A.P.O.
			Collect. 53 remount	
	25th			
	26th		3rd Div Arty men unfit & dismounted to VI Corps for remounts & present M.6 Central (51 a)	A.P.O.
	27th		Lieut Lomas & party returned from Abbeville with 53 remounts. 33 horses & 21 mules.	A.P.O.
			A.1 allotted to Brigades 12 to D.A.C.	
	28th		Orders received that the Divisional Artillery would march to forward area on	A.P.O.
			2nd prox. Training Programme cancelled & Preparation commenced for coming move.	

W Humphreys Colonel R.F.A.
Comdg 3rd D.A.C.

(A7090). Wt. W28159/M1293. 750,000. 1/17. D. D. & L., Ltd. Forms/C.2118/14.

Army Form C. 2118.

WAR DIARY
or
INTELLIGENCE SUMMARY.

(Erase heading not required.)

34 D Aust FA
WD
Jul 27

Place	Date	Hour	Summary of Events and Information	Remarks and references to Appendices
EYRE WARNIN	March 1919 1st		Preparations made for move to forward area.	WD
SOUASTRE	2nd		O.A.C. marched to Killets at SOUASTRE arriving 1.35 pm — LIEUT G LOMAS, 2 LIEUT REID and 2 LIEUT BIRD proceeded on ahead from to HAMELINCOURT to take over Killets and lines from 40th D.A.C. weather cold & snowing.	WD
HAMELINCOURT	3rd		Column marched from SOUASTRE to HAMELINCOURT arriving 11.30am as 40th D.A.C. had not vacated the lines both units occupied the same billets and lines for the night — LIEUT G. LOMAS and 19 O.R's take over 40th Divn W.R.P. on IRRAS-BAPAUME mainroad.	WD
"	4th		Lines and billets taken over from 40th D.A.C. who marched out at 9am — 14 reinforcements reported arrival from base.	WD
"	5th		30 O.R's attached to each of 152 & 160 Bde's from D.A.C. for work in forward area — 1 G.S. wagon attached to H.Q. O.R's each battery of 152 & 160 for duty — 2 G.S. wagons to D.A.M.O. for Ammn supply in forward area — LIEUT L.E. SPIR reported arrival from base. 20 reinforcements reported arrival from base.	WD

Army Form C. 2118.

WAR DIARY
or
INTELLIGENCE SUMMARY.
(Erase heading not required.)

Instructions regarding War Diaries and Intelligence Summaries are contained in F. S. Regs., Part II. and the Staff Manual respectively. Title pages will be prepared in manuscript.

Place	Date	Hour	Summary of Events and Information	Remarks and references to Appendices
HAMELINCOURT	6. Jan 1918		27 G.S. wagons to A.R.P. to collect Ammn for delivery to Ammn Dps. Reserve position of 152 Bde. — Unit reinforcements Parties to Bdes. Weather fine.	
"	7th	9 am	LIEUT. L. ESPIR reported to 160 Bde. — LIEUT. P. APPLEBEE detached as member of Tent Committee for area. — 18 G.S. wagons to A.R.P. to collect Ammn and delivered to Ammn Dps reserve position. 160 Bde. — 8 OR's posted to Trench mortars. 5 E. Skegans units. LIEUT. R. COOPER detached to collect tow bar truck for Bde. Bomb store. — 16000 Rds of S.A.Ammn to R.E.	
"	8th	9 am	15 G.S. wagons for fatigues under an Officer to collect WS rubble for build bomb store. — 4496 F. and 4 600 AT and 5 2400 WS Rds of BX Ammn. delivered to 152 & 160 Bdes. — 158,000 Rds of S.A.Ammn delivered to Infty. Bdes.	
"	9th Jan		LIEUT. R. COOPER and 7 OR's horses by road to Remount Depot. — BELLEVUE by FARM, ALBERT to collect 9 Remounts for S.A.C. & G for Brig. train. — LIEUT H.P. APPLEBEE & 12 OR's horses by road to collect 21 remounts from BIEFVILLERS. — 1 L. Skegans. BOYELLES to collect Tow paper B.D. LIEUT A.E. OWEN proceeds to D.A.C. from Trench mortars.	

H.P. APPLEBEE + 12 OR'

A.8534 Wt W.4973/M687 750,000 8/16 D. D. & L. Ltd. Forms/C.2118/13.

WAR DIARY or INTELLIGENCE SUMMARY.
(Erase heading not required.)

Army Form C. 2118.

Place	Date	Hour	Summary of Events and Information	Remarks and references to Appendices
HAMELINCOURT	March 10 1918		10 G.S. wagons to Sun^t Bomb Store to collect stores for delivery in forward area — 6 G.S. wagons to 102 Inf. Bde for ammunition — W.A.A. Reed. Classed as the discharged. 102 Inf Bde. — 1/Lieut F. COOPER returned arrival with 15 remounts from H. BERT. R.Dmy. HOLMES accidentally injured by his horse falling & rolling on his rt foot.	W.I.
"	11		32 re-inforcements joined from Base — 10 G.S. wagons to 102 Inf Bde. — 8 G.S. wagons to R.F.C.O. to take mounts to 152 Inf Bde new location. — 60 Rds G.S.A. mounts to H.tg. Bde. S.— 435000 Rds.gd. A.Amm. to Inf. Bde.S.	W.I
"	12		12 G.S. wagons to 160 Bde to remove ammun from forward position to reserve position — 1 Turner Loads to 160 Bde — LIEUT. C.G. WOODWARD mos.R.P.rearvo parthor for Bde.S. — 2/Lieut GALT 100P W.S. proceed.S. by rail to BAPAUME to collect 19 Remounts for Bde. — 2/Lieut H.T. BIRD procls to 1/160 Bde. Orders received to stand to ready to move at half an hour's notice — all transport and men collected from Bde.s and others detachts of coynes to Camp — weather fine. —	

A5834 Wt. W4973/M687 750,000 8/16 D. D. & L. Ltd. Forms/C.2118/13.

Army Form C. 2118.

WAR DIARY
or
INTELLIGENCE SUMMARY.
(Erase heading not required.)

Place	Date	Hour	Summary of Events and Information	Remarks and references to Appendices
HAMELINCOURT	March 1918 13th	9 am	20 re-inforcements hooks to 152 & 160 Bdes. - Wheels & Electric hooks to 8" Siege Battery R.G.A. 21/6/17. B.M. arrives with Remnants of "Beer" and 5. 38 for Duct Train - Units in state of readiness for move	W.J.
"	14th	6.30 am	D.A.C. still held in readiness to move at half an hour notice. Driver W. TOWNHILL admitted to 10 KS Amb. with regrets W.A. wounds and placed under arrest. Visit of S.O.S R4 to inspect Billets & lines etc - 110,000 Rds of S.A.Amn. to Inf. Bdes.	W.A.
"	15th	6.30 am	Transport & 6 hrs of mules sent Drivers & Harness to Inf Bns. to deal Agricultural Officer for Agricultural work - 10,000 Rds of S.A.Amn to Inf. Bdes.	W.A.
"	16th	9 am	Column receive orders to hold itself in readiness to move at 5 am hence not to.	W.A.
"	17th	9 am	30 re-inforcements reports from Base - 15,000 Rds of S.A.Amn to Inf. Bdes.	W.A.
"	18th	9 am	1 N.C.O & 5 men to 18 N.F. Pioneers for R.E. Relay & extra in forward area. 1 Corpl. & 3 truth to 18 N.F. to instruct in throwing - 21/6/17. O.C. 5A.94. R W.J. reports arrival from Base - 1 O.R. to 160 Bat.	W.J.

WAR DIARY
or
INTELLIGENCE SUMMARY.

(Erase heading not required.)

Army Form C. 2118.

Place	Date	Hour	Summary of Events and Information	Remarks and references to Appendices
HAMELINCOURT	1918 March 19th	9 a.m.	Signalling class of 24 O.R's from Bdes. & 6 OR's from H.Q. commenced. B.S. wagons with 900 Rds of A/A.A Ammn. from A.P.D. to 153 Bde.	W.H.
"	20th	7 a.m.	Further instructions received to be ready to move at the shortest possible notice. R.E. schelon fetched 9 all animals harnessed up. LIEUT. T. WILLIAMSON reported for duty from Bay Department. 1060 Rds of A/AA Ammn. to Bde.	W.H.
"	21st		Gunner S. OLSEN killed as of Hq. Qrs. A hostile fire commenced about 1 a.m. during which MOYENVILLE and the area around the camps were heavily shelled. LIEUT G.B.SHOP 7.20 OR's sent to 1 P.D. as extra assistance during the passage of wagons due to the enemy attack which has commenced in the early morning. 23 G.S. wagons to forward area to move Ammn. to reserve position. Officer & Personnel of this attached to S.A.C. for duty on through Camp. Bombed at 10.45 pm by enemy air craft. One bomb fell in the lines of No.1 Section no casualties. Area around camp was also shelled from 4 am to 6.30 am. During the heavy all Schelon were kept fully hooked, horses harnessed, and all transport & personnel kept in a state of readiness to move at soon as the order was received.	W.H.

WAR DIARY
or
INTELLIGENCE SUMMARY

(Erase heading not required.)

Army Form C. 2118.

Place	Date	Hour	Summary of Events and Information	Remarks and references to Appendices
HANDICOURT	March 1918 22		Orders received for S.A.C. to march to HENDICOURT, moving at 9.15 am. – A special Armts Group established at By Company MANZINCOURT at which 4000 Rds of .177 Kynoc Reported for use in emergency. 2LT. 6.T. HICKLING, PARKER, VENABLES & GRICE reported arrival from base. 2 OP'S reported moving in forward area – 900 000 Rds A.P.P. S.A.A. with 10 duty Belts LIEUT. G.B. BISHOP & 20 OP'S take over 6 Corps A.P.P. at BOIRY BOTRUDE.	WSA
"	23rd Jan		LIEUT. LOMAS and 50 OR's take over A.R.P. from LT. BISHOP. 2LIEU LLEWELLYN and Ennum T. HOLLINGWORTH Recles in action near from Camp Jules – First N.R. – 100 000 Rds of S.A.A. to transmitterous – During this period there was great demand for ammo. Some difficulty was experienced in keeping the Guns supplied owing to the resistance Lorries had to be brought from supplementary dump.	WSA
"	24th Jan		S.A.A. Sect. marches to BAPAUME area for entraining with duty Base. – 94 reinforcements reported arrival from Base and were trucks dined to Base. – 13.250 Rds of A.P.X. returned to Arty Base and 1,220 S.A.A. to duty Belts in forward area.	WSA

A.5834 Wt.W.4973/M687 750,000 8/16 D. D. & L. Ltd. Forms/C.2118/13.

WAR DIARY
or
INTELLIGENCE SUMMARY.

(Erase heading not required.)

Army Form C. 2118.

Place	Date	Hour	Summary of Events and Information	Remarks and references to Appendices
HAMELINCOURT	March 25 1918	9 am	116. Oy? R.A. attached to S.A.A. – 3 G.S. wagons to R.H.Q. 98 Bty. – 2/Lieut. BALL and VENABLES joined to 160 Bde. 2/Lieut. HICKLING and PARKER joined to 152 Bde. 12 reinforcement (Signallers) arrived from base and joined direct to Bde. – At 7 pm received orders to be held in readiness to march at a moments notice, and orders received to march to BELLACOURT at 11 pm where column arrived at 2 am R.B. and encamped on N. side of village.	Msg
BELLACOURT	26		On accordance with orders from 31st D.A. – D.A.C. started to march to GUIDEMPRE at 11 AM via BERLES AU BOIS & POMMIER but were stopped enroute at HUMBERCAMPS and orders to return via LA HERLIERE & BAVINCOURT to BELLACOURT which was reached at 5.30 pm. – Lt ESPIR ¨ 2/Lt HENRY joined from 160 Bde to No. 142 Echn. respectively. During both the outward & return Journey the vicinity of the road along which the column was marching was shelled.	
"	27		We were standing ready to move – Area around S.Gomet, etc. shelled throughout the day – 8750 Rds of 18 pdr Ammn. delivered to Bdes.	H.A.

WAR DIARY or INTELLIGENCE SUMMARY

Army Form C. 2118.

Place	Date	Hour	Summary of Events and Information	Remarks and references to Appendices
BELLACOURT	March 1918 28th	9pm	Sections attached to Bdes to facilitate the supply of Ammn. The remainder of Column lorries up awaiting orders to move — The ARRAS–DOULLENS road and Camp areas shelled during the morning. Orders received at 2 pm to march to GUIDEMPRE – Column moved off at 2.40 pm and reached Lt BAZEQUE on Enroute at close of recce & have bivouaced at 3.30 pm. H.Q. of Column at V.21.d.1.8 (Sheet 51F). 8.0/5 Res of Ammn to Bdes —	W/T
GUIDEMPRE	29th		4 D.A.C. reports arrived from 6th Corps – 9600 Rds of Ammn to Bdes	W/T
"	30th		2° Lieut. A.V. ADAMS reports arrival from base.	W/T
"	31st		Instructions received that 31 D.A.C are to be relieved by 32nd D.A. on nights 1/2 & 2/3rd – L.P.A forms D.A.C. H.Q. Area covers 5 Camps during the night — no Casualties.	W/T

Total Amnts supplied to Arty & Infantry —

	18 Pdr		4.5 How	6409	L.S. How.	D.W. Grenades
	Shrapnel	Explosive				
Receipts	22160	23160		6409	1,855,000	5281	7600
Issues							

All above totals all except 4 MG machineGun in 6 Camps

Wilkinson Colonel
Comm 31st D.A.C

34th Divisional Artillery

WAR DIARY

34th DIVISIONAL AMMUNITION COLUMN R.F.A.

APRIL 1918

WAR DIARY or INTELLIGENCE SUMMARY

Army Form C. 2118.

Place	Date	Hour	Summary of Events and Information	Remarks and references to Appendices
GUIDEMPRE	1/11	2 am / 9 am	Area round Camp shelled by E.A. from 2 am to 6 am. Reckon camp out of reach even from their Guns	West
"	"	2.30 pm	Orders received to march to BAVINCOURT which had been selected as place of assembly for 38 Ouf [Div?]. Three transports sent for per Army Area. The Column started at 9. R.A.E. arrived to refit a [?] as a [?] to evacuate [?] separation for more equipment. Supplies for men — complete turnout to each of 157 [?] 160 Beds for the nurses.	
"	2/11	9 am	Party of 32nd Siege Hty to march to be on 38th Camp — erecting tents from H.A.C. tent on to new area. BAVINCOURT to erect tents [?] Camp 34 & 38 A.E. engineering teams. R.A.H.Q. marched at 11 am via LA HERIERE arriving at 12.15 am. 3, 34 & 38 A.E. relieved at CHATEAU-[?] in turn on Camp became their B.	
BAVINCOURT	4/11		During the day Sections of 3, 34 & 38 A.E. Batteries were [?] to [?] general was part of hutts. Orders are issued tents to march to RAMECOURT which was to commence the following day.	
"	5/11	9.30 am	Column commenced marched to RAMECOURT at 2.30 am via SAULTY - SOMBRIN - STREE - HAMIN - HOUYIN and SUMORMUEX arriving at 4.30 pm. H Chateau area and [?] [?] (Lt Deval, Cpt Orr) and 3 Other [?] were accommodated in camp. Party of 1 Officer (Lt Priestly APM.30Y) & 3 Ort. were sent under instructions from HQ.R.A.H. to take over billets in HAMPT STEENWERCK the [?] was a Guard to STEENWERCK	

Army Form C. 2118.

WAR DIARY
or
INTELLIGENCE SUMMARY.
(Erase heading not required.)

Instructions regarding War Diaries and Intelligence Summaries are contained in F. S. Regs., Part II. and the Staff Manual respectively. Title pages will be prepared in manuscript.

Place	Date	Hour	Summary of Events and Information	Remarks and references to Appendices
RANCOURT	6/7/15	10.15 am	March was continued S/W Hamy. Marlbeing Rancourt at 10.15 am arriving at ST. HILAIRE AND EQUIDESCQUES at 5 pm via ST. POL - PERNES - FLAMINGHAM - FERFAY - AMES and AINERS. Headquarters and 2 coys were quartered at ST. HILAIRE the other 2 coys at EQUIDESCQUES. Owing to the recent fighting taking over was not easily by long wait for ration.	W/J
ST. HILAIRE and EQUIDESCQUES	7/15	10 am	Headquarters and No 2. Coys. commenced march to HAZEBROUCK via COR BIE at 10 am No 1 Coy from EQUIDESCQUES joined column at 11.30 am the destination was then reached via BUNG? and ST. VENANT at 3 pm - with the exception of 2 coys had to be billeted on side of roads. Billets were few & men had to bivouac being inconvenient barns for accommodation.	W/J
HAZEBROUCK and LA CORBIE	8/6	9.30 am	The march was continued to STEENWERCK at 9.30 am to relieve the 39th /8/16 who had marched out of the area earlier in the day. One time of each of 152 & 160 Div. had marched to stop with the column to show over the billets on arrival of 121 & 122 Bdes. on night of 8/9. The Column moved 1 - 2 km Camp and billets were taken over as LEAN RUSO - FARM A.29.a To NO CO2 NO CAT at LA STRADE B.25.d ^ NO9 C Coy at GALLAMEWEGATE LINE at A.29.c INPUT / OMAS B.5.Ot? nine dispatches to take over parts from 39.4.1 4.5 Routes feateral reserve which have been despatched from base on 24 March show reported arrival under LIEUT. H. CLARK -	W/J

WAR DIARY or INTELLIGENCE SUMMARY

Army Form C. 2118.

Place	Date	Hour	Summary of Events and Information	Remarks and references to Appendices
BEENWERCK	9th [1918]	4-15 a.m.	At 4-15 a.m. a heavy bombardment commenced on front, front and rear lines and on transport throughout the situation. No A.T.B.'s came near Transport HQ. A message received at Brigade referring to the 131st/156 Bdes which was sent on to the O.C. 38th Bn informed him of the general retreat from the 30th N.B.S. and we must now re-establish liaison with 34th Bde in C.M.N. area. The 38th N.B. It was however later reported that message was taken over by the 34th B.I. — M.S., O.P. and Recon. Camp were rapidly mostly being emptied during the early morning. Orders were received to stand by ready to move, and the Column marched to new area A.1.B or 59 N.W. at BEENWERCK at 7.12 men moving at 14 p.m. W.I. Remainder were transport + waggons he had an advance of the road. — 15 P.M. 144 3 O.R. wounded in L.B.H. section — 13 P.M. Sp. 1 W. 7 S. 1 8.1 W. 4/0R were killed + 1 OR wounded. + 30R wounded Sgt not known and 3 OR wounded in 102 Route. 6 horses were killed + 20 rounded during the early bombardment. The new area came under fire immediately on arrival of the B.H.Q. All roads in advance N. of BEENWERCK were shelled and the forenoon morning there were two casualties. T.H.Q. were no H.S. in march shortly all eight ready to move — Pte 12 mg section have been received to move Column to a new named A.B. 2. 13 N.W.B. area 2s at Brewery during the early in the area. N of the retirement ceased relieved up to 30 to 40 trenches of firing into air and to their retreat. Gener Officer O.O. who had 6 cut their units wage commanders by 5 A.C. for the night Transport orderly to Brigade was as ordered and was referred to experience in keeping the Column intact.	WJ

WAR DIARY
or
INTELLIGENCE SUMMARY.

Army Form C. 2118.

(Erase heading not required.)

Instructions regarding War Diaries and Intelligence Summaries are contained in F.S. Regs., Part II. and the Staff Manual respectively. Title pages will be prepared in manuscript.

Place	Date	Hour	Summary of Events and Information	Remarks and references to Appendices
STEENWERCK	10th April 1918	5.30 am	At 5.30 am the Column marched to BLANCHE MAISON F.8.U. (Sheet 36) arriving 7.30am During the morning STEENWERCK was heavily shelled by the enemy and airplanes flew up to the Bn. Boten's dugout found to own transport back when they started the advance to the town. There was a report to be expected many to which there S.M.O. for thirty of 8mm. an M.G. bullets were coming down the roads from the direction of STEENWERCK and information was received that M.G. fire of the enemy were already in the town. The O.C. allowed to withdraw the Column from BLANCHE MAISON towards OUTERSTEEN and a report of the action taken was sent to Bde H.Q. 31st Bn. Reply to this report was received. "Movement of Column to E. of OUTERSTEEN approved." The march of the Column was most unpleasant owing the congested state of the roads which in places too inflicted — many infantry men crowded into transport re military and returning carrying bundles & conveying their belongings in hand carts. perambulators, bicycles, etc, and every point of slow moving transport. The Column eventually reached into billets at farm E. of OUTERSTEEN. On arrival 4 Batmen and Grooms were sent to Battery gun position much quicker than had been sent from Brigades. The transport was derailed and defaulted to the convoy return of the journey in the morning

B.Q.M.S. Pte W. WALTERS wounded on the 9th was reported as having died of wounds. | |

WAR DIARY or INTELLIGENCE SUMMARY

Army Form C. 2118.

Place	Date	Hour	Summary of Events and Information	Remarks and references to Appendices
OVERSEEN	March 1918 11	2 p.m.	Echelons apart from Battery horses at 9am. Orders were now received to stand by ready to move. One of our Aeroplanes was brought down in flames near HP OS by E.A. about noon. Men were seen escaping. 11.30am the order to move the Column to MORBECQUE area was received. Column marched VIA METRIS - PRAZELLE - BURRE and HAZEBROUCK arriving in billets at 9 p.m. Great confusion in this area as to billets to be occupied which was eventually settled by Area Commandant. HAZEBROUCK on account of French wagons being detailed to Gun positions which were in action near BAILLEUL. Afterwards trunks burnt were also established in this area under LIEUT. G JONAS 150 prisoners of munster this unit have to be immediately evacuated owing to many gilt Pois? another ack was found at N.17.B.5.5.(Sheet 27) — 2 Li Winger leading 248 trunk wagons of 18m. R.S.Row trunks were dumped as they arrived during the night. Orders were now received to march 7 18m trunk wagons tonight and all horses teams & others to 121° Base. A.S.C. seem to be now interest in the area. Inness to form fifty base when now at BORRE.	U.9

WAR DIARY
or
INTELLIGENCE SUMMARY.

(Erase heading not required.)

Instructions regarding War Diaries and Intelligence Summaries are contained in F. S. Regs., Part II. and the Staff Manual respectively. Title pages will be prepared in manuscript.

Place	Date	Hour	Summary of Events and Information	Remarks and references to Appendices
NORDBECQUE	12/4/1918		Column arrived in this area during the morning from BOESEGHEM after refilling at the BULLHEAD. A great number of very heavy shells fell around the farms & roads in the area, especially the Column second army transport HEZEBROUCK which was shelled at intervals throughout the day. At 6.30 p.m. orders were received to move the Bn. to St SYLVESTRE-CAPPEL. In column marches at 7 pm and arrived at situation at 8 pm. No accommodation could be found at St SYLVESTRE. Billets were allotted in (area of) CAPPEL and for the 12 men about a mile E of St SYLVESTRE. Band hears continually at a farm about a mile E of St SYLVESTRE. Lands arrived in billets where men having tea, and rations were sent up from Column area and it/were expressed in keeping them together during the normal changes that were taking place. Band & horses had no dinner this evening ————	
St SILVESTRE	13/4/1918	6.30 am	At 6.30 am orders were received to move to St MARIE CAPPEL and to GODEWAERSVELDE. No orders that B and an S arrived in area at 8 a.m. Horses watered at 8 a.m. and then to limbers at camp, to reach the B.H.Q. near horses near road to St. Sylvestre's side of the village — the B.H.Q. near horses and are the church. Billets were nearly allotted to B & H & Band a relief wanted that morning of the ambulance we allotted to 16 P N.J.2 noon and reserve gun was dispatched to being attack has established at FUZEVILLE by St Omas to 20 Off of 2nd Sec. A.C./1st Cdn CAPPEL before to reach after refilling forward was taken as were 5 to Camp as 7.30 am. feeding morning	

WAR DIARY
or
INTELLIGENCE SUMMARY.
(Erase heading not required.)

Place	Date	Hour	Summary of Events and Information	Remarks and references to Appendices
GODENVERSVELD	April 1919 14th	9.30 am	Echelon arrived at Camp at 9.30 am – At 9.30 am orders were given to transfer same and hand in ready to move. Horses were not ready off the animal rest – At midday 29 horse & H.T. wagons to proceed such as return. Animals were ready for sufficient horses owing to the demand for horses and the long journey. Notes to be made to proceed it – Lieut Colonel B.W.M. O.S reported he arrived from 12 Bde: to be attached pending arrangement for his transfer to ENGLAND. Echelon did not return to Camp until following morning.	
"	15th		Horses were returned to Camp at midday. New dump was now established at T.6.c.9.9. – Ammunition was now running short at the dumps and no more could not be obtained from Railhead – Refilling was carried out at CASTRE do what there was been issued up the afternoon –	
"	16th		All reactions sent to forward dumps the 18th Horses were now sent to arise from H3.52.15 and H.5.73.10 which from CASTRE – Horses leaving for CASTRE in the afternoon did not return until 6am following morning	

WAR DIARY
or
INTELLIGENCE SUMMARY.

(Erase heading not required.)

Army Form C. 2118.

Place	Date	Hour	Summary of Events and Information	Remarks and references to Appendices
GODEWAERSVELDE	1918 Aug 17	2.1.30am 7am	Lieut: A.D. GRACE reports to 160 Bde— Echelons returned to Camp at 6am. At 1.20 am the enemy commenced shelling GODEWAERSVELDE STATION & vicinity. Between 2.9.2.30 am 12 shells were dropped into the yard. Were the enemy of H.Q'rs and the N.Y.Y. team were located. The Y.Y.H. team was where of the village was the house occupied by the S.O. Offr. H. Wam an outbuilding received by the Naval establishment next door to H.Q'r was wrecked by a shell. One native and one civilian their Q killed and one native wounded. As there were rumours of the cavaliers amongst the troops & civilians on the message the S.O.Q Troops were moved to a small farm as O.K.L 5.3 (sheet 27.)	W.J.
"	18th	2am	At 2am all Echelons were ordered out to empty its Battery Gun positions— they returned during the morning. At 2 p.m. all B.X. echelons were sent out to dump at L 34.d 3.3 to deliver as much B1 as reports from FUZEVILLE dump—	W.J
"	19th		A total of 4,100 Rds of B.Y.Y. was delivered to dump & Battery position— Area round camp was bombed during the night. There were no casualties.—	W.J.

WAR DIARY
or
INTELLIGENCE SUMMARY.
(Erase heading not required.)

Instructions regarding War Diaries and Intelligence Summaries are contained in F.S. Regs., Part II. and the Staff Manual respectively. Title pages will be prepared in manuscript.

Place	Date	Hour	Summary of Events and Information	Remarks and references to Appendices
GODEWAERSVELDE	20th 19/8		Commenced todays echelons were refilling at dumps L, 3A d, 3, 3 (sheet 27). During the night this refilling began at CUSTRE HAGERS. Packhorse teams had been working in relays of 36 hours. They had very little rest between journeys from the 16 to 20th Inst. In addition the teams were always in a state of readiness to move plenum was not taken off except for very short periods. Camp was bombed from 10 pm to 1 am — no casualties.	
"	21	2 am	Camp was bombed intensely from 2 am till 5 am.	
		7 am	Lt Colonel B.W. MOSS — Seven to Six the 38th S.A.L — 10 R.F. wagons Battery prepared to remove empties to Packhorse — Orders issued to hold in readiness 20 Officers + 73 GPs to proceed to CLAIP to Rd. Rations 145. Remounts for Beer of 38 Bn.	
"	22 nd	1.11 P	R.A.H. Section ordered to move to ALPANGER BIEZEN to join 34 Div. Arty, Bar. 10 R.F. wagons despatched to Bulow Rd.	
			gun positions to collect empties — All echelons emptied at forward dumps.	

WAR DIARY
or
INTELLIGENCE SUMMARY.

(Erase heading not required.)

Instructions regarding War Diaries and Intelligence Summaries are contained in F. S. Regs., Part II. and the Staff Manual respectively. Title pages will be prepared in manuscript.

Army Form C. 2118.

Place	Date	Hour	Summary of Events and Information	Remarks and references to Appendices
GODMANSTEAD	23rd Nov 1918		LIEUT SPURNUR + 2/LIEUT ASHBY 38th Mortar 47th Bty 343rd & 3 horses & CARLIS to collect 145 rounds for 38 bh - 3.5 shrapnel which had been loaned to destroy air outfit of trench mortar returned to S.A.A. Depot - Camp shelled + bombed from 9 pm till 2 am - no casualties -	Ref
"	24th	9am	LIEUT POLLETT & N. ADAMS forces to 152 Btty. Orders were received at 9 pm to move column to HAMMOSK the following day at 10-30am.	Ref
"	25th	10-30 am	Column marches to HAMMOSK at 10-30am - via PUEZLE crossroad - L.17 & 2.1 - Switch road - L.12.O. (Sheet 27) Buffeting harbourage sent forward and the Camp at L.14. 2.9.1. (Sheet 28) was about to the S.A.C. where it arrived at 12-30pm - During the journey Ref to the main road it was constantly under enemy fire - The switch road and Railway adjacent was heavily shelled during the time the column were moving in the direction. There had been numerous casualties amongst troops on the roads - Although the road had been fired on various times the column had no casualties - some shells dropped with the the column - but no damage was done -	

WAR DIARY
or
INTELLIGENCE SUMMARY.

(Erase heading not required.)

Army Form C. 2118.

Place	Date	Hour	Summary of Events and Information	Remarks and references to Appendices
GONDRECOURT	Aug 25 1918		35 Continued	

The Column had been in this area about an hour when orders were given to move to another area. The march commenced at 2.30 p.m. along the roads already reconnoitred for our men at 5 p.m. and we reached Fancheres by FRENCH buses met upon the Column about 5 p.m. near Ruts. Owing to the absence of saddles and 156 Bits & Bridles had down to C.H.Q. with the high sheeting remounts it was impossible to harness up all the vehicles at the same time. A certain number of wagons had therefore to be left behind and were sent out with sufficient harness to send back to their from the portion of the column which had completed its march. This and the counter-march already mentioned occasioned great delay & inconvenience and the last wagons did not reach their destination until 12 midnight. Pickets were also detailed to deliver 2 hundred wagon loads of supplies to each gun in the line about G.24.27. The task was a difficult one owing to the shortage of animals & ? from the wagons — they returned the following day about 10 am.

Army Form C. 2118.

WAR DIARY
or
INTELLIGENCE SUMMARY.
(Erase heading not required.)

Instructions regarding War Diaries and Intelligence Summaries are contained in F. S. Regs., Part II. and the Staff Manual respectively. Title pages will be prepared in manuscript.

Place	Date	Hour	Summary of Events and Information	Remarks and references to Appendices
WATOU area L.9.b.5.5.	17/1/18 26	10 am	Echelons returned to Camp at 10 am. - Men & horses were rested for the day. 145 Remounts arrived from CALAIS for 85 Bde.	K.S.
"	27		8.30 pm echelons were sent to Bucs to obtain 2 pounder lewisgun & 18 pdr 14.5 Shr Ammn to reach gun wheel we are now in possession about G.25.29.28, + G.25.29.30 (sheet 28) - If was war head to be this area about 12 noon by the QMG & Gibson to clean the camp was occupied by the 8.A.L. Hertfordshire, another was sent made pending the decision of the 38th Div.	K.S.
"	28 Jan.		Column harness all ready to move at 8 am awaiting instructions from the 38th that this area to be occupied. Meantime 6 town 166 orders to take over the camp. After reconnoitering the adjacent country the column was much difficulty accommodated in an area about L.7.a (sheet 7) which was made at 1.15 pm. No exact location has been given to the Column as what areas being to occupied consequently other units who generally claiming the camp as being in their area.	K.S.

Army Form C. 2118.

WAR DIARY
or
INTELLIGENCE SUMMARY.
(Erase heading not required.)

Instructions regarding War Diaries and Intelligence Summaries are contained in F. S. Regs., Part II. and the Staff Manual respectively. Title pages will be prepared in manuscript.

Place	Date	Hour	Summary of Events and Information	Remarks and references to Appendices
WATOU L.7.d.	April 29		During the night there was a heavy bombardment — wheel carts throughout the day. The roads about here were shelled. No damage to carts etc in the between. 16 wagons of rounds sent to 124 Bty W.Q at 10 a.m. — lorries on the way 18-18pr & 18-4.5 How wagons sent to empty ad Battery gun positions. Arrangements for 15th & 34th Bat made and nearly all men Battle S. The shoemakers were now divided between the tents of the 34th D.A.C. — One very light shrapnel enroute from Town & hooded to 152 Bde.	
"	30"	9am	"B" FORDON now both sent to have being undersage — 18-18pr & 18-45 "How wagons sent to empty at forward position — One OR wounded in forward area —	

Ammtn received 5" howrs 5 for period 9 to 30 t
18 par	4.5 How		
shrapnel	H.E.		
66.164	25.000	6.500	

97664

C Sunderland R.F.A.
Com: 9 By W.A.C

WAR DIARY or INTELLIGENCE SUMMARY

Army Form C. 2118.

34 D Am Col
Vol 29

Place	Date	Hour	Summary of Events and Information	Remarks and references to Appendices
W.S.O.J (Col 37)	1st May 1917		All 18th and 4.5 How. Echelons emptied at Battery positions — Gun ammunition to hold in readiness 2 Officers & 29 O.R. to proceed to Remount Depôt C.A.S.A. 13 to collect 58 mules. D.R. reported arrival from 34 D.A.C. column for attachments to D.A.C. duty.	W.S.
"	2nd Jan		LIEUT. ESPIR, LIEUT. HENRY and 29 O.R. proceed to CH.I.A.V.C. to collect 58 mules. Echelons refilled by lorry and emptied at Battery gun positions —	W.S.
"	3rd Jan	5 am	D.A.C. sent under the orders of 49th Div. H.Q. from Camp. Echelons emptied at forward dump & lorries supply now run entirely by A.S.C. in conjunction with M.T. Coy	W.S.
"	4th Jan	9 am	All echelons emptied at forward dump — new dump formed at GJ. TANTER. B4125 W to refill echelons.	W.S.
"	5th		The 18pr & 4.5 How. and D.A.C. were now grouped into 337 Bde. Arty — counter engagements inactive —	W.S.

Army Form C. 2118.

WAR DIARY
or
INTELLIGENCE SUMMARY.

(Erase heading not required.)

Place	Date	Hour	Summary of Events and Information	Remarks and references to Appendices
WATOU	1918 7.7.18	6.15am 8am	All O.C. & Echelons to Battery positions at 8 am - the 18th division to forward by train at 2 pm - instructions were by now received that the 34th & 39th D.A.C. were to divisions on 7.5 & 15th, not D.A's to 18th but 6th to march on 7th & no 2 sections to move on 8th at 8am from the 18th D.A.C. column exceed of from 22nd Corps Railhead to replace others moved to 14 Sqn 38 Div D.A.C. Lieut. LOMAS hands over charge to an Officer of 38th Division D.A.C. 57th R.F.A. reports arrival with 56 mules from 14th D.A.C. from march commenced.—	
WATOU	7/5	10am	Headquarters 7th Q.(Sections marched to MOREBECQUE area & from thus sent off at 10 am via WATOU - WINNEZEELE - CASSEL - WALLON CAPPEL to camp at C.13.d. & D.19.a. (Sheet 35A) - Camp R. Billets handed over to Adjutant 38th D.A.C.	
"	8"		No 2 Sections marched from WATOU at 9 am to carry on in Camp at 3.30pm Lieut. Bn Q.M. WITHERS extends QK do D.A.C. from 160 O.R.	

WAR DIARY
or
INTELLIGENCE SUMMARY.
(Erase heading not required.)

Army Form C. 2118.

Instructions regarding War Diaries and Intelligence Summaries are contained in F. S. Regs., Part II. and the Staff Manual respectively. Title pages will be prepared in manuscript.

Place	Date	Hour	Summary of Events and Information	Remarks and references to Appendices
NORDBECQUE	May 1918 9		Overnight Shoes, Jifs & Oilsheets issued to Civilians. Orders for Column to proceed to HESDIN BECQUE via 28 tonner wagons sent to Battery positions 2.50 — W.N.CLARK & 20 O.R. moved to Civs. to collect O/coments	[?]
"	10	9.15	Column marched to HESDINBECQUE area to Farm Langhe 164. TROUPIN to collect 20 elements	
HESDINBECQUE	11		Orders to put 6 horses in each Sect. Efforts to exch[ange?] Battery of 160 Bde. to take Regtl horses. Lieut. C. R. Scott, G.L. arrived with 40 remounts from CALAIS — 25 for wagons & 15 for Battery R.H. to commence training 400 yds of Beauvais rd for 160 Bde.	[?]
"	12	1	Serg¹ O'Donnell head to A.S.C. from particular matter. Tea round Camps parks from P.P. 230 arrived Beauvais	[?]
"	13	1	Capt. Ren. H.T.P. YOUNG proc¹ to 160 Bde — 4 S.L. wagons to R.E. dump AIRE to draw Deauville road	[?]

Army Form C. 2113.

WAR DIARY
or
INTELLIGENCE SUMMARY.
(Erase heading not required.)

Instructions regarding War Diaries and Intelligence Summaries are contained in F. S. Regs., Part II. and the Staff Manual respectively. Title pages will be prepared in manuscript.

Place	Date	Hour	Summary of Events and Information	Remarks and references to Appendices
MBEUBCODE	May 1918			
	14	9 am	4 Wagons to R.E. dump to draw Breuvillerails	ref
"	15	10 "	" " " " "	"
"	16	"	Enemy bombing O.A.R.E. from 10 pm to 1 am.	"
"	17	9.30 "	20 Inf. Reserve to Battery positions —	"
"	18	9 am	2nd Lt. Beaumont to A/R.E. for casualties evac — Eng. O'Donnell Report	ref
"	"		Lt. Hodge to O.C. Duty	"
"	19	9 am	20 O.R. sent to R.E. dump to draw 2m. x 6' Duckwalk	"
"	20	"	Lt. Hurn proceeded to Raish — nothing —	"
"	"		" " " to follow. 2/Capt. T.C. FILLERY, 2/Lieut. F.G. LEAHY	ref
"	"		45 O.R. 51 Natives — No. 1 G.S.O. 24 G.S. O others and 80 Animals to	"
"	"		PEUPLINGHE Camp 2 – CALAIS. Lieut. R. COOPER to remain Coy	"
"	"		arrival, to remain School of Army. Lieut. G. BISHOP	"
"	"		2/Lt. 2 O.R. 112 Natives to R.A. Reinforcement Camp 2 Henny	"
"	"		MILQUES.	"
"	21	"		
"	22	9.30 am	Lt. LOVELL F. O'C. Off Ground visited out lying parade —	ref
"	"		2/Lt. WIRTH Lt. 1 G.O.R. H.Q. wounded —	"

Army Form C. 2118.

WAR DIARY
or
INTELLIGENCE SUMMARY.
(Erase heading not required.)

Instructions regarding War Diaries and Intelligence Summaries are contained in F. S. Regs., Part II. and the Staff Manual respectively. Title pages will be prepared in manuscript.

Place	Date	Hour	Summary of Events and Information	Remarks and references to Appendices
RENDECQUE	23rd	May/18	Inspection of horses [illegible] 23/5/18 destroyed by D.A.D. [illegible]	App
"	24th		Reinforcements arrived from Base	4A
"	25th		" " " " "	4A
"	26th	3	—	
"	27th		Report arrival from Base	4A
"	28th		Inspection of Camp by G.O.C. R.A. 34th Divn at 11 am. Inspection of Camp by G.O.C. XI Corps in the afternoon. 11 re inspection and notice to move. (see note)	6A
"	29th		The Bombardment commenced at 1am — new arrangement Camp — Camp Bombed at 11-55 pm — Out of wounded 2 horse killed an 11 wounded. 2 of which had to be shot — two bombs [illegible] dropped — Our camp + 3 others in a straining [illegible] occupied by WARWICK Regt — 2 men being killed + 4 wounded.	6A
"	30th	1	Loose bugles to C.F. [illegible] PORTUGUESE + Rev Bunkers V.Y. and [illegible] amongst in vicinity	6A
"	31st		ARE	4A

Colonel Cmdg R.A. Corps 34th Div. G.S.

(A7030). Wt. W12859/M1293. 750,000. 1/17. D. D. & L., Ltd. Forms/C.2118/14.

WAR DIARY
or
INTELLIGENCE SUMMARY.

Army Form C. 2118.

34 D Aux Cpl

(Erase heading not required.)

Place	Date	Hour	Summary of Events and Information	Remarks and references to Appendices
STEENBECQUE	June 1918 1st	9 am	24 Re-inforcements posted to 160 Bde.	WJ
"	2nd			WJ
"	3rd			WJ
"	4th			WJ
"	5th	9 am	40 O.R's reported sick with fever.	WJ
"	6th			
"	7th			
"	8th		No 2 Sectn. struck off duty owing to sickness amongst British & native personnel.	WJ
"	9th			
"	10th			
"	11th		An average of 100 O.R's sick daily with fever.	WJ
"	12th			
"	13th			
"	14th		1 Signaller of 38.S sent to Gen. Sec. Prisoners of war from R.A. WOOLWICH. - No 2 Sectn. commence supplying Hutns. WJ from to-day - An increase of sickness in the O.ranks No 1 Section.	

Army Form C. 2118.

WAR DIARY
or
INTELLIGENCE SUMMARY.
(Erase heading not required.)

Instructions regarding War Diaries and Intelligence Summaries are contained in F. S. Regs., Part II. and the Staff Manual respectively. Title pages will be prepared in manuscript.

Place	Date	Hour	Summary of Events and Information	Remarks and references to Appendices
STEENBECQUE	June 1918 15	8 pm	STEENBECQUE area shelled from 8.40 – 8.45 pm — One shell fell in the field occupied by No 1 Section, three lines & 4 in the immediate vicinity – other casements — one shell fell in rear of HQ Off. Officers' billet — no casualties —	K.H.
"	16	9 am	Over 100 men reported sick from No 1 Section with flu.	
"	17	7 am	No 1 Section ; more to new lines & Billets at I.3.6.7.7. (Rhe 26A)	K.H.
"	18			
"	19		3 O.R's. No 1 Section ; wounded in forward area & indeed killed in forward area.	K.H.
"	20			
"	21		3 O.R.S. No 1 Section ; wounded in forward area.	K.H.
"	22			
"	23			K.H.
"	24		LIEUT. P.E.H. FRANKLYN 2/LIEUTS: W. BOUSTRIDGE, G. RILEY and E.D. BEECH with 88 O.R.S including 9 S.M men for reforming Y. Mortars, proceeded from Red from Penny reinforcement Camp.	K.H.

Army Form C. 2118.

WAR DIARY
or
INTELLIGENCE SUMMARY.
(Erase heading not required.)

Instructions regarding War Diaries and Intelligence Summaries are contained in F.S. Regs., Part II. and the Staff Manual respectively. Title pages will be prepared in manuscript.

Place	Date	Hour	Summary of Events and Information	Remarks and references to Appendices
STEENBECQUE	25/6/1918		"Z" & "Y" Batteries 34 & 1 Brit'd Trench Mortars reinforced —	key
"	26		"Z" OP shots to M.E. from E.A.6 — 72 Reinforcement posts to Odes. — 23 Reinforcement posts from 15th Army K.A. Camp. — 2 Lt. G. RILEY and E.O. BEECH posted to 160 Bde. LIEUT FFH FRANKLIN & 2LT M.R.D.CROOKES posted to 34 Brit'd Trench mortars. 2ND LIEUT W. BOOSTRIDGE posted. Do not seem.	K.A.
"	27		23 Reinforcement posted to Odes.	K.A.
"	28		Establishment of all 18 pr & 4.5" How teams reduced to 4 animals — Horse transport increased from 20 to 32. A Mes reduction of 18 Drivers & 36 Animals this Bde. from this date — Area around camp bombed at 11 p.m. one dropped near R.P. doing slight damage to gate & which teeth. Slight damage to civilian property, no casualties —	W.A.

Army Form C. 2118.

WAR DIARY
or
INTELLIGENCE SUMMARY.
(Erase heading not required.)

Instructions regarding War Diaries and Intelligence Summaries are contained in F. S. Regs., Part II. and the Staff Manual respectively. Title pages will be prepared in manuscript.

Place	Date	Hour	Summary of Events and Information	Remarks and references to Appendices
STEENBECQUE	June 1918			
	29		Instructions received re adoption of new establishment concerning of British & native personnel in accordance with war Establishment no 818. Part VII. to come into operation on 6th July 1918.	
	30		Notification received from S.A. to be ready to move to join the remainder of the reinforcements at an early date.	

C.W Sampson? Capt? RAM
Com'g 7 S.A. Gen Hosp

WAR DIARY
or
INTELLIGENCE SUMMARY.

Army Form C. 2118.

34 D Am Col

Vol 31

Place	Date	Hour	Summary of Events and Information	Remarks and references to Appendices
STEENBECQUE	July 1st 1918		Instructions received that 34 D Div Arty will march to join 62nd 2nd Corps 2nd Army on July 3rd —	
—	3rd		Overhaul of Equipt etc prior to march — area Pouzones Rue 45 Rely Scheme, Cl. Staff Capts R.Q., 59 Sgr. visit 34 lines to ensure accommodation prior to marching in —	
—	3rd			
—	"	4h 9.30.	S.A.C. commenced march to HONDEKOT area at 9.30 en route arriving in fields at RUBROUCK at 4pm	
RUBROUCK	5th	10.30	Column continued march to 2 Army area. 10.30 am via WORMHOUDT and HERZEELE arriving Camp at 5 pm. Bd at PONTYPOOL CAMP. 2/1 Section at PUSSY CAMP, Hd Qrs at PATIALA CAMP. D.A.M. Vehns were now reforming at CLIFFORD CAMP.	

WAR DIARY
or
INTELLIGENCE SUMMARY.

Army Form C. 2118.

Place	Date	Hour	Summary of Events and Information	Remarks and references to Appendices
PROVEN (PoperingheCan)	July 1918	6.	LIEUT COCKS, 2ⁿᵈ LIEUTS. MORRIS & POTHECARY and 120 O.R. report for duty with 34 & 2nd Siege Artillery, at G.H.Q. Reserve, which was now reforming under the orders of G.H.Q. — 196 Animals unit horses casualty. E.S. 7/13 L.G. wagons taken over from party which had heavy loss from Gas — LIEUT COCKS assumes temporary command of G.H.Q. Reserve.	W.A.
"	"	7.		W.A.
"	"	8.	2ⁿᵈ LIEUT BOLSTRIDGE proceeds to M.M. team.	
"	"	9.	Colonel E. N. Humphrey A.S.O. proceeds leave to ENGLAND to 22nd inst. — CAPT A. N. MORTON assumes command of the B.H.Q.	W.A.
"	"	10.		
"	"	11.		W.A.
"	"	12.		
"	"	13.	Warning Order that Division is or G.H.Q. Reserve and to be ready to move at very short notice.	W.A.
"	"	14.	Same arrangement received.	W.A.
"	"	15.	Orders received that Division will move by rail from HEIDEBEEK PROVEN WAYENBURG and REXPOEDE riding, commencing at 14.10 on 16th — LIEUT N.D. CROOKS & 2ⁿᵈ LIEUT W.A. HENRY sent forward by lorries for billeting — T.S. to 4 remain in camp for heavy van and frontwagons to travel next, balance for entraining. LIEUT J. WILLIAMSON attached to "B" Battery for duty.	W.A.

Army Form C. 2113.

WAR DIARY
or
INTELLIGENCE SUMMARY.

(Erase heading not required.)

Place	Date	Hour	Summary of Events and Information	Remarks and references to Appendices
PROVEN	16/8/18		1st Gp R.A. A. Cmd. (acting) train entraining at 3 pm at PROVEN - this completes the entraining of the 2nd Hy. How Bty. HQ which was moved by train 25 & 30 under the ordrs of 102 Corps Bde - from REXPOEDE.	HQ
CHANTILLY	17	7.	1st A.A. Actus entrained at REXPOEDE at 6 am. HQ & 1st Gp R.A. (acting) arrived at CHANTILLY at 3.30 pm. Detraining commenced at 4.30 pm. 1st A.A. marched to billets at SURVILLIERS. 1st Actus arriving into, were billeted at THIERS.	
SURVILLIERS	18		Capt G. SAMWAYS assumes command of 1st A. Actus - Orders received to be ready to move early on the morning of the 19th.	HQ
"	19		Orders received at 1.20 pm to march to VIC-SUR-AISNE area - Starting hour 2 pm. Route 6.5 am - Via FRESNOY VILE - MONTAGY - NANTEUIL-LE-HAUDOUIN - ORMY - CREPY. arriving LA FRESNOY at 7.30 pm.	HQ
LA FRESNOY	20		Brig. Atty. moved in General Reuse of Allied forces. Instructions that small moves were early & very short moves. One officer at 2 O.R's reps. to meet 1 C.R.A. for instructions in reconnoitering route to follow. - instructions - Btys under verbal orders received to move to FONTENOY arr. FEUIL then moving to FORT BONNEVIL at 12.55 am.	HQ

Army Form C. 2118.

WAR DIARY
or
INTELLIGENCE SUMMARY.
(Erase heading not required.)

Instructions regarding War Diaries and Intelligence Summaries are contained in F.S. Regs., Part II. and the Staff Manual respectively. Title pages will be prepared in manuscript.

Place	Date	Hour	Summary of Events and Information	Remarks and references to Appendices
VIVIERS	July 1918 21st		Commenced march to VIVIERS at 1.10 am via BONNEUIL arriving new area at 5 am. Officers sent forward to CHAVIGNY FARM for instructions regarding camps etc occupied and to act as guides to units on arrival in la GRILLE FARM area.	KA
"	22nd		Orders received for No. 2 section to move forward as 2/Lieut SKELTON was still there to make independently at 4 pm to position in forward area. No 2 & No 1 section to move to new area at 8 am on 23rd – 34 horses and commenced operation at 11 am supply to 10th FRENCH CORPS. No 2 Section commenced delivery of amm to Gun positions.	KA
"	23rd	8 am	No. 2 & No 1 section commenced march to forward area via RIND-dela-REINE – TOUR-DOUMONT – CARRE- PONT-au-SHOT-DUCEP?– arriving la GRILLE FARM at 11 am. – LIEUT. W.A. HENRY attached to Strength of N.A. for instruction – COLONEL C.N. SIMPSON D.S.O. returned from leave to ENGLAND and assumed command of the D.M.E. Operating with FRENCH CORPS continue. No 1 section commenced delivery of ammto Gun positions 152 Bde.	KA
la GRILLE FARM	24th		LIEUT H.S. SPENCER reported arrival from base. Section continue supply of amn to Guns for 300 Bde for 12 pm 13 pm 2 pm for Troops & materials.	
"	25th	9 am	Two Officers sent forward to meet S.G.R.A. arriving every hour from VILLIERS-HELON at 9 am – for information regarding forward position for supply of ammn.
LIEUT H.S. SPENCER proceeds to D/160 Bde.	KA

Army Form C. 2118.

WAR DIARY
or
INTELLIGENCE SUMMARY.
(Erase heading not required.)

Instructions regarding War Diaries and Intelligence Summaries are contained in F. S. Regs., Part II. and the Staff Manual respectively. Title pages will be prepared in manuscript.

Place	Date	Hour	Summary of Events and Information	Remarks and references to Appendices
LA BRIQUE FARM	26th July 1917		Advance of 10th & FRENCH CORPS continues - Batteries moved forward.	
"	27th		12 mules to 15th Bde to replace casualties - Motor ambulances on 10/7 to clear them from lines hooked by batteries of ammunition, gun & rifle returned to A.R.R. during the night & returned to A.R.R.	
"	28th		10th & FRENCH CORPS continued the advance. A.R. received orders to move forward to ROZET WOOD - Owing to the advance the Bridges of enemy is now commenced to form dumps near ST JULIEN. 3rd Section with 5 lorries urgently wanted for return eastwards to the Corps tomorrow to be ready to move into the new position. One S.R. commander remained at duty.	
ROZET WOOD	29th		Owing to the pressure of work by keeping up the supply of ammunition 30 O.R. detailed to return from hospital & present at hand. at A.R.R.	
"	30th		Advance dumps having been formed at BALLISTE the supply of ammunition to Batteries was carried on from this point.	wish
"	31st		15 Gunner forks to Bn. to replace casualties.	

C.H. Humphreys Colonel R.F.A.
Commander & Adc

WAR DIARY
or
INTELLIGENCE SUMMARY

Army Form C. 2118.

34 D Au Cd / SL 32

Place	Date	Hour	Summary of Events and Information	Remarks and references to Appendices
ROZET WOOD	Aug 1/18	3pm	Orders received in the afternoon to be ready to move forward probably in the evening – Brigades continue their advance –	
– " –	2nd		Held in readiness to move forward. Orders for march received. B.H.Q. marched to OULCHY-LA-VILLE at 9.15 pm and bivouacked by 11.30 pm. a. la BAILLETTE at 1 am – Brigades were now advancing in pursuit – Column held in readiness for further advance –	
OULCHY-LA-VILLE	3rd		Column standing by until 12 noon when orders were received to march to L'EPROLLE and VICHEL ara at 2 pm – B.H.Q marched to L'EPROLIE FARM and bivouacked. B.H.Q. moved to ROZET WOOD at 4.30 pm left. During the afternoon congratulatory messages were received from FRENCH Commander on the 34 Divn work done by the 34 Div'n. Instructions were now given to be prepared to march to entraining stations on the 4th.	
ROZET WOOD	4 & 5		Orders received in the early morning to march to BOULLARRE en route for entraining stations. B.H.Q. left starting point at 9 am via NEUILLY-ST-FRONT – DINHARD – MOREUIL-SUR-OURCQ arriving BOULLARRE at 4 pm. B.H.Q. have entraining arrangements and march table for the 5th & 6th made.	

Army Form C. 2118.

WAR DIARY
or
INTELLIGENCE SUMMARY.
(Erase heading not required.)

Place	Date	Hour	Summary of Events and Information	Remarks and references to Appendices
BOULARRE	Nov 5th 1918	6am	Batteries of Brigade despatched to Batteries with Brigades. B Ex. marched to LE PLESSIS BELLEVILLE at 4 p.m. Entrained at 10 p.m. – No 1 Echn marched to NANTEUIL via HAUDOUIN. No 2 Echn marched to DAMMARTIN and a half of D.A.A. Echn marched to ORNOY-VILLERS all for entraining	KS
LA PLESSIS	6th	3 am	B. Gp. R.A., HQ Gp. R.A. and no 1 & 2 Train left LA PLESSIS by train at 3 a.m. Remaining portion of D.A.A. Echn marched to NANTEUIL for entraining at 11 a.m. with army Bder.	KS
ESQUELBECQ	7th	7am	H.Q. train arrived ESQUELBECQ at 3am. Detraining was commenced at once & D.A.C marched to DROGLANDT area near WATOU arriving at 6am. Detached portions of Brigr arrived in camp during the day having detrained as soon as ...	KA
WATOU	8th	1	Settling in billets. General overhauling of equipment and stores. The remaining half of D.A. Echn never having entrained on the 6th now reported its arrival.	KA
"	9th	8pm	Presentation of CROIX de GUERRE to Officers 4 O.R.S by H.Q.G 34 Army Corps A.W. NOLINDINIA LIEUT. G. LOMAS and DRIVER T. SIMPSON. No 2 Echn having arrived & received its food park which the division was on the line with the 10th FRENCH CORPS from 22nd Sep to 2nd August. O.S return to H.Q Section – arrival from Indian Cash ROUEN and kits	KS

WAR DIARY
or
INTELLIGENCE SUMMARY

Army Form C. 2118.

Place	Date	Hour	Summary of Events and Information	Remarks and references to Appendices
WATOU	Feb 10/18		Warning orders that Bde Arty H.Q. would move to HANDEKOT area on the 12th.	
"	11	5	Preparations for march. Church Parade for His Majesty the King at TERDEGHEM — two representatives sent from the R.A.C.	
"	12	8.30 am	B.A.C. marched to new area at HANDEKOT at 8.30 am. H.Q. Bde at S/27. E.17. b. 9.7. – Batteries and new road covering the C POPERINGHE line.	
HANDEKOT	13	9 am	12 L.S. Wagons sent to R.E. Dump to collect Helio Flick H4 refs for Brigades.	
"	14		LIEUT. R. COOPER (Horse) to B.A.C. from 33rd Divn Arty — LIEUT W.A. HENRY (Horse) to "A" R.A. Battery for duty. —	
"	15		GUNNER DAHLMAN Proc'd to his Home from 160 Bar. — BOMBR. WILKINS A.A. Instructor Proceeded to Remount Depot CALAIS for course in horse management.	
"	16		Warning Order for move to forward area in relieving Divn. — 4 Infanteer?? Brigades.	

WAR DIARY or INTELLIGENCE SUMMARY

Army Form C. 2118.

(Erase heading not required.)

Instructions regarding War Diaries and Intelligence Summaries are contained in F.S. Regs., Part II. and the Staff Manual respectively. Title pages will be prepared in manuscript.

Place	Date	Hour	Summary of Events and Information	Remarks and references to Appendices
MANDEKOT	17/8/18	—	39 Re inforcements posted from base —	64
"	18.	—	8 S.L. wagons to R.G. in depôt in front area — 7 S.L. wagons to S/W Bde to move dumps to forward positions in the line. Lieut R. LOWIS and CROOKS with 20 ORs take over A.R.D. from 49 2nd Divn —	64
"	19.	—	15 S.L. wagons to empty site — 9 S.L. 1 G.S. Pol. 6 R.E. 6 M.T. wagons at CAVANAGH Rd dump — Lieut T. WILLIAMSON (Roads) to E.P. 44 Battery.	64
"	20.	—	Lieut LANDER 30 MAN PWR labour Coy report his arrival from base and attack to S.P.R. Keen — Lieut 30 NTN wagons to S.P.R. from 160 Bde — Lieut REID (roads) to 160 Bde. — 8 S.L. wagons to R.E. & 7 S.L. wagons to 102 Infy Bde. suspension for move to forward position — Driver T. HUDSON killed Gunner J. RIDDINGTON Gunner KEMPSON and Driver D. PARSLEY wounded on forward area.	64
"	21.	—	Column march to new area in relief of 495 Divn Arty Col at 8.30 am — Lieut Colonel H. ALLCARD attached to 38 Divn R.A.C. finding pushing to a R.F.A. Bde.	64

Army Form C. 2118.

WAR DIARY
or
INTELLIGENCE SUMMARY.
(Erase heading not required.)

Instructions regarding War Diaries and Intelligence Summaries are contained in F. S. Regs., Part II. and the Staff Manual respectively. Title pages will be prepared in manuscript.

Place	Date	Hour	Summary of Events and Information	Remarks and references to Appendices
HAMMOEL	27 Jun 9	8	Warning orders for S.S.T.'s section to be prepared to move to S/27 - K.21 at 9.8. L.B.S. wagons send to cast of Light Rec. T.M.B. Station - Finishing party of 20 men to CHATEAU dump - 6.50 wagons forward over to more new huts.	
"	28	7am	S.B. wagons to R.E. — CAPT. G. CANWAY and LIEUT. R. COOPER M.C. K.S.A admitted to hospital.	
"	29		W.D. Dets. move to new area with Coy G.P. Pkv. — 22 miles from Ramouel Rept. Coys 3 Prio to D.H.B. — 15 B. wheremaps families from base — 6 B.S. wagon to forward area to collect huts. —	K.S.A
"	30		LIEUT. COLONEL HARCOURT proceeded to join 256. L. Bn. 5th Pion. — 15 B. reinforcements to Bwer — 8 E.S. wagons to R.E. — area around LOVIE CHATEAU (huts) during the evening.	K.S.A
"	31		Warning orders to be ready to move at short notice — 9 Refugees report arrived from Indian Lest. Base — Inded to Reft Pm. K.A.	

C.H. Lunderfunland VK
Cm 93h K.E.6

Army Form C. 2118.

WAR DIARY
or
INTELLIGENCE SUMMARY.
(Erase heading not required.)

Place	Date	Hour	Summary of Events and Information	Remarks and references to Appendices
HAMHOEK	Aug 8/18		54 mules 15 D. horses 1 G. horse and 1 charge received from Remount Depot CALAIS.	
"	22nd			
"	23rd		LIEUT. H.S. WHITE, BELGIAN Liaison Officer, and LIEUT NUNN M.C. II Corps dump Officer attached to S.A.E. Heavarm. Camp. Several H.A. during the night and bombs dropped near camp at 12 mn & at 2 a.m.	
"	24th		8 G.S. wagons to R.E. for fatigues and 6 for Area Commdt. E.S. (Repairs of standings commenced).	E.S.
"	25th		1 O.R. (M and) 19 O.R. to CALAIS to collect remounts — 32. reinforcements reported arrival from Base — 8 G.S. wagons to R.E. for fatigues. Unknown forward area —	H.S
"	26th		8 G.S. wagons to R.E. & to the Commdt. to collect material & for reconstruction of standings — Repairs commenced to Gun positions on E POPERINGHE line — Amm to CHATEAU dump. 24 r.e. reinforcements to Base.	

WAR DIARY or INTELLIGENCE SUMMARY

Army Form C. 2118.
34 D.A.C.
WD 33

Place	Date	Hour	Summary of Events and Information	Remarks and references to Appendices
HANNOEK (27) K.23.d.h.h.	July 1918 1.		Warning Order has D.A.C. (could) march to PATRICKOT area (27) K.23.d.h.h. on 2nd Inst — A.A.A. Scots caught novice at Eligh 818 - of practically French & totally Mobile personnel —	A/1
-"-	2nd	8am	Column marched to PATRICKOT area at 8am, running 10am and take over camp from 6 Div. — A.A.A. Stragglers handed over to 36 F Regiment — No 1 & 2 Sections were wheated by Lieut. Senn to Batteries for purposes of trans supply.	A/1
PATRICKOT 27/K29.a.d.u.u	3rd	1	Three O.R.'s A.F.A. Scots verged on punish'ble deeds whilst on with in forward area.	A/1
-"-	4th		A.A.A. Scots marched to new area near ABEELE by Rly Station — LIEUT. RILEY posted to no 1 Section form 30/6/18 A/1 Bde.	A/1
-"-	5th	10am	Column marches to POPERINGHE area (27/L.16.d.54) — new R.P. established at G.34.d.u.u. — Instructions for exchange of wagon lines from locations between 34.F.A.A. & A. F.A. Brown received.	

WAR DIARY
or
INTELLIGENCE SUMMARY.

Army Form C. 2118.

(Erase heading not required.)

Place	Date	Hour	Summary of Events and Information	Remarks and references to Appendices
POPERINGHE	Sept 6		Capt the Rev. F.T.G. 14 D.1.3 R.O. we proceeded to D.A.C. from R.A.H.Q.	
"		7½	3 E.S. wagons to D.A.M.O. for duty —	
"		7¾	Orders received that Column would move to RENINGHELST in relief of 41 Dn. Div:— Party of 1 N.C.O. 10 O.R.'s to relieve personnel — 4 B.S. wagons to H.Q. R.S.O. to move Ammunition forward	
"		8¾ 10am	D.A.C. moved to RENINGHELST at 10 am: stable over G.29.A.G.H.6. Lines — 2 Lieut Low as takes over Ammunition Dump at G.29.d.20.80 —	
RENINGHELST	9¾		Party of 1 Officer & 20 O.R.'s to STEEN AKKER dump to clear 64	
			French "stores" — 8 Agnelles lorries from Base —	
"		10¾	2 B.S. wagons to D.A.M.O. for 1st. 4 ni. pound area — 1 N.C.O. &	
			and 10 men to lorries Officer for taking burden —	
			Party of 1 Officer & 20 O.R's on leave work at STEEN AKKER.	
"		11.5	2 Lieut L.S. Vause reports arrival from Base and is attached to No 2 Section	

Army Form C. 2118.

WAR DIARY
or
INTELLIGENCE SUMMARY.
(Erase heading not required.)

Instructions regarding War Diaries and Intelligence Summaries are contained in F. S. Regs., Part II. and the Staff Manual respectively. Title pages will be prepared in manuscript.

Place	Date	Hour	Summary of Events and Information	Remarks and references to Appendices
RENINGHELST	Sept (?) 1917		Work on STEEN AKKER pump continued – 20 Drivers Horses do 41 St Divn – 17 Drivers Horses to 9 Divn – 7 Drivers Horses to 2nd Brigade – ammunition delivery by men was carried out – ammunition stores 818 – 9/1917 that material personnel & ammunition & reinforcements moved to 15 & 160 Batts R. – S.I.& learnt & truck removed when run by 32 m.E. Battalion – between moments to ann– amount. LOVE and STEEN AKKER.	[illegible]
LOVE	13th		LIEUT. L.S. VALE hooked to 160 Bde. LIEUT. R.D. CROOKS hooked to WH. No 2 Secto from several matters –	[illegible]
"	14th		2/LIEUTS. F. COOK and R.C. OTHER reports arrived from leave.	WH
"	15th			
"	16		Area around Nos 1 & 2 Sectors at STEEN-AKKER shelled from 5 to 7.30 pm. — no casualties.	
"	17th		Camp of Nos 1 & 2 Sectors were again shelled from 12 m. to 2 am 18th — no casualties —	

WAR DIARY
or
INTELLIGENCE SUMMARY.

(Erase heading not required.)

Army Form C. 2118.

Place	Date	Hour	Summary of Events and Information	Remarks and references to Appendices
LOVIE	July 13 1917		Reconnaissance of forward area pushed to DEPOT. LIEUT. OWEN to locate wrecked guns and equipment for salvage. No 2 team (with horses) also at 6 p.m. 2 G.S. wagons were despatched to the pit. LIEUT. Y. CLARKE (Junior) in Car Louie.	A/4
		19.V	LIEUT. OWEN & 2 parties of 10 men each commenced salvage work forward. 3.18 "A" Team & Carriages returned to Park (having returned). No 2 team more (new move) to new area at L.33 C.L.3. vicinity to enemy shell fire.	K/9
		20.V	LIEUT. T. HEARTY proceeded to "H.H." Battery from no. 6 & 1. wagons to D.A.R. Gun, 5th Brigade & 2 limbers. 2 G.S. wagons to salvage. 5 G.S. wagons to H.Q. to turn. Returned to new depth 10 S. Trade guns to H.Q. & P.L. elect. Ammn.— Salvage party collected 2.75 Guns and 2 carriages & aluminium to salvage & also reverts items again wheels form 7 to 8. 30 Suz.	A/7

WAR DIARY
or
INTELLIGENCE SUMMARY.
(Erase heading not required.)

Army Form C. 2118.

Place	Date	Hour	Summary of Events and Information	Remarks and references to Appendices
NOYELLE	21		LIEUT. SPENCER reports to D.A.D. form B/160 Rev — 2 4 wagons to Railhead to collect 21 main nits — E.F.C. to H.Q. — there — talog heavy rockets 1-18 p — Juice — 8 loads of another 18 pr — sent 1-75 ton lorries.	63
"	22		1 lose 2 F wagons of junk to 160 Bac — 970 Rds of 18 collected from POBSONS Dum Rithing — reserve rations party collected 1-18 hr carriage from forward area.	64
"	23		12 pounder wagons to "A" B/160 — 1-18 pr carriage refit + 6 spare kigs — 2 German Heavy 170 value from list. forward area + send to salvage.	65
"	24		Orders for Colonel E.M. Graham 8.50. to proceed to England on duty. 6 munition wagons to B/160 - 6 Rds "A"/152 and 6 to 123/152 Rec — 300 Rds of 4.7 from 10-1 Carts BELMONT DUMP + Salvage party collect 1-45 How Zice and buffer- 5 wheels + spare parts + refitted to Salvage.	

WAR DIARY
or
INTELLIGENCE SUMMARY.
(Erase heading not required.)

Army Form C. 2118.

Place	Date	Hour	Summary of Events and Information	Remarks and references to Appendices
LOVIE	April 25th	9 p.m.	Handing over command of S.A.C. to MAJOR F.A. WILLIAMS. 2-4.5 Howitzers – 1-75 cwt Rng 2 – 1 German Trench M. Bart occupy position Gun – 1-6 Cwt German Gun 9.1-45 How L mtr orders to return to base Siege Bt.	1
"	26		12 mtn unpour to 152/Bde – 6 Inch unpour to 4/5.6. storage of Equipt etc from forward area continued –	
"	27		Handed over S.A.C. to Major F.A. WILLIAMS and proceeded to ENGLAND. R.S.M. PAIN with his arrival from base – no R.S.M. of smoke BX to 5 1/160 –	
"	28		R.S.M. CRUICKSHANK reports to HO Gp. 160 Bde form HQ O.S.A.C. Evening of returns to plans of ready forming forward to HQ. Battery wagon lines – Area around HQ Gp. very heavily bombed throughout the night – no casualties –	

WAR DIARY
or
INTELLIGENCE SUMMARY.
(Erase heading not required.)

Army Form C. 2118.

Instructions regarding War Diaries and Intelligence Summaries are contained in F.S. Regs, Part II. and the Staff Manual respectively. Title pages will be prepared in manuscript.

Place	Date	Hour	Summary of Events and Information	Remarks and references to Appendices
LOYE	Sept. 29th 1918		Ordered to move Column forward to KEMMEL VILLAGE at 6 pm – D.A.C. arrived at 11 pm and bivouaced on the roads around KEMMEL – Rein' throughout the night –	95 R.A.
KEMMEL	30th		Reparations for another move forward – Orders received to move to ZANDVOORDE area with Brigades at 2.30 pm on 1st of Oct:	R.J.
			Total Salvage for month	
			4 – 18 pr with Carriage – 1 – 18 pr piece spare –	
			2 – 4.5 How with Carriage – 1 – 4.5 How piece & buffer	
			1 – 4.5 How Carriage – 1 – 6 cm German gun complete.	
			1 – German Hotz. Hand carriage without gun –	
			2 – Heavy German Guns – 1 – 75 complete –	
			1 – Carriage & buffer of 18 h – 8 Howitzer bods of 18 pr	
			6 – wheels – 1 Carriage & other essential parts of a 75. –	

F.J. Meurs
Major RFA
c/o 34 D.A.C.

Army Form C. 2118.

34th D.U.C.
Vol 34

WAR DIARY
or
INTELLIGENCE SUMMARY.
(Erase heading not required.)

Place	Date	Hour	Summary of Events and Information	Remarks and references to Appendices
KENNEL	Sept 1918 1st	9.30	Under instructions received on 1st Aug. the 8.46 marches to KIRKWILDE at 10 a.m. Owing to congestion of traffic the column did not arrive until 10 a.m. on 2nd inst.	nil
KIRKWILDE	2nd	10 a.m.	Column arrives KIRKWILDE at 10 a.m. – At 2.30 p.m. the camp was heavily shelled and has to be evacuated temporarily. Shelling commenced again at 4 p.m. and several casualties occurred – one native driver killed, two British & one native driver wounded – 20 animals were killed, 12 wounded. The camp was picked automatically throughout the night. Instructions were received to move the column at dawn to CAFÉ BELGICA.	nil
KIRKWILDE	3rd	6 a.m.	Column marches to CAFÉ BELGICA arrives at 6 a.m. and was encamped at 38/S.29 Central. Forward troops dump at NIEUPORT was heavily shelled – no casualties –	nil
CAFÉ BELGICA	4th		New forward dump was now formed at CAFÉ BELGICA and the forward relief from DUNKIRK and old gun positions – officers & 60 O.R.s from French Motors 5 a.m. & 15 lorries were detailed for this work. A new dump was also established at HOUSE S.E.	nil

Army Form C. 2118.

WAR DIARY
or
INTELLIGENCE SUMMARY.
(Erase heading not required.)

34th D.A.C.

Place	Date	Hour	Summary of Events and Information	Remarks and references to Appendices
CAFEBERG	Oct 4 1918	5th	Salvage party under Lt Sugden + 15 others with 4 limbers went out.	W.H.
-"-		6th	Work on Salvage continued - B.S. formed before supplying forward dumps - 96 & 7 A Bde.	W.H.
-"-		7th		W.H.
-"-		8th	Salvage continued - Instructions that Column moves more to area S.of DICKEBUSCH on 9th	W.H.
-"-		9th	Column marched to HALLEBAST CORNER - (N.3.2.20.10.) 26 sets of fish nets collected for 152 Bde. Found it was now decided to form packets of 160 Bde; the Journeys dumps maintained for 152 Bde only.	W.H.
HALLEBAST CORNER		10th	A new dump was formed at this location.	W.H.
-"-		11th	Salvage work continued - 96 & Bde. were now supplies with them in from A.R.P. at HALLEBAST	W.H.
-"-		12th	A new A.R.P. was formed at (28/0.2.A.3.8.) BUSHHOUSE under LIEUT LOMAS -	W.H.
-"-		13th	Front from CAFEBERG and HALLEBAST CORNER relieved to BUSHHOUSE dump -	W.H.

Army Form C. 2118.

WAR DIARY
or
INTELLIGENCE SUMMARY.
(Erase heading not required.)

*Instructions regarding War Diaries and Intelligence Summaries are contained in F.S. Regs., Part II. and the Staff Manual respectively. Title pages will be prepared in manuscript.

Place	Date	Hour	Summary of Events and Information	Remarks and references to Appendices
HOLLEBAST CORNER	9/24/918 14		Salvage of Ammn continued — 12 re-inforcement horses to 15th Bde —	
"	15		Column marches to GHELUVELT (28.T.23.d.8.8.) —	
"	16		Eleven remount horses to Column	
GHELUVELT	17		"	
"	18		"	
"	19		Column + 96 R.F.A. Bde. march to E. of MENIN (R.10.c.5.6)	
MENIN	20		12 re-inforcements reported arrived from base —	
"	21		B.A. Guns & 96 & 11 F.A. move to LAUWE (N.14.E.) —	
LAUWE	22		12 re-inforcement horses to R.H.Q. + 3 Bdes —	
"	23		"	
"	24		Column 96 & 3 sec. 1½ mi march to KUITGAT —	
KUITGAT	25		Reinforcing R.B.P. formed at T.2.0.3.3. — with Remount Labels from 100 Gun positions at LAUWE — 19 Remount horses to R.A. & 3 Bdes. —	
"	26		6 B.L. wagons sent to HOLLEBEKE dump to collect B. Smoke. —	
"	27		Vicinity of above shelled about 01.00 with H.V. — LIEUT LOKE & 18 horses nor. wounds from 36th Divm —	

Army Form C. 2118.

WAR DIARY
or
INTELLIGENCE SUMMARY.
(Erase heading not required.)

Instructions regarding War Diaries and Intelligence
Summaries are contained in F. S. Regs., Part II.
and the Staff Manual respectively. Title pages
will be prepared in manuscript.

Place	Date	Hour	Summary of Events and Information	Remarks and references to Appendices
KUTTGAT	28		Column marches to BESVEREN and take over lines by beech vacates by 36th A.C. - Area around Buscheides by enemy A.V. guns at 19.00. -	
BEVEREN	29			
"	30		Area sented about 15.00. - 6 mules wounded	

Oct 1918

Total Ammunition Salves from O.C. Brigade in the month

R.		A.A.	B.X.	B.S.	Bde.T.
20,740	17,270	1342	27,706	3,126	240

Total 70,424

A.W. Thorburn Capt.
Comdg. 34 DAC

Army Form C. 2118.

34 OTC

WAR DIARY
or
INTELLIGENCE SUMMARY.
(Erase heading not required.)

Place	Date	Hour	Summary of Events and Information	Remarks and references to Appendices
BEVEREN	Nov 1918 1st		Forward R.P.'s (6 stations) at 28/J.19 with 4 metres. Intake from old Battery position - Camp tondes - from 06.30 to 09.30 hrs. Three OP's Briky'l one OP Shaver Wounded. Lieut Mackie killed, and 4 wounded.	
"	2nd		Instructions for OP's BG 16 move to MOORSEELE area on 3rd.	
"	3rd		Column marched to MOORSEELE area at 10.30 am VIA HARLE BEKE - COURTRAI passing KLOEFHOEK - where biloett were arranged at 1.30 pm - taken N.W. of LINDNIA Assumed command of column during the absence on leave of MAJOR F.A. WILLIAMS.	
KLOEFHOEK	4.5		Overhaul of Equipt and stores. Scheme of training put into operation.	
"	5th		Orders to stand ready to move to XX Corps area on 6th. Training on Race Course in suspension.	
"	6th		Orders for No 182 team to move forward to 6.9.c.00. and R.F. and join 152.Y/bo Bder on the 7th.	
"	7th		No. 6 + 2 R teams march to St Louis at 9 am - HQ. Offr staff Reman + OR at KLOEFHOEK.	

(A7092). Wt. W12859/M1293 750,000. 1/17. D.D. & L. Ltd. Forms C.2118.

WAR DIARY
INTELLIGENCE SUMMARY

Army Form C. 2118.

34 STA

Place	Date Nov 1918	Hour	Summary of Events and Information	Remarks and references to Appendices
KLOEFHOEK	8	—	J.M. Batteries commenced re-organising on mobile Batteries	A
"	9	—	H.Q. (Op) marched to ST LOUIS area to join Battery and were	A
"	10	—	billeted at ESSCHER.	A
ESSCHER	11	—	Armistice signed — Hostilities ceased at 11.00 hrs	A
"	12	—	Column marched to MOORSEELE & billeted as HERTHOEK	A
"	13	—	Orders for probable move forward on 15th	A
HERTHOEK	13	—	24 L.D. Horses & 16 horses from Remount Dep.	A
"	14	—	B.H.C. marched to ST GENOIS at 10.30 via WELVEGHEM—LAUWE	A
"	15	—	HERSEKE—ROLLEGHEM arriving 3.30 P.M. — Horses & transport reported arrival from base.	A
ST GENOIS	16	—	march continued to ELLIGNIES LES-FRASNE P area at 17.00. via HELCHIN and CELLES — Column was now moving with 2nd Army II Corps as part of Army of Occupation in Germany.	A

WAR DIARY or INTELLIGENCE SUMMARY

Army Form C. 2118.

Place	Date	Hour	Summary of Events and Information	Remarks and references to Appendices
EUGNIES LES-BROSNES	Nov 17		Sunday. Column resting. Thanksgiving service held near camp for our great victory. General Wallace CMG DSO in command. Service conducted by Senior Chaplain. The G.O.C. Rd. Head's warm tribute to the Officers & men of the Division at the conclusion of the service.	K53
—	18		R.A.C. entrained its march to LARANAYDE area covering STOCP at 03.30 hrs.	K54
BOUISSONS	19		Baths, change of clothing etc from LESQUIEP.	K55
—	20		MAJOR F.A. WILLIAMS reported arrival from base 20/6/14 and assumes command of the Division.	K54
—	21		Troops were unable to move forward during this period owing to difficulties of supplies.	
—	22			
—	23			
—	24		Service overhaul of equipment etc in preparation for inspection by Genl. Genderson on 4th Dec.	K
—	25			
—	26			
—	27			
—	28			
—	29			
—	30			

R.W.Vincent
Lt. Col. RFA

Army Form C. 2118.

WAR DIARY
or
INTELLIGENCE SUMMARY.
(Erase heading not required.)

34 D Au Col
Vol 36

Instructions regarding War Diaries and Intelligence Summaries are contained in F. S. Regs., Part II. and the Staff Manual respectively. Title pages will be prepared in manuscript.

Place	Date	Hour	Summary of Events and Information	Remarks and references to Appendices
BOUSSON OEUDEGHIAN	Dec 7.1918		Shaving, arrangements for Divl Surrender, preparation	
		3 pm	on 4 E.	
"		4 pm	Inspection by the Divisional Commander.	
"		5 pm	Seeing the horses arrangements were made for	
"	10		Officer down to head BRUSSELS	
"	11	10 am	Moving with march table for extension of move	
			on B. day.	
"	11		Instructions that B day will be 13th	
"	12	noon	D.A.C marched to BLASKLY and OUDGHNIES area and	
			billeted at DORDEZENES.	
BOLS-de- LESINES	13		"Entry nothing as DORDEZENES."	

WAR DIARY or INTELLIGENCE SUMMARY

Army Form C. 2118.

Place	Date	Hour	Summary of Events and Information	Remarks and references to Appendices
BOIS du LESCHES	Sept 1918 13th		March continued to SOIGNIES via BOURLON - ILLY - O/S Billets at NEUSART - LONGPONT and HORNVES.	
SOIGNIES	15th		Resting — Instruction that Battalions march via KURREY to SOIGNIES.	
"	16th		Column marched from SOIGNIES to Lt LOUVIÈRE - via LA ROUEX and Billets at HOUDENG - AIMERIES.	
HOUDENG	17th		March continued to ROUX - via LA TESTRE - CHAPELLE - LES HERLAIMONT - TRAZEGNIES - Billets new found at LA GASSE.	
LA GASSE	18th		Marched to CHÂTELINEAU from LA GASSE via LODELINSART - GILLY.	
CHATELIN AU	19th		Continued march to final area St GERARDS via CHATALET - PRESLES St VITRIVAL - FOSSE.	

WAR DIARY or INTELLIGENCE SUMMARY

Army Form C. 2118.

(Erase heading not required.)

Instructions regarding War Diaries and Intelligence Summaries are contained in F.S. Regs., Part II. and the Staff Manual respectively. Title pages will be prepared in manuscript.

Place	Date	Hour	Summary of Events and Information	Remarks and references to Appendices
GERARD	20		No entry of any events.	
"	21		Orders to reconnoitre area at MORMONT FARM and FILIPOLLE for Billeting BHQ & move instructions to move to these areas on 23rd	
"	22		Column moved to MORMONT area at 09.30 hr. — H.Q. & Kenn'l & "B" mess & T/M Battery located at FILIPOLLE. — Demobilization commences 24 men & 2 Demobilized deputed to dispersal area.	48
MORNING	23		20 minors other ranks men to dispersal area.	48
"	24		3 men to dispersal area.	69
"	25		6 men to dispersal area.	
"	26		29 miners (incl.) R.eng service men to dispersal area.	

WAR DIARY
INTELLIGENCE SUMMARY

Army Form C. 2118.

Place	Date	Hour	Summary of Events and Information	Remarks and references to Appendices
MORNIMONT	Oct 27 1918		O.C. Major de Beaupré supplies Lieut R. TANNER appointed Second Major of PARK FORCE and LIEUT W.T. WTS LANDER Junr Major of MORNIMONT 7 & 4 M.	
"	28			
"	29		Areas occupied to first reconnoitres for stores, vehicles & measurement being by first reconnoitres.	
"	30			
"	31		Total Vehicles, Stock and Animals:- 73 Motors & Ambulances 8 Lorries (Approx) 600 Depo of Trucks	

H. Vincent
Major R.F.A.

copy

Army Form C. 2118.

34 D Aux Col

WAR DIARY
or
INTELLIGENCE SUMMARY.
(Erase heading not required.)

Instructions regarding War Diaries and Intelligence Summaries are contained in F.S. Regs., Part II. and the Staff Manual respectively. Title pages will be prepared in manuscript.

Place	Date Jany. 1919	Hour	Summary of Events and Information	Remarks and references to Appendices
MORNIMONT	1st.	—	Peace routine of Animal a/cs commenced	Initials WSA
"	2nd.	—	6 G.O. Wagons to 103 Infy Bde. for duty.	WSA
"	3rd.	—	The names of CAPT. W. HOLDEN, R.S.M. G. CRUICKSHANK and B.S.M. C. CAYLOR appeared in despatches dated 24th Decr. 1918 as "mentioned".	WSA
"	4th.	—	"	WSA
"	5th.	—	"	WSA
"	6th.	—	2 Demobilisers, 2 Pivotal men & 2 miners despatched to Concentration Camp.	WSA
"	7th.	—	60 O.R's attached to D.A.C. from 103rd Infy. Bde. for instn. in Riding and Driving.	WSA
"	8th.	—	6 German Lorries sent to Divnl. Dump.	WSA
"	9th.	—	"	WSA
"	10th.	—	Inspection of Billets, Animals etc. by the Divnl. Commander and the E.R.O. The Divnl. Commdt. expressed his great pleasure with the interior arrangements of No. 2 Section. Lieut. R. COOPER proceeds to GERMANY as billeting officer.	WSA
"	11th.	—	Major F.A. WILLIAMS proceeds on leave to PARIS – Capt. G. SAMWAYS assumes command of the column. 2 WATFORD details and 3 Students despatched to Concentration camp.	WSA
"	12th.	—	"	WSA

Copy

WAR DIARY
or
INTELLIGENCE SUMMARY.
(Erase heading not required.)

Army Form C. 2118.

Instructions regarding War Diaries and Intelligence Summaries are contained in F. S. Regs., Part II. and the Staff Manual respectively. Title pages will be prepared in manuscript.

Place	Date	Hour	Summary of Events and Information	Remarks and references to Appendices
MORNIMONT	Jany 1919 13th	—	5 miners to Concentration Camp.	W.S.A.
"	14th	—	"	W.S.A.
"	15th	—	Warning Order that Divnl. Ortty would probably commence entraining on 23rd. for GERMANY.	W.S.A.
"	16th	—	20 OR's attached to 113 Army F.A. Bde. from D.A.C. and I.M. Batteries	W.S.A.
"	17th	—	Train arrangements for move to GERMANY received — One man per Section to act as guide sent on by Serial No. 2.	W.S.A.
"	18th	—	"	W.S.A.
"	19th	—		W.S.A.
"	20th	—	Classification of all animals by W.A.D.S.S, 34th Divn.	W.S.A.
"	21st	—		W.S.A.
"	22nd	—	Major F.A. WILLIAMS returned from leave to PARIS & assumes command of D.A.C.	W.S.A.
"	23rd	—	A.Q., D.A.C. and half of SAA Section entrain at TAMINES, Serial No. 19 Half S.A.A. Section, 2 G.S. wagons, and 8 Ammn. wagons, No.1 Section entrain at AUVELAIS on serial No. 20 for GERMANY.	W.S.A.
MORNIMONT and SIEGLAR	24th	—	A.Q., D.A.C., S.A.A. Section and portion of No.1 Section arrive TROISDORF at 16.00 hours. Detraining completed about 20 hours and units marched to SIEGLAR	W.S.A.

Army Form C. 2118.

WAR DIARY
or
INTELLIGENCE SUMMARY.
(Erase heading not required.)

Place	Date	Hour	Summary of Events and Information	Remarks and references to Appendices
SIEGLAR	Jan'y 1919 25th. 26th. 27th. 28th.	—	Detached portions of Sections arrived with Brigades during this period. No.1 Section billeted at MULLEKOVEN and No.2 Section at SPICH. These arrangements being temporary, pending move of 2nd CANADIAN D.A.C. Orders received to move column to ZUNDORF, LULSDORF and LIEBOUR. Reconnaissance of these areas prior to move on 29th. was carried out.	
—	29th.	—	H.Q. D.A.C., SAA Section and J.M. Batteries march to ZUNDORF, No.1 Section to LULSDORF. No.2 Section remain at SPICH pending further instructions. Last portion of No.2 Section arrive at detraining station at 19:00 hours.	
LULSDORF and ZUNDORF	30th. 31st.			

(Signed) F.A. Williams.
Major. R.F.A.
Comdg. 34th. D.A.C.

B.P. Humphreys? Lt. R.A.
Adjt. 34th D.A.C.

Army Form C. 2118.

WAR DIARY
or
INTELLIGENCE SUMMARY.
(Erase heading not required.)

34th Div. Ammtn. Column

Vol 36

FEBRUARY 1919.

Instructions regarding War Diaries and Intelligence Summaries are contained in F.S. Regs., Part II and the Staff Manual respectively. Title pages will be prepared in manuscript.

Place	Date	Hour	Summary of Events and Information	Remarks and references to Appendices
ZUNDORF SPICH LULSDORF	1st		Inspection of Animals by Capt. Horse Masters	
	2nd		✓	
	3rd		2/Lt. Angell X/34 TMB attached No.1 E Section for duty. Capt. W. Holden attached R.A.H.Q. for duty as "Staff Captain". Capt. C.S. Youngs X/34 TMB atta 34th DAC as Adjutant	
	4th			
	5th		5 men to Concentration camp at COLOGNE for Demobilization	
	6th			
	7th		Lt. A.S. Spencer struck off the strength on from 21-1-19. Lt. G. Lomas struck off the strength on from 19-1-19.	
	8th		34th D.A.C. ordered to select officers as Town Majors in ZUNDORF and LULSDORF.	
	9th		Captain G.H. McEwen DCM returned from leave to U.K.	
	10th			
	11th		Drivers Crough + Mackie tried by F.G.C.M. C.R.A. visited the Column. Capt. D.L. Carmichael RAMC proceeded on leave to U.K. 15th/2 – 14th 1/3/19	
	12th		Lt. S. Angell atta No 2 Section. No 2 Section move from SPICH to LIEBOUR and RANZEL. Lt./Lt. J.I. D'Arcy joined to take over Command	

(A7092). Wt. W12839/M1293. 750,000. 1/17. D. D. & L., Ltd. Forms/C.2118/14.

WAR DIARY or INTELLIGENCE SUMMARY

Army Form C. 2118.

(Erase heading not required.)

Place	Date	Hour	Summary of Events and Information	Remarks and references to Appendices
ZUNDORF LULSDORF LIEBOUR RATZEL & LANGEL	13th		Lieut. N.R. Crookes to Concentration Camp at COLOGNE for demobilization. No.1 Section moves 1 Subsection to LANGEL.	
	14th		Lieut. F.E.H. FRANKLYN. T.M.B. attached to No.2 Section (for duty).	
	15th		Capt. A.W. MATHER. R.A.M.C. attached for duty. 2nd Lieut. W.H. CLARK admitted hospital	
	16th		Lieut. R. COOPER, M.A. and 15 other ranks to Concentration Camp COLOGNE for Demobilization	
	17th		Lt.Col. J.I. DARCY R.F.A. assumed command of D.A.C.	
	18th		Major F.A. WILLIAMS, proceeds home on demobilization	
	19th			
	20th			
	21st			
	22nd		8 men to concentration Camp COLOGNE on demobilization	
	23rd		2nd Lt. T.H. Mems and 1 man to Concentration camp for demobilization. Wire from 2nd Army — No more demobilization until R.A. units are up to 90% of establishment.	
	24th		2nd Lt. W.H. Clarke discharged from Hospital, and granted leave from 25/2/19 – 11/3/19	
	25th		Captain MALLIN DINIA granted leave from 27/2/19 – 13/3/19 Lt. C.G. HODWARD takes temporary command of No.2 Section	

Army Form C. 2118.

WAR DIARY
or
INTELLIGENCE SUMMARY.
(Erase heading not required.)

Instructions regarding War Diaries and Intelligence Summaries are contained in F. S. Regs., Part II. and the Staff Manual respectively. Title pages will be prepared in manuscript.

Place	Date	Hour	Summary of Events and Information	Remarks and references to Appendices
ZONDORF	3 July 1917		34th D.A.C. ordered to send all D Animals to 44th M.V.S., and others of B strength.	
LULSDORF	26th			
LIEBUR	27th			
RANZEL &	28th		2LT Jameso 7/34 T.M.B. attached S.A.A Section for duty.	
LANGEL				

J. J. Shaw LT COL RFA
Commanding 34th D.A.C.

Army Form C. 2118.

WAR DIARY
or
INTELLIGENCE SUMMARY.

(Erase heading not required.) 34th D.A.C.

March 1919

Nil 39

Place	Date	Hour	Summary of Events and Information	Remarks and references to Appendices
ZUYNDORP LANGEL LUISDORP RANZEL LIEBOUR	1st	—	Horse Master & 4 Corps inspects animals of H.R. & S.A.A. for re-classification	
	3rd	—	" " " " " No 1 & No 2 Sects.	
	7th	—	Gunner Ridgely tried by F.G.C.M.	
	8th	—	10 G.S. Wagons loaned to Infantry Brigade	
	10th	—	Inspection by Divnl. Commander and C.R.A.	
	12th	—	25 "Z" Animals sent to Animal Collecting Camp	
	13th	—	18 Reinforcements arrive from R.A. 28 "X" Animals received from Collecting Camp	
	14th	—	Visit of S.C. R.A. and Major Tempest to discuss arrangements for accommodation.	
	16th	—	Lieut. W. Fanlane R.F.A. and 27 Reinforcements from R.A.	
	17th	—	16 Otherranks returned from 113th F.A. Bde.	
	18th	—	30 L.D. Horses to Animal Collecting Camp	
	21st	—	2 men to concentration Camp for demobilization. Lt. T. Pethecary conducting officer, & others grant leave. 30 Mules and 2 Riders from Remounts.	
	22nd	—	15 men to concentration camp for demobilization, but at last carried away Out leave & demobilization stopped.	
	24th	—	26 Otherranks to concentration Camp for demobilization. Capt. W. Holden proceeds on leave.	
	25th	—	Capt. E.S. Young applies a/Adjutant. 23 Reinforcements arrive from R.A.	
	28th	—	Capt. Birkenshaw 9/lc R.A.V.C. attached D.A.C. 16 L.D. Horses changed for 16 Mules and 182 Bde. 979. 18 "X" Mules posted to D.A.C.	
	29th	—	9 men to concentration Camp for demobilization	
	30th	—	54 "Z" Mules and 6 "Z" Horses to animal collecting camp.	
	31st	—	Summary Court Martial on Native 2nd Range Field. Sentenced to 6 months rigorous imprisonment	

J.J. O'Neill
Major R.F.A.
Commdg Aviation
D.A.C.

Army Form C. 2118.

WAR DIARY
or
INTELLIGENCE SUMMARY.
(Erase heading not required.)

Eastern D.A.C.

May 1

Instructions regarding War Diaries and Intelligence Summaries are contained in F. S. Regs., Part II. and the Staff Manual respectively. Title pages will be prepared in manuscript.

Place	Date 1919	Hour	Summary of Events and Information	Remarks and references to Appendices
ZUNDORF LULSDORF RANZEL	May 2nd		A.D.V.S. Xth Corps Inspects animals of Column	APP 1
	3rd		3 men to concentration camp for demobilization. Divisional Gas Officer inspects H.Q. and S.A.A. Section	APP
	5th		Lt. R.R. Bantan granted leave 5-5-19 to 19-5-19	APP
	6th		Divisional Gas officer inspects Gas masks of No 1 and 2 Sections	APP
	7th		Capt. Jameson proceeds to concentration Camp for demobilization. Armourer Sergt. Beckett examines revolvers and rifles of H.Q. and S.A.A. Section	APP
	8th		Lt. Potheary to concentration camp for Demobilization. Armourer Sergt. Beckett examines revolvers and rifles No.1 Section	APP
	"		Lt. T. Hayes posted to D.A.C. Surplus animals inspected by D.A.D.V.S.	APP
	9th		Armourer Sergt. Beckett inspects rifles and revolvers No 2 Section	APP
	"		Lieut B.D. Holt posted to D.A.C.	APP
	"		2/Lt. J.W. Thompson posted to D.A.C.	APP
	10th		1 Havildar and 2 L/Naicks posted from 3rd D.A.C. to S.A.A. Section	APP
	11th		Bdr. Last returns from medical course.	APP
	13th		Lt. Porter returns from leave	APP
	"		Capt. G. Samsurup granted leave from 13th to 27th May.	APP
	14th		8 reinforcements arrive and posted to S.A.A. Section	APP
	16th		10 reinforcements to arrive and posted to S.A.A. Section	APP
	"		A.A. & M.G. visits Column	
	"		Capt. C.S. Youngs returns from leave	
	"		Lt. G. Burgess returns from leave	APP

WAR DIARY
or
INTELLIGENCE SUMMARY.
(Erase heading not required.)

Army Form C. 2118.

Eastern D.A.C. May continued 2

Place	Date 1919	Hour	Summary of Events and Information	Remarks and references to Appendices
	May			
	17th		Lt H.T Couchman returns from leave	AA
	19th		Lt Jenkins granted leave from 21st May to June 4th	AA
	22nd		Surplus stores and ammunition from No I & 2 Subsecs returned. C.O. X Corps	AA
	23rd		Lt C.C. Rees posted to Lowland Divnl Arty. 23 Native reinforcements arrive 12 to No 1 Sec. 11 to No 2.	AA
	24th		Lt R.L. Machan + Lt J.B. Garland posted to D.A.C. Capt Bacon RAMC rejoins 102 Field Ambulance. M.O. to visit sections daily in future.	AA
	25th		Lt L.H. Chaldecott posted D.A.C. (1-5-19)	AA
	26th		Capt C.S. Youngs appointed Adjutant Eastern D.A.C. vice Wilson Anstey X Corps No 1354/A d/22-5-19	AA
			Lt C. Wilson posted Southern D.A.	AA
	28th		Capt G. Sannarey returns from leave. D.D.V.S. inspects animals of Column	AA
	31st		Capt. Inc Ewen granted leave 2/6/19 to 16/6/19 Lt Dunbar granted 8 days leave in France. 10 men c/o reinforcements from 104 I.A. Bde. 2 to H.Q. 36 No 2 Sec. 5 to S.A.A. Sec	AA

A.H. Wiley Lt Col RDA
Commy Eastern DAC

Army Form C. 2118.

WAR DIARY
or
INTELLIGENCE SUMMARY.

(Erase heading not required.)

Eastern DAC JUNE 1919

Instructions regarding War Diaries and Intelligence Summaries are contained in F. S. Regs., Part II. and the Staff Manual respectively. Title pages will be prepared in manuscript.

Place	Date	Hour	Summary of Events and Information	Remarks and references to Appendices
LULSDORF ZUNDORF & RANZEL	1st		1 O.R. posted from D/161 Bde.	
	3rd		Eastern Divnl. Commander paid a visit to D.A.C. Headquarters.	
	5th		Capt. Mirtlindiuis granted leave 7-21/6/19	
	"		Lt. Bull posted S.A.A. Section	
	6th		Lt. Jarvis tried by F.G.C.M.	
	"		2/Lt E.J. Jonko rejoined from leave	
	"		1 O.R. to Concentration Camp for demobilization	
	7th		3 O.R. to Concentration Camp for demobilization	
	12th		Lieut. Tuckey proceeds to England to report to War Office	
	13th		Regt. Lancs and 4th mules from Ammunition Collecting Camp	
	14th		2 Fitters posted to D.A.C. 2 O.R's. to Concentration Camp for demobilization	
	"		Inspection by C.R.A.	
	17th		10 Natives posted from Lancashire D.A.	
	18th		4/Capt R.R. Banham proceeds to England to report to War Office.	
	"		H.Q., No 1 and S.A.A. Section move to join Col. Kinnairds Column, and camp for the night at SIEGBURG	
	19th		H.Q., No 1 and S.A.A. Section march to HENNEF Race Course and camp there.	
HENNEF & DONRATH	"		No 2 Section march to DONRATH, and are attached to 160th Bde.	
	20th		Inspection of camp at HENNEF by C.R.A.	
	23rd		do by X Corps Commander.	

Z. Army Form C. 2118.

WAR DIARY
or
INTELLIGENCE SUMMARY.

(Erase heading not required.)

Title pages **EASTERN D.A.C.** June 1919

Instructions regarding War Diaries and Intelligence Summaries are contained in F. S. Regs., Part II. and the Staff Manual respectively. Title pages will be prepared in manuscript.

Place	Date	Hour	Summary of Events and Information	Remarks and references to Appendices
HENNEF	23rd		Mounted Sports at HENNEF	
"	25th		Divisional Commander inspects No 2 Section	
DONRATH	26th		Lt Gilbert proceeds on leave for 1 month. I.O.R. to Concentration Camp for demobilization	
"	30th		Divisional Commander inspects H.Qs No 1 & S.A.A. Sections in marching order. D.A.C. march to former billets in ZUNDORF area.	

Ashley Lieut Col R.A.A.
Commanding Eastern D.A.C.

Army Form C. 2118.

WAR DIARY
or
INTELLIGENCE SUMMARY.
(Erase heading not required.) Eastern D.A.C. July 1919.

Instructions regarding War Diaries and Intelligence Summaries are contained in F. S. Regs, Part II. and the Staff Manual respectively. Title pages will be prepared in manuscript.

Place	Date	Hour	Summary of Events and Information	Remarks and references to Appendices
ZUNDORF LVLSDORF RANZEL	1/7/19		2 Officers, 36 O.R's and 34 Horses attached Practice Camp WAHN for duty. 4 G.S. Wagons from No. 2 Section attached 160 Bde.	
	3rd		Lt.Col. J.H.G. Riley granted leave from 4.7.18. Capt. G. Lammrup resumed command of Column.	
			General holiday for Peace celebrations. Concert at ZUNDORF. Lieut. Burgess ordered to join party at WAHN Practice Camp	
	7th		10 reinforcements posted from R.A. Lt Stott proceeds on leave.	
			1 man despatched to Cologne en route for Paris Victory Parade.	
	8th		8 G.S. Wagons attached to 152 Brigade	
	10th		Lieut Gordons proceeds on leave. Lieut Pollen reports to R.A. vice "Gordon"	
	13th		1 Officer & 1 N.C.O. proceed to Paris to witness Victory march.	
	14th		Cricket match with 52nd Bn. Sussex Regt (lost)	
	15th		5 men posted 5th Bde R.H.A.	
	16th		Inspection of animals for reclassification	
	18th		Party attached Practice Camp return to Sections	
	19th		General holiday 1 Officer, 1 Sergt. 15 O.R's to Animal collecting Camp BONN for duty.	
	23rd		Concert in ZUNDORF by No I Section	

Army Form C. 2118.

2

WAR DIARY
or
INTELLIGENCE SUMMARY.
(Erase heading not required.) Eastern D.A.C. July 1919.

Instructions regarding War Diaries and Intelligence Summaries are contained in F. S. Regs., Part II. and the Staff Manual respectively. Title pages will be prepared in manuscript.

Place	Date	Hour	Summary of Events and Information	Remarks and references to Appendices
ZUNDORF	24/7		Revd Stott returns from leave.	AA
LVISDORF &	25th		Lt Holt proceeds on duty with leave party, and granted leave 27/7/19 to 10/8/19.	AA
RANZEL	26th		45 Indian O.R's posted to D.A.C.	AA
			A.C.L. J.H.G. Riley returns from leave.	AA
	29th		Lt England returns from leave	AA
	31st		Divisional Horse Shows. Lt Gilbert returns from leave.	AA

K.S. Murray Capt. & Adjt
for Lt Col R.F.A.
Commdg Eastern D.A.C.

www.ingramcontent.com/pod-product-compliance
Lightning Source LLC
Chambersburg PA
CBHW081425300426
44108CB00016BA/2305